AMERICA DANCES

AGNES DE MILLE

AMERICA DANCES

A HELENE OBOLENSKY ENTERPRISES, INC. BOOK

MACMILLAN PUBLISHING CO., INC. New York
COLLIER MACMILLAN PUBLISHERS London

Isadora at the Parthenon. CREDIT: *Edward Steichen. Reprinted with the permission of Joanna T. Steichen.*

Also by Agnes de Mille:

Where the Wings Grow
Speak to Me, Dance with Me
Dance in America
Russian Journals
Lizzie Borden: A Dance of Death
The Book of the Dance
To a Young Dancer
And Promenade Home
Dance to the Piper

Macmillan Publishing Co., Inc.
866 Third Avenue, New York, N.Y. 10022
Collier Macmillan Canada, Ltd.

Library of Congress Cataloging in Publication Data
De Mille, Agnes.
    America dances.
    Bibliography: p. 215
    Includes index.
    1. Dancing—United States—History.   I. Title.
GV1623.D36 1980   793.3'0973   80-17025
ISBN 0-02-530730-4
10 9 8 7 6 5 4 3 2 1
PRINTED IN THE UNITED STATES OF AMERICA

Design by Antler & Baldwin, Inc.

To Mary Green

CONTENTS

Foreword   ix
Acknowledgments   x
Historical Chronology   xi

1.
ORIGINALS   1

2.
ETHNIC AND POPULAR FORMS   13

3.
EARLY BALLET   23

4.
POPULAR THEATER BEFORE 1900   37

5.
ISADORA DUNCAN   43

6.
EARLY REVOLUTIONARIES   51

7.
POPULAR THEATER 1900–1930   59

8.
TWENTIETH-CENTURY BALLET   71

9.
DANCE IN EARLY FILMS   81

10.
MODERN REVOLUTIONARIES   91

11.
THE MAVERICKS   111

12.
THE INHERITORS OF THE BALLET   123

13.
THE NEW MODERNS   159

14.
THE NEW BALLET COMPANIES   177

15.
BROADWAY   187

16.
DANCE IN FILMS AFTER 1950   197

17.
THE MECHANICALS: TELEVISION,
    VIDEO AND SOUND TAPE   201

18.
STATE ENDOWMENT AND
    THE UNIONS   203

Bibliography   213
Index   215

FOREWORD

THIS book represents a personal and highly subjective outline of the facts of our dance history. I have chosen those episodes and personalities which, in my view, have shaped and influenced our modes of expression, our styles of movement, our qualities of delight and preference in entertainment. I have made no attempt to catalogue exhaustively the hundreds of interesting, even distinguished, figures. This is the merest outline. When the story reaches the twentieth century and lies, more or less, within living memory, I have quite arbitrarily chosen to write about: first, the people I saw, not others; second, the people I liked, and this does not include all the people who have been singled out by critics for praise.

I feel that this is my privilege as author, and I also know that since I was present at many of the dance occurrences and followed the development of careers with living eyes, I have a certain knowledge of the reasons behind the contemporary appraisals, very few of which were objective. The reader, therefore, will find to his surprise, certain names totally omitted and others seemingly slighted. This was a deliberate choice and possibly blameworthy, but it is my choice and represents my tastes. I do not expect universal agreement, indeed there may be a certain amount of outrage.

I have attempted to record faithfully the facts in regard to dates, places, and measurable success.

ACKNOWL-EDGMENTS

I wish to acknowledge gratefully the faithful help of:

Mary Green, for six years of typing, fetching and carrying, hunting and researching, correlating and correcting, and for patience;

Barbara Barker, for research on the nineteenth century, the verifying of dates, and for the Chronology;

Barbara Cohen, for a first assembling of pictures;

Lisa Phillips, who typed, sorted pictures, obtained permissions and rights, telephoned all over the world, and with great patience and sweetness behaved as *bonne à tout fais*;

John Martin and Zachary Solov, and Gwendolyn Rudell for the lending of rare pictures;

The staff of the Dance Archives of the New York Public Library;

Francis Robinson, who gave me information about the old opera house;

And Elisabeth Scharlatt, for skillful editing under difficult conditions.

HISTORICAL CHRONOLOGY

1607   English settlement established at Jamestown

1620   Arrival of Puritans at Plymouth

1624   Dutch West India Company establishes New Netherland on Manhattan Island; in 1664 the English capture the island and rename it New York

1670   Charleston, South Carolina, established by English colonists

1685   Increase Mather's "An Arrow Against Profane and Promiscuous Dancing, Drawne out of the Quiver of the Scriptures" published in Boston

1695   The site on which Alexandria, Virginia, now stands is settled; a community known as Belhaven is founded in 1731 and in 1749 is renamed for John Alexander

1718   New Orleans established by French traders

1739   Laws are passed in American Colonies forbidding blacks to use drums, the native instrument, lest these arouse slaves to insurrection

1774   Two dancing teachers, Pietro Sodi and Signor Tioli, establish schools in Philadelphia

1776   Declaration of Independence

1777   Articles of Confederation adopted by Congress

1783   Treaty of Paris—England officially recognizes independence of United States

1785   Itinerant ballroom dancing teacher Monsieur Roussel introduces the "Pigeon Wing" to polite society in Philadelphia

1790   John Durang, first American professional dancer, makes his stage debut with the Old American Theatre Company at the Baltimore Theatre

1791   Pierre Tastel, a French dancing master, establishes an academy of dance in Charleston, South Carolina

        French dancer Alexandre Placide and his wife arrive in Charleston; he becomes manager of the Charleston Theatre from 1798 to 1812

1792   The Placides present *The Bird Catcher, a Dancing Ballet* in New York City; John Durang is listed in cast

1794   Mme. Gardie, a dancer from Santo Domingo who had performed in Paris, appears in *Le Forêt Noire* at the New Theatre, Philadelphia

1796   James Byrne, English dancer and mime, whose specialty is Harlequin, makes his American debut in Philadelphia in the Grand Serious Pantomime, "The Death of Captain Cook, with Native Dances of the Hawaiian Islands"

      M. Francisquy of the Paris Opera Ballet arrives in New York with a small troupe of French dancers; they produce ballets at the John Street Theatre

1821   Park Theatre, New York City, engages French ballet master Claudius Labasse to perform and stage dances

1822   Marie Taglioni makes her debut in Vienna in a ballet especially staged by her father for the occasion; her future rival, Fanny Elssler, is listed in the corps de ballet

1825   Mr. and Mrs. Conway, English dancers, appear in New York City

1827   Park Theatre burns down May 24 and is rebuilt in the same location

      A French dancing troupe arrives in New York for an engagement at the Bowery Theatre; dancers include M. and Mme. Achille, M. Labasse, and Mlle. Celeste

1828   Thomas Dartmouth (Daddy) Rice presents "Jim Crow" characterization for the first time at the Columbia Street Theatre in Cincinnati

      Charles and Ronzi Vestris arrive in New York for a one-year engagement at the Bowery Theatre

1832   Italian musician and dancer Signor Papanti establishes a dancing school on Boston's Tremont Row and is appointed master of deportment and dancing at West Point

      Maria Taglioni creates title role in *La Sylphide* at the Paris Opéra

      The Ravel family of pantomimists, rope dancers, and acrobats arrives in America; they tour until their retirement to France in 1866

1833   Lorenzo da Ponte brings a troupe of opera singers to New York City and builds an Italian opera house

1836   Fanny Elssler performs the Cachucha in Jean Coralli's *Le Diable Boiteux* at the Paris Opera

      M. Hazard, a dancer from the Paris Opera, establishes a ballet school in Philadelphia where child prodigies Augusta Maywood and Mary Anne Lee receive their early training

1837   Augusta Maywood and Mary Anne Lee make their debuts in *The Maid of Cashmere* at the Chestnut Street Theatre, Philadelphia

1839   Marius and Jean Petipa, as members of the Lecomte troupe, dance in New York and then tour New Orleans, St. Louis, and Mobile in 1840

      Augusta Maywood makes her Paris Opera debut

      Paul Taglioni and his wife Amelie perform in *La Sylphide, Le Dieu et la Bayadère*, and *Nathalie, La Laitière Suisse* at the Park Theatre, New York

1840–   Fanny Elssler tours America
42

1841   When James Sylvain, Elssler's partner, returns to Europe, American dancer George Washington Smith assumes his roles

1845–   Potato famine in Ireland causes Irish
46   immigration to United States

1846   Edwin P. Christy founds Christy's Minstrel Troupe

      French dancer Mlle. Blangy performs first American Giselle, at the Arch Street Theatre, Philadelphia

      George Washington Smith appears in Boston at the National Theatre with Mary Anne Lee and at the Bowery Ampitheater in *Harlequin Toad in the Hole*

1847–   Hyppolite and Adele Montplaisir and
48   their French troupe tour the United States; the company includes twelve corps de ballet members, sixteen supernumeraries, and six children; *Esmeralda* and *Le Diable à Quatre* are in the repertory.

1847 Augusta Maywood becomes Prima Ballerina Assoluta at La Scala, Milan

John Durang's *Terpsichore, or Ballroom Guide* is published in Philadelphia

1848 Park Street Theatre burns to the ground a second time

"Juba" (William Henry Lane) goes to London to perform with a blackface minstrel troupe, Pell's Ethiopian Serenaders

1850 Leon Espinosa, father of a famous English family of dancing teachers and performers, makes his New York debut in *Le Diable à Quatre*

1852 George Washington Smith and Lola Montez appear at Boston Athenaeum Theatre

1854 Academy of Music opens on 14th Street in New York City

1857 The Ronzani Ballet Company from La Scala appears at the Academy of Music in Philadelphia; among the troupe are Cesare and Pia Cecchetti and their son Enrico

1860– Duration of the Civil War
65

1866 *The Black Crook* opens in Niblo's Garden Theatre in New York City, featuring Italian Prima Ballerinas Rita Sangalli and Maria Bonfanti

1867 Italian ballerina Giuseppina Morlacchi arrives in New York to star in *The Devil's Auction* at Banvard's Opera House

1868 Lydia Thompson and her British Blondes appear in New York in *Ixion, or the Man at the Wheel*

1869 Transcontinental Railway completed, allowing easier access to Western audiences

1883 Metropolitan Opera House opens at corner of 39th and Broadway, New York City; Malvina Cavalazzi is first ballerina

1884 Steele Mackaye begins an acting training program at his Lyceum Theatre in New York; the school, which becomes the American Academy of Dramatic Art, spreads Delsarte's system

1891 Loie Fuller makes her debut in a dance titled "Serpentine" at the Casino Theatre in New York City

1904 Isadora Duncan opens a dancing school for children in Germany

1905 Juilliard School of Music founded in New York City

Premiere of Isadora Duncan's *Iphigenia in Aulis* at the Krystall-Palast, Berlin

1906 Ruth St. Denis choreographs *Cobras, Incense,* and *Rhada,* the dance she considered her masterpiece

1908 Adeline Genée appears in Florenz Ziegfeld's review *The Soul Kiss*

Gertrude Hoffman dances *The Dance of the Seven Veils* in Oscar Hammerstein's production of Richard Strauss's opera *Salome*

1909 First Paris season of Diaghilev's Ballets Russes

Metropolitan Opera House establishes a school of ballet under Malvina Cavalazzi

Anna Pavlova and Mikhail Mordkin hire the Metropolitan Opera House for midnight performances featuring members of their own company

1910 Emile Jacques Dalcroze establishes school at Hellerau, Germany, dedicated to expression of rhythm in music, dance, and theater

1911 Irene and Vernon Castle become the rage of Paris, performing exhibition ballroom dances in the Café de Paris

1912 Gertrude Hoffman presents "La Saison des Ballets Russes" at the Winter Garden, New York City, with pirated Diaghilev ballets *Les Sylphides, Cleopatre,* and *Scheherazade*

1913 Roshanara, an English dancer specializing in East Indian dances, appears in a series of concerts in New York City

Margaret Curtis assumes leadership of Metropolitan Opera House ballet school

1914– Duration of World War I
18

1914 Ted Shawn joins Ruth St. Denis's company, and they marry

1915 Denishawn School opens in Los Angeles

Isadora Duncan premieres *La Marseillaise*

at the Trocadero in Paris and later the same year performs it at the Metropolitan Opera House

1916 Diaghilev's Ballets Russes tour United States and conclude their first season in this country with a series of concerts at the Metropolitan Opera House; Otto Kahn is the financial backer

Sol Hurok presents Anna Pavlova in *The Sleeping Beauty* at the Hippodrome, New York City

The Dumb Girl of Portici is filmed in Hollywood, starring Pavlova

1919 Capital Theatre, one of the early cinema houses, is built on Broadway in New York City

Rudolph Valentino dances the tango in *The Four Horsemen of the Apocalypse*

Michel Fokine and his wife Vera Fokina arrive in New York to give a series of concerts; Fokine tries to establish a ballet company of his own

Adolph Bohm organizes Ballet Intime in Chicago

1922 Fred and Adele Astaire achieve national fame in *For Goodness Sake*, a Broadway show written especially for them

Grauman's Egyptian Theatre built in Hollywood

1923 Albertina Rasch opens her own school in New York City and a year later organizes the Albertina Rasch Girls

1924 Angna Enters gives her first series of dance-mime performances in New York City

Martha Graham School established in New York City

The "Charleston" achieves popularity

Martha Graham appears in Greenwich Village Follies as a solo dancer; the cast includes Roshanara

1926 Sound film invented

Paramount Building constructed in New York City

The "Black Bottom" introduced by Ann Pennington in *George White's Scandals*

1927 Roxy Theatre built on 7th Avenue in New York City; the precision troupe, Roxyettes, introduced; theater demolished in 1961

Humphrey and Weidman leave Denishawn and begin giving their own concerts

Grauman's Chinese Theatre built in Hollywood

The "Varsity Drag" introduced by Zelda O'Neil in *Good News*

1928 Bill "Bojangles" Robinson establishes his reputation as a tapdancer in *Blackbirds of 1928*

1929 Léonide Massine is appointed choreographer for the Roxy Theatre

Martha Graham choreographs *Heretic*

1930 Massine stages *Le Sacre du Printemps* for the League of New York Composers

Carmelita Maracci makes her professional concert debut in Los Angeles; her New York debut is in 1939

Martha Graham choreographs *Primitive Mysteries*

1931 Hanya Holm opens a New York branch of the Mary Wigman School; in 1936 she forms her own concert dance company and changes the name of the school to the Hanya Holm Studio

Final performance of the Denishawn company, at Lewisohn Stadium concert in New York City

1932 Sophie Maslow, Jane Dudley, and William Bales form the New Dance Group in New York

Fred Astaire and Ginger Rogers star in the film *Flying Down to Rio*

Flying Colors, a Broadway show with separate black and white choruses (the first show to hire both racial troupes), opens

1933 Ted Shawn organizes a company of male dancers which tours the United States and Europe until disbanding in 1940

Ruby Keeler is featured dancer in Busby Berkeley's *Gold Diggers of 1933*

The New York City Ballet is founded by Lincoln Kirstein; the School of American Ballet starts in 1934

1934 Sol Hurok brings Colonel de Basil's

Ballet Russe to New York with Léonide Massine as artistic director and principal choreographer; the company tours United States from 1934 to 1944

Ruth Page begins her association with the Chicago Opera ballet as first dancer and choreographer

Lester Horton forms his own company in Los Angeles

1935 George Balanchine choreographs the Ziegfeld Follies

Catherine Littlefield and her sister Dorothy found the Philadelphia Ballet Company, which disbands in 1942

George Gershwin creates the first American folk opera, *Porgy and Bess*

Premiere of *Serenade*, the first ballet choreographed by Balanchine for the newly formed American Ballet Company

George Balanchine is appointed ballet master at the Metropolitan Opera House, a position he resigns at the end of the 1935–36 season

1936 Lincoln Kirstein founds Ballet Caravan, featuring works by American artists; the company tours until 1941

Ray Bolger is leading male dancer in *On Your Toes*, choreographed by Balanchine; Bolger is especially commended for his dancing in the ballet-within-the show, "Slaughter on Tenth Avenue"

Doris Humphrey choreographs *With My Red Fires*

1937 Hanya Holm choreographs *Trend* at the Bennington Festival

Mikhail Mordkin founds the Mordkin Ballet Company in New York City

1939 Eugene Loring choreographs *Billy the Kid*, to a score by Aaron Copland, for Ballet Caravan

Ballet Theatre founded by Richard Pleasant and Lucia Chase

The opening season at Radio City's Center Theatre presented the work of eleven choreographers with eighty-five dancers in a repertory of twenty-one ballets

1940 Martha Graham choreographs *Letter to the World*

Katherine Dunham choreographs *Tropics* and *Le Jazz Hot* (Pins and Needles Revue, produced by The Garment Trade)

1941– Duration of World War II
45

1941 Hanya Holm establishes The Center of Dance in the West at Colorado College and teaches summer courses there for over thirty years

Sybil Shearer begins her career as a solo concert dancer

San Francisco Ballet founded by Lew Christensen

Ted Shawn becomes director of Jacob's Pillow Dance Festival and University of Dance at Lee, Massachusetts

Antony Tudor choreographs *Pillar of Fire*, starring dancers Nora Kaye and Hugh Laing, for Ballet Theatre

1942 Agnes de Mille choreographs *Rodeo*, to music by Aaron Copland, for Ballet Russe de Monte Carlo

Jack Cole choreographs the Broadway musical *Something for the Boys*

1943 Agnes de Mille choreographs *Oklahoma!*

Katherine Dunham, eminent exponent of black dance, choreographs her first Broadway production, *Tropical Revue*, to be followed in 1945 by *Carib Song* and *Blue Holiday*, and in 1946 by *Bal Nègre*

1944 Jerome Robbins choreographs *Fancy Free* for Ballet Theatre, with settings by Oliver Smith and music by Leonard Bernstein

1945 Michael Kidd choreographs *On Stage!*, in which he creates the role of Handyman; in 1947 he stages dances and musical numbers in the Broadway musical *Finian's Rainbow*

Oliver Smith becomes co-director of Ballet Theatre with Lucia Chase

1946 Antony Tudor is appointed choreographer-in-chief and artistic administrator for Ballet Theatre

George Balanchine and Lincoln Kirstein organize The Ballet Society

1947 Agnes de Mille directs and choreographs *Allegro* by Rodgers and Hammerstein on Broadway, the first dance director to fill the dual function

Jerome Robbins choreographs *High Button Shoes*, including the Mack Sennett ballet, on Broadway

1948 Black dancer-choreographer Pearl Primus makes her first trip to Africa to study native dance forms and to perform

The Ballet Society becomes the resident company at New York City's Center for Drama and Music; the company, under the direction of Balanchine and Kirstein, is renamed The New York City Ballet

The British film, *The Red Shoes*, with Moira Shearer, Robert Helpman, and Leonide Massine, premieres

Agnes de Mille choreographs *Fall River Legend* for Ballet Theatre, with settings by Oliver Smith

1949 Jerome Robbins becomes co-director, with Balanchine, of New York City Ballet

José Limón choreographs *The Moor's Pavane*, based on *Othello*

1950 Donald McKayle choreographs *Games*, based on the joys and terrors of urban black children

Herbert Ross choreographs *Caprichos*, based on Goya's etchings, for Ballet Theatre

1951 American Ballet Theatre School established

1952 Omnibus television series first dance presentation, *Rodeo*, is broadcast

Merce Cunningham presents *Collage*, the first production of "musique concrète" in America

Department of dance is added to Juilliard School of Music

Robert Joffrey's school, The American Ballet Center, founded

1954 Filming of *Oklahoma!*, directed by Fred Zimmerman with Agnes de Mille creating the choreography

Hanya Holm choreographs the Broadway musical comedy *The Golden Apple*

Virginia Williams founds the Boston Ballet

1955 Bob Fosse choreographs *Damn Yankees* on Broadway

John Butler Dance Theatre is organized and continues through 1961

1956 Robert Joffrey Ballet founded

Merce Cunningham choreographs *Suite for Five in Space and Time*, with music by John Cage and costumes by Robert Rauschenberg

Anna Sokolow choreographs for the New York City Opera

Ballet Theatre adopts the title American Ballet Theatre

1957 Jerome Robbins choreographs and directs *West Side Story* on Broadway, with Leonard Bernstein's score and Oliver Smith's settings

Balanchine choreographs *Agon* for the New York City Ballet Company

1958 José Limón's *Missa Brevis* is performed in Washington's National Cathedral

Premiere of Martha Graham's *Clytemnestra*

Alvin Ailey's Company founded

1959 Teacher-choreographer-dancer Doris Humphrey's book *The Art of Making Dances* is published posthumously

1960 Peter Gennaro choreographs Meredith Wilson's *The Unsinkable Molly Brown* on Broadway

Alvin Ailey, black dancer and choreographer, creates *Revelations*, based on spirituals and folk songs

Gower Champion directs and choreographs *Bye Bye Birdie* on Broadway

1961 Paul Taylor Dance Company formed

Roxy Theatre demolished

New York State Assembly votes $450,000 to aid the arts outside New York City

1963 Alwin Nikolais choreographs, designs, and lights one of his best-known theater pieces, *Imago*

Balanchine's New York City Ballet receives a seven-million-dollar grant from the Ford Foundation

1964 The New York State Theatre is completed at Lincoln Center, and New York City Ballet takes up residence

Pennsylvania Ballet, under the direction of Barbara Weissberger, is started with a grant from the Ford Foundation

1965 President Lyndon B. Johnson signs a bill for the first National Endowment for the Arts

American Ballet Theatre celebrates its twenty-fifth anniversay with a gala at Lincoln Center

1967 Eliot Feld's choreographic debut, *Harbinger*, is presented by American Ballet Theatre

Metropolitan Opera House demolished

1968 American Ballet Theatre is named resident company at the John F. Kennedy Center for the Performing Arts, Washington, D.C.

Antony Tudor and Margaret Craske are named co-directors of the Metropolitan Opera Ballet School

1971 Pilobolus Dance Theatre formed by Moses Pendleton and Jonathan Wolken

1973 Twyla Tharp choreographs *Deuce Coupe* for the City Center Joffrey Ballet

Agnes de Mille starts Heritage Dance Theatre in conjunction with the North Carolina School of the Arts at Winston-Salem

1974 American choreographer Glen Tetley is named director of the Stuttgart Ballet, succeeding the late John Cranko

1975 The "Dance in America" series, directed by Jac Venza, begins on the Public Broadcasting System

1976 Martha Graham is awarded the Medal of Freedom, this country's highest civilian award, by President Gerald Ford

1977 Graham choreographs Hawthorne's *The Scarlet Letter*

1978– *The Bartered Bride*, directed by John
79 Dexter, designed by Josef Svoboda and choreographed by Pavel Smuck, is produced at the Metropolitan Opera House

1978 Bob Fosse choreographs the Broadway revue *Dancin'*

Herbert Ross directs the film *The Turning Point*

1979 Mikhail Baryshnikov announces his appointment as director of American Ballet Theatre, succeeding Lucia Chase

—

1.
ORIGINALS

EVERY group of people that has lived on the North American continent, anthropologists tell us, even the supposedly stoic Indians, has been restless and explosive in expression. This shows in the migration of entire peoples, the moving about of individuals, as well as in the tension and dynamics of dancing—in other words, their pace.

There are many good reasons for dancing. The first have to do with survival—with the control of the elements, with food, with procreation.

The American Indians danced for courage, control, and power. They danced to chants of one or more voices, without harmony and without development of any sort, for musical harmony was unknown to them. They danced to drums, dead beat, unvarying, unaccented, never accelerating, for hours, even days, without surcease and without climax. On an average the drumbeat was a little quicker than the human heartbeat, and the dancer's pulse adjusted to it. The climax occurred outside the dancers; for example, rain dances often ended in a downpour, the direct result, the dancers believed, of their efforts. The Indians, however, were canny; they performed rain dances, for example, during the rainy season. Since the elements were not always docile or quickly obedient, most of the dances were of long duration. It was not unusual for a buffalo dance to last nineteen days, at the end of which time the young men, in a state of semi-hypnosis, actually believed themselves to be buffalo and so found it an easy matter to go out on the plains and call the herd in to be slaughtered.

The steps were simple, with scant deviation and no individual invention, because the Indians felt deviation was displeasing to the gods. Occasionally the ministrants danced through fire or with hoops, or with live rattlesnakes in their mouths, as in certain Hopi dances. Not infrequently there were special displays of torture, even mutilation. The Mandan ceremonies were notably cruel.

Hunting and fighting skills were taught through dancing; so was bravery, in the Mandan torture dances, for example; so was potency. Men and women seldom performed together, not even in mating dances such as the Navaho Eagle Dance, where the role of the female bird was taken by a man. Inasmuch as the dances were magic and involved the safety and continuity of the tribe, the men felt they could certainly not be entrusted to women, although the women were invariably present, but only as a chorus and supportive background, as encouragers, a sort of cheering section. Except in a few dances like the Navaho Squaw Dance, they very seldom participated actively.

The dancers rarely touched one another or joined hands. They were, rather, an ensemble of soloists. They danced on their own but within rigid rules. Since the purpose of their dancing was often magical or religious, the slightest improvisation was always under very strict auspices.

The dances were often, though not invariably, pantomimic. The dancers' bodies were stretched in ecstatic appeals for power or crouched in imitation of animals or set in fighting postures that involved weapons and the protection of viscera, for these dances were always the the prelude to real-life action.

The dancers used paint and masks, but never as frivolous or optional decoration. The symbols were ordained and potent, just as a priest's stole is potent and not merely a decorative neckpiece, or as crowns and uniforms, which have no intrinsic power of themselves but are the symbols of power, are potent. (The crowning of a queen in Westminster Abbey is not to be thought of as a display

of headgear.) So with the Indians; every mark on their faces or bodies was important and powerful.

In the Cherokee ant dance, sixteen dancers looked each other squarely in the eye and did not move except to flick their fingers and mark time with their feet. But in most of their dances, the Indians rarely used their hands for symbolic or aesthetic gestures; they used them for clutching totems or weapons. Their feet were shod in moccasins as soft as gloves. The foot felt the earth, caressed it, made love to it—the whole foot, like the palm of the hand. The Indian foot and the earth are like two voices in a duet. The white man who wears hard leather soles cannot approximate this manner of moving and stepping. The Indian foot talks.

The early settlers saw plenty of Indian dances wherever they went, but they feared and scorned them, considering them the goings-on of heathens and savages, which generally foreboded trouble. The Europeans took kindly to the Indians' tobacco, maize, potatoes, leatherwork, and furs, but not to any of their art forms. Accordingly the races shared little except—and then only during beneficent interludes—cooking recipes. When the settlers heard

Above, *Buffalo Dancer*. Monore Tsa-To-Ke, c. 1930. Right, *Deer Dancer*. Theodore Suina, c. 1935. Left, *Taos Turtle Dance*. Vincent Mirabel, 1938. CREDIT: *U.S. Department of the Interior, Indian Arts and Crafts Board, William and Leslie Van Ness Denman Collection.*

the Indian drums, they closed their windows, got out the fire buckets, and hid the children. They did not observe Indian dances with the slightest aesthetic or anthropological curiosity. Instead, the two groups traded firewater, gunpowder, scalping knives, and, of course, smallpox and syphilis, a wretched basis for cultural exchange.

The first permanent settlers who came to America from England were Calvinists, Puritans who practiced a harsh and merciless religion that forbade all pleasure: the theater (they closed the theater back home for twenty years under Cromwell), dancing certainly, and graven images (they knocked the faces off their stone saints in their beautiful cathedrals), and music, except for sacred hymns. Frivolities of dress and luxuries for the table were obviously not available in early Massachusetts, but they would have been forbidden even if they had been. The rigors of their discipline, however, probably toughened the settlers up to withstand the climate and hunger in New England and enabled them later to fight the Indians, whom they most certainly provoked. Other colonists followed—Anglicans in Virginia and the Carolinas, Dutch Protestants in New York (New Amsterdam, then), Quakers in Pennsylvania, Huguenots in North Carolina, Moravians in Pennsylvania and North Carolina, French and Spanish Catholics in Louisiana. The dominant influence, however, was then and remained English and largely Puritan, and the general approach of the Puritans toward all art was disapproving if not condemnatory. The idea of dancing as part of religion was unthinkable throughout Christendom at the time, it is true, but in America even the social value of dancing was barely accepted and then only in certain restricted classes and areas of communal life.

What music the colonists did bring to America was of a highly developed nature. There were five thousand years of cultural evolution between the Stone Age Indian tom-tom beat and the Elizabethan madrigal. The colonists had dynamics, the twelve-tone scale, melody in tonal modes, harmony, and counterpoint. The sound of their music would help to change the history of the New World, along with that other sound, gunshot. A gun had never been fired on the North American continent before the Spaniards and Englishmen came.

For centuries after the Christian Church threw dancing out of its ritual in the thirteenth century, the only uses for dancing accepted in Christian Europe were in courtship and jollity, the releases of happy animal spirits. "Dancing is practiced to make manifest whether lovers are in good health and sound in all their limbs, after which it is permitted them to kiss their mistresses, whereby they may perceive if either has an unpleasant breath or exhales a disagreeable odor as that of bad meat," wrote the French monk Thoinot Arbeau in 1588, "so that, in addition to divers other merits attendant on dancing, it has become essential to the well-being of society."

The dance floor, then, whether parquet or trodden earth, was for centuries the only ground on which young Christian men and women could meet socially with communal sanction. It was the presentation spot for prospective lovers, and occasions with dancing were treated, if not as ceremonial, at the very least as festive. The participants dressed up and minded their manners, for at these times the most important life decisions were determined. It made no matter what a parent (or a dynasty) had negotiated beforehand. The young principals had to stand up face to face, and first impressions were extremely important. On the dance floor, in your best clothes and airing your best deportment—that was the one spot, outside of a blood-soaked battleground, to get ahead. A distinguished manner at court or in the ballroom, therefore a fair suit and jewels, as well as a good leg—these were once as important to the political aspirant as a strong lobby in Washington is today.

Sexual differences were strongly emphasized. If the bodice clung, the woman stood revealed, lovely and sensuous. If the doublet was short and the legs were in hose, the back, thigh, and calf of the man were favored. In the next four centuries, bosoms were bared, waists were narrowed, hips were exaggerated by farthingale or hoop, and skirts were looped to show the dainty instep. Likewise, males wore ruffs, breeches, and heels to display the carriage of the head, the gentleman's hands, the strong thigh of the rider, the trained foot of the swordsman. But whatever the style, the clothes worn on a dance floor or in a ballroom were always the best the owner could afford.

The ability to dance well was as indispensable

Square dancing as illustrated by students of the North Carolina School of the Arts for the Agnes de Mille Heritage Dance Theater.
CREDIT: *Peter Garick.*

to an ambitious gentleman as the ability to fence well, swordsmanship being not only sport but the direct means of preserving life. Courtiers danced or they did not go to court. And the seat of government, both in the old country and in the New World, was the hub of power. So gentlemen danced, and the best swordsmen danced the best, because the one exercise complemented and strengthened the other. The colonial gentry in America studied assiduously under dancing masters all the French forms—the voltas, galliards, canaries—and the citizenry followed the examples set on the estates and in the great halls. All the arts and instruments of coquetry were in these French dances—handkerchiefs, fans, veils, and swaying skirts, posturing and preening. The men danced erect, because they fought with steel weapons and they wore armor and so could afford to expose their bodies.

By far the most preponderant of the dances to reach America, in influence as well as pervasiveness, were the English country dances—longways, rounds, and squares. They underwent little adjustment in the new environment, except that they spread out and became quicker, longer, and harder. Over here they were raced; there was more room. Here they were shouted or called; there was more vocal energy in them. Here the figurations progressed counterclockwise, whereas in the old country the patterns always moved clockwise. And here some of the dance sets lasted fifteen minutes— of steady running. The Americans were strong people who could stay the course of an evening's dancing after a day's plowing.

The American running set or square dance, which was popular as early as the seventeenth century, consists of four couples standing facing one another in a square. The steps are unvarying— simple running, forward or back, and turning or spinning in place, or buzzing, as it is called. But from these few ingredients, the intricacy, variety, and beauty of patterns that can be achieved are astonishing. All the different figurations have names: the grapevine twist, roll the barrel, the ocean wave, shoot the owl, chase the squirrel, box the gnat, wind up the ball of yarn, unwind the ball of yarn, a hundred years later, rattle snake twist, Texas star, California show basket.

The steps or patterns are generally arranged in a definite order, but they can be reassembled at the will of the caller. All the steps are "called" by a man who is sometimes also the fiddler or one of the dancers. These callers often became famous for their wit and humor and for their ability to catch the rhythm and give the commands just in time for the dancers to know exactly what to do.

Honor your partner. [Bow to your partner.]
Honor your corner. [Bow to your nearest adjacent neighbor.]

All hands 'round and circle left.

Allemande west and allemande east.

[Allemande is a corruption of the French *à la main*, "by the hand."]

Away we go and do, si, do.
[Circling with the back presented to the partner, from a corruption of the French *dos à dos*, "back to back."]

Sashay here and sashay there.
[Sliding the foot without raising the heel, from the French ballet term *chassé*.]

Ladies to the center and back to the bar,

Gents to the center in a right-hand star.

Ladies to the center and the gents bow under.

Away we go and we go like thunder.

Running up the river Indian-style,

The ladies in the lead and gents plumb wild.

Give your arm to your girl,

Give your arm to your honey.

Double up, boys,

Get the worth of your money.

The ladies lead out and the gents foller.

Thank the fiddler and kiss the caller.

Take her out and give her air,

You know where and I don't care,

'Cause now I'm through and so are you.

These dances are still our country forms, current in all rural areas of the United States.

In the eighteenth century ballroom dancing became more subtle and more delicate. Men no longer fought with swords; they used the rapier, which involved tiptoe, fingertip fighting, graceful but deadly. And their feet were like ballet dancers'. They danced rigaudons, passepieds, bourrées, gigues, and still later, minuets and gavottes, as well as the Virginia reel, the American dance derived from the Sir Roger de Coverley, an English country dance.

The ballroom dances stressed elaborate foot patterns, the lacings and interlacings of arms, and deportment, or manner. Decorum in those days was a strength and not a nuisance, and was cultivated carefully. The eighteenth-century people were fastidious. They touched only fingertips or waists. They did not handle one another or even use first

An Easy Introduction to Dancing. George Bickham, 1738. CREDIT: *George Bickham, 1758. The Dance Collection, The New York Public Library at Lincoln Center. Astor, Lenox, and Tilden Foundations. (Hereafter referred to as The Dance Collection.)*

The Art of Dancing. Kellan Tomlinson, 1735. Note that the hands are held in formal 18th-century dancing position, with the thumb and forefinger joined in a circle. CREDIT: *Kellan Tomlinson, 1735. The Dance Collection.*

names. They dressed in their finest, they liked form, and they guarded privacy. Washington, the father of our country, always stood with his right hand behind his back lest he be trapped into shaking hands with his guests and neighbors.

People soon realized that in America, with its frontier opportunities, there were many ways of getting ahead besides cutting a fine leg, and the Revolution changed the Americans' notions of décorum radically. Benjamin Franklin, unpowdered, unembroidered, unstrutting, unbejeweled, and with no ornament but his gorgeous wit and wisdom, dramatized his cause at the court of Louis XVI by dressing as more and more of his peers were beginning to dress, simply and soberly.

The popular dances at this time in America tended more and more to be country-style ones like the Roger de Coverley, but we were still snobs. We kept importing dancing masters because we still thought of ourselves as colonials, and although we were now an independent country, we were in no hurry to trust our natural ways. New ways of dancing and new forms of expression were certainly being introduced here, but the gentry continued to copy the accepted European dances.

All European dances, court and country alike, had one common characteristic—the pronounced lack of physical intimacy. What went on in the bushes or behind the screen was one thing—and it did, of course, go on because we're here—but on the dance floor or in the parlor, there was emphatically no embracing. Casual handling was simply considered too risky; men and women being too hot-blooded for it. And although the American dances may have been a little rougher than the European forms, with more vigorous swingings and liftings ("If that ain't hugging, I don't know how"); these polite and gallant conventions persisted, among the gentry and particularly on the frontier where women were scarce.

Suddenly, in Europe after the Napoleonic Wars there was a great change. On the dance floor, the relationship of bodies quickly altered, and the man embraced the woman, face to face, body to body, for better or worse. And we followed suit. Swiftly. Why not? We had always borrowed all the arts and gentilities of the Old World, our revolution having been political and not social. But this was no light matter. This new dancing marked

Valse à Trois Temps, 1844. CREDIT: *London, 1844. The Dance Collection.*

a profound change in attitude. It amounted, in fact, to a sexual revolution.

The nineteenth century was to see the cracking of all social molds, the emergence of the individual, the freeing of romantic expression in science and art. Among other things, men and women began to dance as they liked, and apparently what they liked was being intimate. Moralists railed, but to no purpose. Dancing partners embraced. This was the only public way a boy could touch a girl, the only permissible way he could get his arms around her. Of course, there were restrictions. The bodies did not *really* touch. They teased. Between the partners there was always a thin line of candlelight or gaslight. No bare hand actually touched bare flesh; a handkerchief or a glove always intervened.

Furthermore, women's clothes in the nineteenth century were a kind of carapace, as yielding as a lobster's, so tightly laced that the wearers often fainted, not because they were the weaker sex, as they so obligingly allowed themselves to be called, but because they simply could not breathe. The fourteen-inch waist was a fact. Whenever their viscera were released they generally managed to outlast their men. These nineteenth century women consented to the torturous lacing for the same reason that Chinese women consented to the breaking and binding of their feet—because it made them more attractive to their men by most wonderfully heightening the male sense of power.

The toilettes of the female rich were from Paris in the nineteenth century, Worth dresses if possible, set off by a display of family jewels that served as advertisement and come-on. Less affluent women made their own dresses, putting weeks and months of loving toil into ruffles and flounces, all, of course, hand-sewn. Girls were encased in kid to the armpit, and though gloves cost a fortune even then, brand-new ones were used for each occasion.

The dances of the period were not as refined or as intricate as those of the eighteenth century, although many were to exciting new rhythms—the waltz, the schottische, the polka, the mazurka, and the galop. Then as before, balls were the great social occasions, where one made the prime decisions of life. This was where one got engaged or broke off engagements; and engagements were heavy decisions, marriages being for life. This is where one made business deals as well. No young man could have a career in the army, in diplomacy, in the professions, or even in business; no young lady

The Hunt Ball. Stewart. CREDIT: *Stewart. From La Danse by Gaston Vuillard, ©1898, Hachette Freres/Photo: Braun Clement & Cie, Paris.*

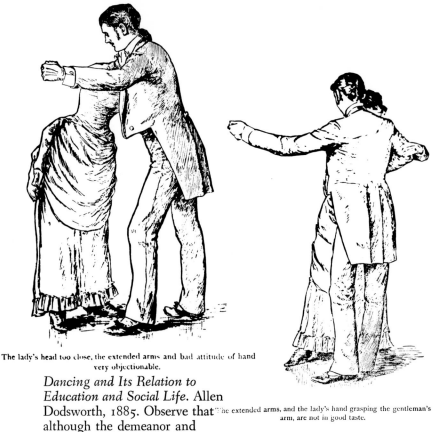

The lady's head too close, the extended arms and bad attitude of hand very objectionable.

Dancing and Its Relation to Education and Social Life. Allen Dodsworth, 1885. Observe that although the demeanor and conduct may have been vulgar, the wearing of gloves throughout is exemplary. CREDIT: *Allen Dodsworth, 1885. The Dance Collection.*

The extended arms, and the lady's hand grasping the gentleman's arm, are not in good taste.

Extremely vulgar.

could "come out" in society, without being a fine and elegant dancer. They had lessons all through their youth. The genteel dancing teacher William de Rham once told his twentieth-century New York City pupils what it was like when their grandparents were young.

> In the old days gentlemen carried (to dancing school) little bags with their pumps in them. I don't ask you to do that, but I want your shoes polished sometime between your last football game and here. I want your hands out of your pockets and nothing in them except a clean, white, folded handkerchief in your handkerchief pocket. I don't want any sprawling. The first thing you are going to learn to do is to sit. You sit still and you sit straight and you sit up. None of you can sit any more because none of you have decent family meals—you just run into some kitchenette in some modern ranch house and run

out again. I want you to choose a girl, offer her your right arm, and march into the ballroom and stop with your heels together . . . (Afterwards) you take the girl to her seat, and if there is a seat, sit beside her. And you don't leave her until she gets another partner or gets married.*

Whether in crinolines, hoops, or bustles, social dances did not vary much in America for seventy-five years; waltzes, German polkas, lancers, varsoviennes, in varying rhythms but with exact steps, followed one another in a carefully ordered plan throughout the evening right up to the final galop. These dances did not change until the beginning of this century, and of course they were all European. But at the same time certain indigenous dance styles, quite unexpected and quite wonderful, were developing right under our feet.

* Cleveland Amory, *Who Killed Society?* (New York: Harper & Brothers, 1960).

2.
ETHNIC AND POPULAR FORMS

IN the seventeenth and eighteenth centuries, over eight million Africans were brought to America as slaves. They came from a wide variety of territories and represented many kinds and degrees of culture. These people brought with them a remarkably developed sense of rhythm and body technique unlike anything the European had practiced. Their use of the naked foot, their body rhythms, their endurance, and their ecstasy were akin to those the Indians displayed, but whereas the Indian danced for power and magical assistance, the slave danced for escape and forgetfulness. And since the slave had no entertainment except of his own devising, he danced for fun. The Indian danced toward spiritual integration, the marshaling of his powers for endurance and ordeal; the black, however, danced for release, abandon, and comfort.

The black changed much of the artistic expression in the United States, particularly in music and dance. The Indian was kept apart from the white settlements and was, except for brief interludes, hostile. He was either feared or despised, but certainly never copied. The black, however, lived on the premises and sang and danced before the house steps, in the yard, over work in the washhouse, in the bakehouse, in the weaving room, at the forge. The white children watched, picked up the rhythms, and joined in. The white child's nurses and playmates were black. He was instructed more deeply by them than anyone realized. A new kind of lilt took over in the nation's songs and dances; the accent was placed, not on the downbeat as in Europe, *one*-two, but on the the upbeat, or offbeat, one-*two*. This was African, but it became American.

Rhythmic beats began to be missed, and the accent slipped to unexpected counts. We call this syncopation. While it had long been known and practiced by great musicians, it was not generally used in Europe by ordinary people. Now the Americans were clapping and stamping their dances on the offbeat.

After an unsuccessful but alarming uprising of slaves in 1739, laws were enacted forbidding Negroes to use drums, their native instrument, for any purpose at all, even for dancing. So the slaves transferred the drum rhythms, the message-giving rhythms, to their feet. They rattled tambourines (borrowed probably from the Spanish Creoles of the South) and they clacked bones together like

13

The Old Plantation, c. 1800. CREDIT: *The Abby Aldrich Rockefeller Folk Art Center, Williamsburg, Virginia.*

castanets. They turned the bonja, an African gourd with strings, into the banjo. It became their stringed instrument. It is native American, found nowhere else in the world.

By 1830 they had developed a highly complicated and brilliant form of rhythmic dancing, brand-new and all their own. They let go, in body, in face, in voice, in fun. And while they danced they yelped, called, giggled, laughed, and moaned. This was a great lesson to the white folks, who had been taught that ladies and gentlemen did not yell or wiggle when dancing. The black folks danced with more personal expression and invention, and they enjoyed themselves while they were at it.

In the mid-nineteenth century there was another tremendous immigration, this time by the Irish, who came voluntarily but in desperation. They came by the thousands because there was a potato famine at home and whole villages were starving. The Irish tinkers traveled everywhere in the South in encampments, and they performed their jigs and reels and clog dances wherever they went. Their foot rhythms delighted the black slaves and they took over learning them quickly, changing the Irish downbeat to the syncopated off-rhythms, and added African emphasis and the free loose swing of body movement. The Irish dance permitted almost no arm or body movement; with head and torso always held rigid. The Irish dancer seemed to live only through his feet, performing as though rooted in the ground, in a starved, rocky kind of way beating defiant tattoos on the hard, bare earth (they frequently clogged at the crossroads where the ground was hard and without grass) or on barn doors laid flat. It was a stiff kind of dancing, but the music for it was jolly and the rhythm of it was irresistible. The black threw away all the restraints, until the decorous hornpipe and the Irish clog be-

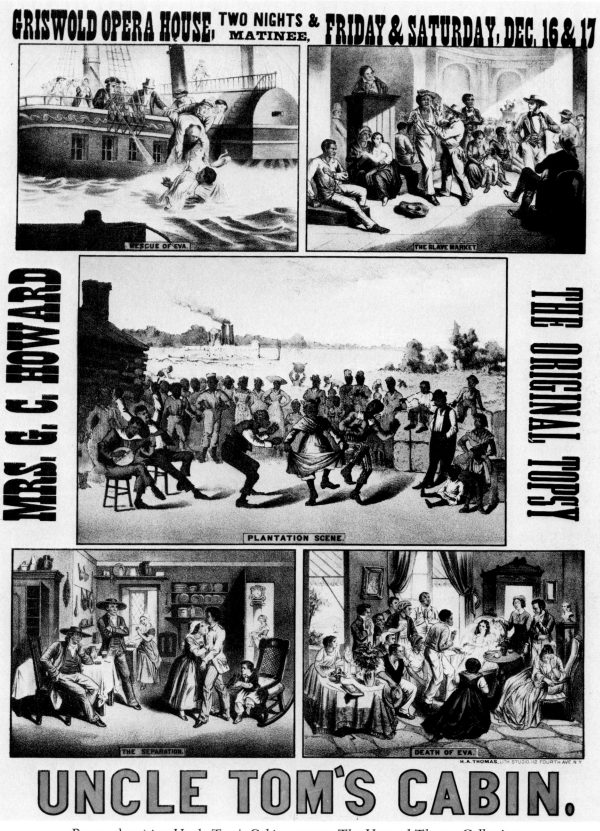

Poster advertising *Uncle Tom's Cabin*. CREDIT: *The Harvard Theatre Collection.*

came the exuberant American buck-and-wing, tap, and jazz.

A new contribution to our folk vocabulary was born. The blacks' creativity never ceased, and their flair for performing made the new dances popular—the Cakewalk, Balling the Jack, the Charleston. In the twentieth century the whites have consistently copied the body rhythms and the rank sexuality of the blacks in such dances as the one-step, the two-step, the fox-trot, the Black Bottom, the Varsity Drag, the Lindy-Hop, the jitterbug, the Shag, the Susie Q, the Big Apple, rock 'n roll, the Twist, the Frug, and the Watusi.

The early ethnic dances were rougher, less respectful, less kindly or gallant than European courting dances. Reformers kept referring to them as "African" or "jungle" or "primitive." They were, of course, nothing of the sort. In their roughness and lack of courtesy these dances may be crude, for they are the expression of a tortured people and they bear the mark of the cage, but on the other hand they are full of invention and humor.

The Turkey Trot and Bunny Hug actually were devised by a white man, Joseph Smith, the son of George Washington Smith, America's first great ballet dancer. He watched blacks at work and copied their body positions and rhythms; then he polished the steps and performed them first in vaudeville. They were later taken up as social dances all over the country and for a time became the ballroom vogue.

These steps, whether invented or inspired by blacks, are as original and as expressive as the gavotte or minuet, but their most astonishing aspect is the rapidity with which they develop. The English and French required two hundred fifty years to change the Elizabethan volta into the waltz. The exuberant and prolific blacks produce a new form each decade. No other ethnic group boils up constantly in such rich, spontaneous gesture. From the beginning, blacks not only mimicked the white steps but invented steps of their own, which were more fun. The blacks had not lost the gift of improvisation, as had many others.

Social dances, like social habits, usually emerge slowly and anonymously. It is rare that a single person effects a new style. But at the beginning of the twentieth century one man did. Vernon Castle (1887–1918), long-legged, slim, and divinely skillful, together with his willowy and lissome wife, Irene (1893–1969), became the rage of the Western world, first in Paris in 1911, then in New York in 1912. They invented many new steps and advertised them in public exhibitions of ballroom dancing. Although they were professional entertainers, their dances were designed to be copied by ordinary people and to be danced everywhere. And they were. The Castles were marvelous performers, inventive and tasteful, and they changed the whole style of social dancing over the Western world. They popularized the one-step, the fox-trot, the Castle walk, and the glide; they introduced the South American maxixe. The tango, a close-clutching, body-to-body dance from Argentina, had already been introduced in the United States by Joseph Smith, but the Castles revised it and popularized it. The old social dances—the waltz, the German, the schottische, and the polka—rapidly lost popularity until today they are as obsolete as handmade buttonholes or plackets. Very few people in the United States now can waltz well, not even highly trained performers.

The Castles danced in contemporary clothes, not in costumes; they were the first performers in one hundred fifty years to do this. Irene Castle was svelte, light, and graceful, and so much more attractive than the overstuffed, pudgy women of her generation that she made dieting popular. Refusing to wear the artificial and uncomfortable corsets that had been stylish in one form or another since the time of Queen Elizabeth I, she unlaced. She wore light girdles and knickers and full, floating skirts of light materials. She was not the first woman to do this, but she was the first fashionable one. She was considered the best-dressed woman of her time and set a style for women everywhere. They even bobbed their hair when Irene Castle's had to be clipped for an operation. Her gowns were ravishing, usually by Lucille of London.*

In dance styles of this period, the early 1900s, the man still led—with the woman moving backward—but the entire body posture of both partners, the spread of step, the speed and zip, the grace and seemliness, belonged to the new century. Everything was more natural, more vigorous, and less artificial

* One of her beautiful dance dresses is owned by the Metropolitan Museum of Art; it is gray chiffon with bands of light gray fox fur on the wide sleeves.

Vernon and Irene Castle. The position, which formerly had been called "extremely vulgar," is now standard for the one- and two-steps. The adaptation of the Dutch cap Irene wears became the vogue for theater attendance, because the street hats of the time were so enormous they blocked everyone's view. CREDIT: *Castle Publication/ The Dance Collection.*

than any dancing done in the previous four hundred years. Of course, no woman in a hoop or bustle *could* have moved the way Irene Castle moved.

The Castles' music arranger was a black, Ford T. Dabney, who had been the official pianist of the president of Haiti. Dabnev helped the Castles change from old nineteenth-century rhythms to the gay Negro jazz beats. In so doing, he spread the influence of black music over three continents.

Since the Castles, nearly all couple dances have been without pattern or rules, something any eighteenth-century lady or gentleman would have considered disorderly in the extreme. The new steps permitted a high degree of improvisation. Within certain limits, each man did as he liked, and the woman, sensitive to his hints of pressure and direction, followed obediently. The skill of leading and following became the tricky part, and an unfamiliar partner presented all kinds of problems to a dancer.

Inspired by the Castles, grown-ups now turned to dancing schools. Descriptions of new steps were printed in ladies' magazines, and people could rehearse in their parlors for the phonograph had just become available. There were thés dansants,

The Charleston. CREDIT: *Mattias Santoyo/The Billy Rose Theater Collection. The Dance Collection.*

and people even danced in restaurants. Europe and America went dance-mad in the period between 1909 and 1913, just before World War I. It is interesting to note that there has always been a dance mania just before a war.

Jitterbugs from the 1939 film *The Jones Family in Hollywood.* This is the kind of step that was performed by jitterbugs in the ballrooms. It was the height of gymnastic exuberance and required the energy of the very young. The middle-aged did not attempt it. CREDIT: © *1939, Twentieth Century-Fox Film Corp./The Penguin Collection.*

The dance marathons were a peculiar manifestation that broke out generally at the height of the Depression, 1932–1933. They were contests solely of endurance in which the dancers had to stay active and awake until they dropped and were counted out. They were allowed to sleep 15 minutes of every hour and they were allowed to sleep in their partners' arms as long as one of them kept moving. The dance floors were full of sluggish partners, one of them unconscious, "squirrely," the other pushing around doggedly. The damage to feet, knees, spine, and internal organs was marked. There was a doctor always in attendance. The aspect of the exercises became grimmer with each succeeding day. The prizes were paltry, but in those days of absolute poverty, of soup kitchens and apple sellers, they did provide warmth, a modicum of excitement, and a little money. And they were, of course, in a grotesque and limited way, attention-getting. CREDIT: *Lawrence Matthew scrapbook/The Dance Collection.*

After the war, there were the grapplings and clutchings of the twenties. The girls parked their corsets in the cloakroom and wore makeup, which up to then was forbidden for decent women. The boys sported hip flasks. And the kids went at it without plan or sequence, just grabbing and grinding. The music, when not a Victrola, was a jazz combo, with saxophone, bull fiddle, and traps. Fraternity houses began to set up a style of their own. A friend of my father's described a dance at a Cornell fraternity house, where the guests, growing impatient of chaperonage, broke all the light bulbs on the floor and danced for the rest of the evening in the dark on crushed glass and the rolling bodies of their brothers and their dates.

About 1924 the Charleston appeared, straight off the wharves of South Carolina. This was a difficult dance, but zesty and humorous and full of wonderful invention. It swept the campuses, and soon there were contests at endless Saturday night dinner dances. Joan Crawford won every one in Los Angeles. Then came the Black Bottom, danced by Ann Pennington in *George White's Scandals* of 1926, and the Varsity Drag, introduced by Zelma O'Neil in *Good News* in 1927, and with them dancing became the property of the young. Anyone over thirty simply could not stand up to the demands of these dances. The older generation just pushed around in a friendly hug and got drunk sitting in cars.

But the young! They rampaged. The thirties brought the apples big and little, the boogie-woogie, the jitterbug, and the Lindy, all extremely difficult, semiacrobatic dances. You had to be healthy just to get through any of them. These were show-off pieces without gallantry of any sort. The boys seemed either to pull the girls to pieces or to throw them away. Sex became a contest of quick riposte and speed. But the American dance steps were marvels, and all the world copied them.

The romanticism engendered by World War II outlasted the event by some years, and with release from rationing, fashion burgeoned into delicious attractiveness, the first alluring style since World War I. Not surprisingly, it was accompanied by a great baby boom.

These babies came of age in the sixties to experience disintegration, revolt on the campuses, wildcat or runaway wars, filial disobedience as an act of faith, contrariness as a way of life, and sexual chaos. The young dressed in trick-or-treat garments, went unshaven and unshod, and discarded all courtesies. They danced whatever they had not seen done before. Their dancing was not new, but it was unlike their parents' style: the jerking of the head to produce vertigo, the swaying and pumping of the pelvis to produce sexual release, repetition as in Oriental rites—all this had been done before but not by them.

But they felt free and new, and in the spirit of freedom the individual fragmented off even from his own partner and danced quite alone, rarely looking at her or touching. Since quite enough touching was permitted elsewhere, the girls and boys may have found the impersonality of the dance floor a genuine relief.

By the seventies the boys and girls did not dance with one another; they danced in spite of one another. I remember watching my son dancing at a club on a Saturday night.

"Don't you like your partner?" I asked.

"Of course I like her."

"Then why don't you look at her?"

"I've seen her."

What seems to be gone from our social practice is the delightful art of flirting. There is nothing today between "hulloa" and "enough." Does no one remember how delicious "perhaps" could be?

There was no courtship now. Was there then mystery? Very little. Was there jollity? Some, but quite different from what we previously knew.

Why do people dance today? Presumably today's dancers have bedded long ago and all questions have been answered before they squeeze onto their discotheque floors.

Today (oh, strange! oh, marvelous) the boys and girls look alike. Except that men have hair on their faces and bony wrists and Adam's apples and longer skeletons. The women now boast gigantic feet and hands, rough voices, and aggressive stances. As to dress, they are identical, even as to adornment—beads, necklaces, bracelets, rings, earrings, hairdos. The women, hitherto, always dressed to be exquisite and vulnerable but, above all, different. Latterly, it has not been so. For the first time in the history of the world, they pretend to be brothers, younger, perhaps, and underdeveloped, the secondary sexual attributes are similar, the primary all but obliterated. And the gestures are in every way alike. In Europe, the gestures have been equal or complementary, but they have never before been exactly the same. This was a manner of dancing without precedent or antecedent in recorded history. Obviously, in our time, the difference in sex is not valued.

There developed in the sixties an air of addiction. The wonderful Beatles had popularized rock music, then others less musical exploded the idea into bombardments of sound. Mechanics improved, and the music grew deafening. (Indeed, many of our young have impaired hearing.) Noise can be a kind of narcotic, a sort of aural sauna, for a bath of sound is more insulating than silence. It may stimulate, but it also numbs and encapsulates the individual. Our discotheques have become an exercise in mass loneliness.

If the discothequers never touched, they also rarely moved from one spot. Space did not exist for them. We took this whole continent and now we had no space. The dancers remained stationary in caged confrontation: couple by couple pulsing and lurching. It is true the waltz could also be hypnotic, but the couples took note of the other couples and they moved about freely. With the alternation of style, of rhythms, however slight, there ensued variety. But now they embraced monotony, the same beat, endless, relentless; and by jettisoning

The Wobble. Susan Perl. CREDIT: © 1962, *The New York Times Co./Susan Perl.*

the safety of planned patterns, the young kidded themselves that they were free as never before. There were no rules to follow, there were no rules to break. There was company only, which was all they wanted. And so they huddled like puppies in a basket for body warmth and generated mass excitement. But it was also mass imitation, almost to the point of protective coloring. The dancers functioned as a group, not for group purpose as in primitive rituals, but for group excitement, as in mobs.

This has lately been our jollity.

Bodies never lie. Therefore the truest expression of a people is in its dances and its music, its earth castings.

In the sixties and early seventies, the names of the steps were the Twist, the Horse, the Hully-Gully, the Dishrag, Jack-the-Ripper, the Mashed Potato, the Watusi, the Frug, the Boogaloo, the Bump (a version of the old Cockney favorite "One, two, three and boomps a 'daisy"), and the Kung Fu, a fighting dance between man and woman, an antecedent to punk rock, a sadistic pantomime in Halloween getup, involving eye-gouging, groin-kneeing, biting, hitting, and choking, reminiscent of the

ferocity of the 1913 Apache dances of Paris which heralded World War I. Punk rock is a frightening omen.

The recent beat has been African and chosen because it is African, not only by the blacks but by everyone. In following this cult, the whites repudiated their own traditions of organized pattern, of formal address, to copy a more primitive, a less evolved expression, precisely because it was less evolved. It was counterestablishment, counterhereditary, counterrule.

Our only indigenous steps, the only dances not imported (saving, of course, the Indians), have always been the dances of the blacks. Their influence (unlike that of the Indians) has impinged on the whites with ragtime, jazz, and blues. It proved overwhelming after World War I, when the vogue for Harlem and the Cotton Club captivated all youth. In the thirties it included Caribbean forms. Now again we were copying the black continent. We went back to the source, and all the world copied us. This was where the dynamics, the thrust, was manifest, not in our white heritage.

Like it or not, this is a fact. We can read the

weather. The dancing was solo, autoerotic, without discipline, manner, or style: a quite suitable expression for the time.

Quite plainly what all this meant was bewilderment as to direction, as to social function, even as to sex; the children were revenging themselves against order, against each other, against us. They were untrusting. They were alone and they were obviously desperate, since this is the dancing of fear. It spelled fragmentation of the moral fabric, a loss of family structure, religion, purpose, and belief, while ahead loomed, and still looms always, the undefined horror of annihilation, the atomic end.

And yet, not quite . . . not quite.

The signs are beginning to be different. For dances live. They change. Today in the discotheques, although the noise there is at full decibel, there begin to be real patterns, real steps, the recognition of partners, the need for friends, for neighbors; and when we call to neighbors, we leave the wilderness and step toward survival.

There are even square dances, many, many running sets, clogs, and reels, done in teams that compete for prizes and draw audiences of thousands. The old cry goes up:

Honor your partner.

Honor your corner.

All hands round and circle left.

And under the torture lights and dizzying electronics, gallantry raises its head.

Give your arm to your honey.

Give your arm to your sweetie.

Swing her once high, and swing her once low,

One, two, three, and away we go.

Then home again, back home, and let go.

3. EARLY BALLET

UNLIKE most civilized countries, early America had very little theater and no official support of the arts.

In seventeenth-century America there had been no theater at all and practically no music except hymns. The people were kept busy enough just staying alive, and their religion forbade frivolous pleasure, particularly theater. This was especially true in New England. Even social dancing was rigorously restricted. Increase Mather's *An Arrow against Profane and Promiscuous Dancing, Drawne out of the Quiver of the Scriptures* (by ("promiscuous" he meant dancing between men and women) condemned only dancing that aroused the passions. But the church fathers had long ago found that just holding hands did that, and what the Puritan preachers thought permissible for boys and girls would today not be considered fun. All theater was a trap of the devil, of "old ugly."

Furthermore, theater presupposes not only leisure but congregations of people. For the most part our communities were sparse and scattered.

What diversions there were were fairly savage: ducking, flogging, pillorying, tarring and feathering, or listening to hair-raising sermons on the tortures of hell. There was also for a time the trying and hanging of wizards and witches.

With the growth of cities during the eighteenth century, troupes of English players began to arrive and perform in New York, Philadelphia, Alexandria and even Boston. There was also French opera in New Orleans. George Washington, for example, was a great theatergoer.

Native dancing was, for the most part, displays of acrobatics or jigs, reels, and hornpipes. (Hornpipe is a generic term for a type of dance and it has nothing to do specifically with the sea, as is popularly supposed. The term derives from the musical accompaniment.) Finally, in the eighteenth century, there arrived in the colonies a troupe of ballet dancers and wire walkers, with one good French choreographer, Alexandre Placide (d. 1812). But they had to work with untrained native talent for choruses.

The best dancers, however, stayed in Europe. A trip across the Atlantic in those days was perilous and lengthy, and the financial rewards for performers in colonial America were negligible.

Teachers came, settling for the most part in

Philadelphia. They were at first French émigrés, trained at the Théâtre Royale de Musique et de la Danse, whose careers had been brought to an untimely halt by the French Revolution and the Napoleonic upsets. They had lost their audience because their patrons, the aristocrats, had lost their taste for dancing along with their heads. And they were welcomed in America because, after the American Revolution, the prejudice against English performers was understandably acute and lasted until well after the War of 1812.

But people will be entertained, and in the nineteenth century theater, even in this wilderness, began to develop. Traveling players took to the boards with Shakespeare and the standard European classics, giving performances wherever there was a platform and a row of benches. Families of native actors, like the Booths, became famous. There were soon good theaters in all the eastern cities, some with fine repertory companies. European stars then consented to brave the seas and the uncouth local manners; America was growing rich and could pay for treats.

Philadelphia became the leading theatrical city, surpassing even New York, with several theaters and regular seasons that included every kind of show: Shakespeare, musical extravaganzas, animal acts, pantomimes, acrobatic displays, and attempts at ballet and opera, frequently all on the same bill.

Since the beginning of the republic there had been sporadic attempts at producing grand opera, particularly in New Orleans. Philadelphia and New York now began to try the form with increasing frequency. But the greatest of the European divas, Maria Malibran (1808–1836) and Giulia Grisi (1811–1869), had to bring or form their own companies. Jenny Lind (1820–1887), the most famous singer of all, appeared only in concert. The opera productions and casts available obviously did not tempt her.

There were, outside of New Orleans, no lasting opera or ballet companies, no official lyric theaters or endowed schools. Every manager and teacher worked on his own. But they kept working. And they kept sending invitations abroad.

In Europe, especially Paris, once Napoleon was out of the way, extraordinary things had been happening. Opera dancing, which is what ballet used to be called, had developed into a fine art, quite on a par with bel canto. Maria Taglioni (1804–1884), the Italian-Swedish daughter of Filippo Taglioni (1777–1871), a pupil of Jean François Coulon and Auguste Vestris, internationally famous stars and dancing masters at the close of the eighteenth century, introduced a new style and technique and almost in one night became the most famous dancer in history. She debuted in Vienna in 1822 and in Paris at the Opéra in 1827.

Her personal style on stage was so exquisite that she changed the entire aspect of her art forever. Ballet dancing had taken to the air. She seemed all gauze and vapor, and she perfected the lovely trick of dancing on the ends of her toes. She was a great jumper, not in the brisk lively sense that Camargo (1710–1770), the eighteenth-century favorite of Louis XV had been, but as we know jumpers today—soaring, commanding, winged. All the critics speak of her enormous stride and her long horizontal leaps, or jetés; she could cross the Paris Opéra stage in three bounds. She could lift herself into the air and float with greater loveliness than any woman in recorded history.

"In all my movements I remained straight without strain," she was to write later. "You could not hear me descend, because it was always my toe which struck first, the heel following gently upon the ground." Her father swore that no one had ever heard her foot fall, and that if anyone ever did he would disown her.

"I adored all of those steps in which I experienced an elevation which kept me almost from feeling the earth. Literally I vibrated in the air. My hands and feet were spiritual," she said.

In order to dance on point, the arch had to be developed to support the weight of the body. This involved a new technique for the foot and a tremendous strengthening of the ankle, knee and back.

Taglioni and her contemporaries wore slippers without stiffening, as fragile as silk gloves, made of light strips of silk ribbon and weighing six ounces. She had support only from the darning of the toes and the binding of the ribbons around her ankles, and could therefore only mount to her toes for poses and take a few short steps on point. The sustained traveling steps and grinding pirouettes done today were not possible for the first point dancers.

Taglioni had a new pair of slippers for every act of her ballets. The stage of the opera house was purposely dirty to prevent slipping. Today, for the same reason, the floor is either wet lightly with a watering pot or dusted with rosin. Every stage has a rosin box in the corner. Slipping is the dancer's nightmare.

She dropped all weighty costumes, because she was really dancing, riding, striding the air, beating her legs like a hummingbird's wings, lighting and balancing on point. She discarded also the too revealing and often immodest tunic of the Empire period. In its place she had Lami design for her a special skirt of gauze that has become the standard ballet uniform. She parted her hair straight in the center and kept the curls and bun tight to her head; this also has become traditional. Her arms were ungainly and long. Her father taught her to cross her arms on her breast or hold them low with crossed wrists to keep them out of the way. This attempt to conceal what her teacher considered a defect influenced balletic style for the next seventy years.

But Maria Taglioni's contribution went beyond elevation and toe dancing, beyond style. She changed the performer's point of view and with it, of course, the audience's. She demonstrated that dancing could express something more than mere sensuous delight. Her quality was predominantly chaste and spiritual. Her father boasted that any gentleman could bring his wife to see her without blushing. The czar, unable to believe that her knees would remain invisible in her great soaring leaps, left the imperial box and went down into the stalls to see. Even from this vantage, she appeared modest and exquisite, her knees mysteriously not in view!

She took all Europe by storm with her indescribable mixture of artlessness and boldness. "She was," said the great actress Fanny Kemble, "like a dancing flower." Wherever she went, new ballet styles and techniques sprang up, even in the far and savage Russias.

This caliber of performer gave rise to the professional critic and the informed audience. The novelist Théophile Gautier (1811–1872) was an important early critic. From him and his newspaper friends, we have for the first time in the history of dancing contemporary critical descriptions by writers who are concerned with individual technique and performing style and who are trained to observe the differences.

There is much more material on the women than on the men because male dancers were despised, and while the critics were condescending even to the females, they found them attractive. They wrote as though they were making love to the ladies which, in fact, they very often were. This critical approach is no longer thought to be in good taste.

There suddenly appeared a rival, and the competition between these two great ladies became deadly. It was followed with excited curiosity even in America, a month away by steamship, by readers who had never seen anything but the hornpipe and the cakewalk and had no conception what dancers could be doing to cause such an uproar.

The newcomer was Fanny Elssler (1810–1884), a Viennese, the daughter of Joseph Haydn's copyist. She was a great beauty and a superb technician, and she resembled the eighteenth-century dancers in their voluptuous appeal. This was not surprising, for she had trained under the eighteenth-century star Auguste Vestris. She became famous for her stylized Andalusian and European folk dances as well as for her brilliant point work. She set the style, later followed by nearly all ballerinas, of including fancy versions of folk dances in repertory.

She was not a jumper like Taglioni, but a dancer *terre à terre*, brilliant, *taquetée*, with a style consisting of quick steps, precise, close together, and digging into the stage. Her points were marvelous, the beauty of her arms and hands unequaled. Gautier says : "She is the dancer for men as Mlle. Taglioni was the dancer for women." (Taglioni was neither dead nor retired; she was dancing at this time in Russia, and the use of the past tense represents a typically Parisian reproach for paying attention to any city but the French capital.) "Elssler has elegance, beauty, a bold and petulant vigor, a sparkling smile, an air of Spanish vivacity tempered by her German artlessness. Mlle. Taglioni is a Christian dancer. . . . Fanny is quite a pagan dancer. . . . She dances with the whole of her body, from the crown of her head to the tips of her toes. . . . It is not the aerial and virginal grace of Taglioni, it is something more human, more appealing to the senses. . . . At the tips of her

Mr. and Mrs. Conway, Miss Dublin performing at Park Theater. CREDIT: *Lithograph, 1827/The Dance Collection.*

rosy fingers ["too heavily rouged," said English critic Chorley of the weekly *Atheneum*] quiver ebony castenets; now she darts forward, the castenets begin their sonorous chatter. With her hands she seems to shake down great clusters of rhythm. How she twists! How she bends! What fire! What voluptuousness! What precision! Her swooning arms toss about her drooping head, her body curves backward, her white shoulders seem almost to graze the ground."

It was said by less enraptured critics that Elssler's Spanish dances were pallid beside the originals, but they were the only Spanish steps most of her audiences had ever seen. She ravished Paris. Chorley wrote: "If Mme. Taglioni flew, she (Elssler) flashed. The one floated onto the stage like a nymph, the other showered every sparkling fascination around her like a sorceress." Jules Janin (1804–1874) commented: "Elssler's steps are so finished, her dancing so correct, her feet so agile, that one wonders whether she really dances or is standing still."

All of this means, in simple language, that Taglioni was one of the lightest and most aerial dancers that ever trod the stage, that her manner was quiet and restrained, and that she was a limited actress. Elssler, on the other hand, had a supple back and brilliant feet, danced with enormous rhythm and verve, was a past mistress of dynamics, and used every trick of personality and coquetry at

her disposal. She obviously could not jump and never tried to, except once when, without much success, she attempted to follow Taglioni in the role of *La Sylphide.*

All the critics spoke of Elssler's acting powers. Gautier says flatly: "As a mime she is unrivaled."

Taglioni's version of her rival is different and somewhat ungenerous. "We owe the beginning of bad taste to the Elssler sisters . . . their joint efforts produced considerable effect; but one could not call this art."

But there were many other voices, and important ones, to the contrary.

In the meantime America was preparing a seedbed; America was getting ready.

In 1833 Lorenzo Da Ponte (1749–1838), Mozart's sometime librettist and later, among other things, a storekeeper in Elizabethtown, New Jersey, brought over an entire troupe of Italian singers and built an opera house for them in New York. Thereafter, there were regular opera performances and ballets in this theater. Here there had been from the beginning of the century steady ballet training under the French émigrés, and although they could not know the latest developments, notably Taglioni's point work and style, their teaching was sound. Reproduction of foreign works became the fashion, however inaccurately obtained, and bits and pieces of different ballets were inserted or taken out or interchanged at will.

The Park Theatre was adjacent to the City Hall Park between Park Row and Broadway. This was the hub of New York in the 1820s and 1830s. It burned down on May 24, 1827, was rebuilt, and burned down again in 1848, not to be rebuilt again. But while it lasted, the Park Theatre imported European dancers annually, as the National and Bowery did later.

In 1839 at the Park Theatre, Maria Taglioni's brother Paul (1808–1884) and his German wife, Amalia (1801–1884), danced most of the works that Paul's father had created for Maria. Everyone hastened to copy them. The local dancers must have sat wide-eyed.

That same year, Jean Petipa and his son, Marius (1822–1910), the future great choreographer, followed.

Paul and Amalie Taglioni, Berlin, 1828. Paul Taglioni was the younger brother of Marie and, like his father Filippo Taglioni, an able choreographer and dancer. But unlike his father and his illustrious contemporary, Perrot, he set no style, choosing to follow in distinguished footsteps carefully and exactly. He made a real hit in his New York visits but returned to Vienna, Paris, and Berlin with evident relief, where he did routine work with great success. His German wife, Amalie, was a charming dancer and highly successful in her New York appearances, but on returning home, she faded into anonymity when brought into competition with her blazing rivals Grisi, Grahn, Elssler, Cerrito, and Duvermay. CREDIT: *Kruger/Berlin National Galleries.*

Marie Paul Taglioni in the Mazurka from *La Gitana*. Marie Paul was the daughter of Paul and Amalie Taglioni. CREDIT: *Music cover by N. Currier/The Dance Collection.*

In the end, all of these proud, distinguished visitors, Paul Taglioni and his wife, and the two Petipas, father and son, as well as the famous French dancer and choreographer Joseph Mazilier (1797–1868), went home, disgruntled, having found neither companies nor audiences to their satisfaction. But no matter how personally disappointed they felt, they had done something; they had paved the way for Fanny Elssler, an

Fanny Elssler in her dressing room on an American tour. This portrait shows the wonderful development of her foot and arch. Elssler was the daughter of Joseph Haydn's copyist. CREDIT: *The Dance Collection.*

achievement, no doubt, quite outside their original intent.

In 1840 the United States was ready for a star. There were enough students to watch with understanding and enough dancers to fill out a company. At least one young dancer was waiting for Elssler with agile legs and hungry eyes. He was George Washington Smith (1820–1899), our first great male ballet star. He had up to then performed ballets remembered by his teacher, Hazard, from his own days at the Paris Opéra. Smith excelled in many styles and was an able actor and pantomimist in the classic English tradition, having studied the harlequin attitudes from the great English clown James Byrne of Drury Lane. He joined Edwin Booth's company, playing bits and dancing hornpipes between the acts of *Hamlet.* An idea of his technical ability can be grasped from the fact that he often and easily performed the *entrechat dix* and was a master of triple turns in the air.

Elssler came to America out of pure greed. But she earned her money. She brought eight full ballets and a number of her most famous variations (short dances). She brought an Irishman, James Sylvain (né Sullivan), as partner and regisseur, and several solists. She added the best American performers she could find, Julia Turnbull and George Washington Smith among others, and recruited local talent to fill out the corps. She turned them over to her Irishman to be whipped into shape, sometimes in only a matter of hours.

The costumes were usually rented and had little to do with each other. But so starved for beauty were the audiences and so devoid of grounds for comparison that they would rise in a mass and stamp and call out their grateful amazement. They took the horses from her carriage and pulled her through the streets to her hotel, a performance that was duplicated by United States senators when she danced in Washington. Indeed, Congress was forced to recess for want of a quorum on the nights she performed.

American artists and intellectuals, even such austere and nontheatrical people as Margaret Fuller and Ralph Waldo Emerson, were deeply impressed. "This is poetry," breathed Miss Fuller in awe. "This is religion," Emerson replied. Who could have thought a dancer in a rose satin skirt could have provoked such a remark from a New England philosopher?

Elssler went home very happy and very, very, rich. She was guaranteed $500 per performance (the equivalent today of $9,000), a vast sum in those days, and she toured quite steadily for two years. There were then no income taxes. She could

Fanny Elssler. CREDIT: *The Dance Collection.*

keep and enjoy every penny she earned. She left behind enduring and fruitful impressions.

As with any colonial nation (and, though independent politically, we believed ourselves still children in the arts), our entire artistic energy went into copying European achievements. There was no true creativity in our theater. Mary Ann Lee, who had been to Paris to study, reproduced *Giselle* and several more of the great ballets. She worked entirely from memory, so they may not have been exact, but she did bring back the scores and the scenarios, as well as the style and many of the steps. Both Mary Ann Lee and George Washington Smith had memorized all the dances and ballets Elssler had performed here.

Young Smith seems to have been an expert at

Augusta Maywood, 1852. CREDIT: *1852 Lithograph/ The Dance Collection.*

George Washington Smith. This photograph was made in the earliest days of photography and the exposure required at least three minutes of immobility to make a good image. The braces used to support his arms can be seen distorting the sleeves of his jacket. CREDIT: *The Dance Collection.*

the carpentry of ballets, and while he never developed any great originality, his skill at manipulating and adapting was to serve visiting Europeans to good effect.

Smith became, with time, sufficiently versatile to partner every great female star who came to America for the next fifty years, including several leading Spanish dancers, Pepita Soto among others.

Augusta Maywood (1825–1879), was perhaps the greatest American virtuoso of her day. At the age of thirteen she left Philadelphia for Paris to study at the Opéra under Mazilier and Coralli (1779–1854). She made her debut there at the age of fifteen. She was an immediate hit and went on from glory to glory, being compared to, and ranked with, Fanny Elssler, Fanny Cerrito (1817–

1909), Lucile Grahn (1819–1907), and Carlotta Grisi (1819–1899), even in their own great roles. Important works were created for her. She performed as ballerina in most of the European opera houses and was partnered by the greatest male dancers. She settled at last in Italy, starring at La Scala for years and touring the country with her own splendid little troupe, the first traveling ballet company. She was probably our first true ballerina, but she performed entirely in Europe, never returning to America.

Her technique was apparently prodigious; her jumps, entrechats, and pirouettes were compared to those of male stars like Perrot (1811–1892). She was also vivacious and an excellent actress.

"Abrupt, unexpected, bizarre . . . sinews of steel, joints of a jaguar, and an agility approaching that of clowns . . . In two or three bounds, she cleared this great theater from backdrop to prompter's box, making those almost horizontal bal pénches which made the fame of Perrot the Aeriel; and then she began to gambol, to turn in the air against herself. You would have said a rubber ball bouncing on a racquet she has such elevation and spring; her little legs of a wild doe make steps as long as those of Mlle. Taglioni," wrote Gautier in 1839.

But Augusta Maywood was exceptional in not touring America. For after Elssler, the European parade was on. Any dancer who had a year to spare and was not doing too well at home hurried over. Ballet reached its peak here in the late 1850s. But although many notables visited us, including the troupe of Dominico Ronzani (1800–1868; later the leading choreographer at La Scala), all their efforts came to nothing in the way of provoking a permanent opera or ballet in the New World.

Ballet as it was practiced in Europe was not a natural American means of expression any more than grand opera was. We did not have the houses or institutions for it, or the state schools or the government patronage, and therefore we did not have the means of cultivating public taste.

There has always been in the United States a breach between the so-called highbrow, or artistic, dancers and popular entertainers.

During and after the Civil War there were financial panics that cut all theater attendance drastically, but the real trouble with native ballet lay principally with the artists, who were often of poor quality. Although George Washington Smith and his colleagues strove mightily to maintain the standards of the great days, it was to no avail. Ballet did not take root here and flourish. It faded and cheapened. The audience became aware of this and stopped attending. Fancy flyway dancing was not for us.

We kept on from habit buying European talent to satisfy our snobbishness. But the paying public forms no habits—or none it will not readily break—and it stopped liking ballet, in spite of such temporary excitements as *The Black Crook* (1866), an enormously successful extravaganza performed with a full complement of dancers headed by two Italians, Maria Bonfanti (1840–1921) and Rita Sangalli (1851–1909).

Bonfanti was a pupil of Carlo Blasis (1797–1878), the great Italian dancing master who preserved the classic school of Taglioni and Elssler. Bonfanti herself seems to have been an exquisite though cool dancer, not relying on point work for effect and feeble with jumps and beats, but remarkably graceful and tasteful. For this reason she stood out among her athletic competitors.

The success of the great New York musicals, however, was due as much to the remarkable scenery, the marching Amazons in tights, the flying fairies on wires (aerial dancing was a whole technique in itself) and the parades of pygmies (children) as it was to any genuine dancing or choreography. Especially notable was an 1869 spectacle called *The Forty Thieves, or Stealing Oil in Family Jars,* "in which a formation of forty females put cigarettes in their mouths, lifted one foot, struck matches on their heels, and lit their forty cigarettes."*

This is perhaps the place to note that the accident rate and mortality among young dancers was tragically high. Girls caught and tangled in or dropped from wires, smashed or mangled in trapdoors and flying scenery, burnt or hopelessly scarred in the gas flames numbered in the hundreds. There was no legal redress or protection by insurance. These were the hazards of the trade, and the dancers took their chances. Moreover, the pay was beneath subsistence, and out of their paltry stipends the poor little things had to furnish their own cos-

* Barbara Barker—Doctoral thesis 1980.

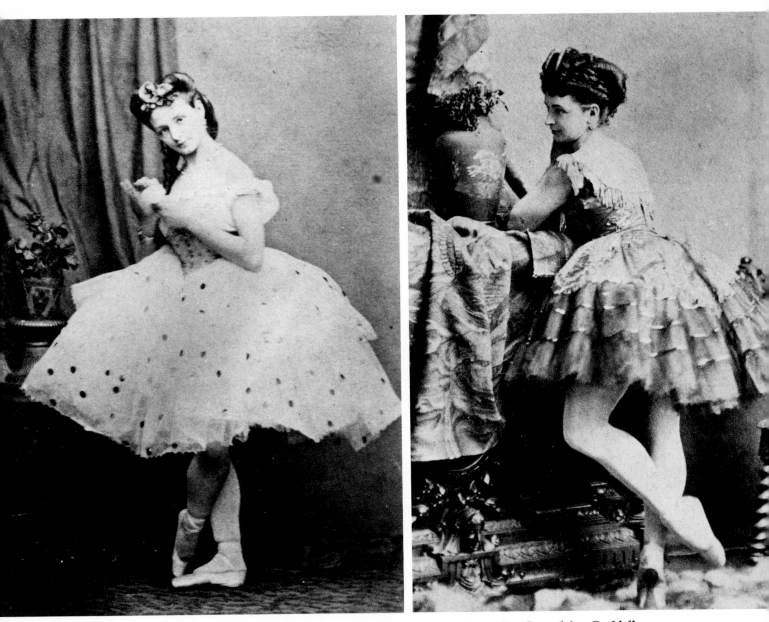

Maria Bonfanti. CREDIT: *Courtesy of her granddaughter, Mrs. Gwendolyn Ruddell.*

tumes and maintain them. To make matters worse, there was a total sense of dishonor and degradation attached to the business.

In 1869 the Transcontinental Railway was completed. The two great lengths of track were joined up and in Summit, Utah, the golden spike was driven into place with full ceremony. The trains could now go without great gaps of stage-coach travel between locations and the way was clear for ballet dancers, rascals and other riffraff to journey to the West and bring culture to the honest folk digging the plains and the mountains out

there. The dancers who went out at that time were intrepid and faced every possible kind of danger and discomfort. How they managed to pull the curtain up on anything is a marvel to think about since in many places there were no accommodations of any sort, either for themselves and the people they had to make use of in their arduous travels or for their work.

Bonfanti and Sangalli and the Ronzani troupes and Morlacchi (1843–1886) stalwartly toured the South and the West, penetrating places that had been inaccessible before the opening of the Transcontinental Railway. And they worked prodigies. They carried with them only a token group of dancers and musicians and recruited what they needed where they happened to find themselves. In some cases they had to resort to brothels and whorehouses to get women who were willing to appear on the stage with them in tights, since "good women" refused. (One bordello owner in Omaha forced his whores to sit on the lawn in rocking chairs dressed in ballet skirts as advertisement.) The ballerinas had to carry all their props and music with them as well as their costumes. Bonfanti carried twelve dozen ballet slippers made in Paris for her and bolts and bolts of gauze and tarlatan

Loüret de Ducale, Pedestal Clog Dancer, in *The Black Crook*, Niblo's Garden, New York, 1886. CREDIT: *The Agnes de Mille Collection.*

Stalacta's Grotto. This was one of the great transformation scenes in the second act of *The Black Crook* in which the entire visual image changed before the eyes of the beholder. This was accomplished by depth on depth of stage and many layers of scenery, finely cut-out effects mounted on gauze, and carefully hidden gaslights. CREDIT: *The Harvard Theatre Collection.*

which was not procurable in rugged, out-of-the-way places. Ballet skirts were not then made of nylon but of tarlatan and fine net which wilted very quickly and had to be replaced after two or three performances. But she and the others were successes because somehow, under these strenuous and exacting circumstances, she managed to maintain style, grace and an aura of ethereal nobility. The rest of the performance was given over to blatant spectacle and was, one can imagine, patently shabbier the farther west the troupe traveled. But she must have made a certain lasting impression, because Rita Sangalli followed her to the same mining town some time later and was given a gold brick as a token of appreciation. "The miners were," writes Barbara Barker in her biography of Bonfanti "nonplussed." All the other guests were showered not with bouquets, of which the miners and cattle rustlers had none and knew nothing, but gold nuggets and handfuls of gold dust, which they said was hard on the eyes and difficult to get out of their hair. On her return to Paris, Sangalli gave picturesque interviews about her adventures in the West. Unhampered by the truth, they sounded as though they had come from the pen of Merrimé. She carried little of the necessities of life, she said, but she always carried a gun to "protect her girls from the savages."

Giuseppina Morlacchi (1843–1886), another of the intrepids, was a pupil of Augusta Maywood in Milan and so had naturally heard a good bit about America. She became the beloved of New York and had a sizable reputation in Europe and the East, but she left it for a decade of frontier dancing and cut quite a swathe in Texas. She married Texas Jack, the Indian fighter, whom she met in a road show and retired a rich and beloved widow to Billerica, Massachusetts, where she died at forty-three.

These young women were valiant not only in physical courage, but in persistent, daily arduousness. These young, beautiful and foreign women with their very strange troupes appeared like passing meteors from time to time, but as they were not followed up by any consistent teaching, although they may have been remembered personally, their art was lost in myth.

Grand opera had been housed always in New

The proscenium, stage, and gold curtain of the Metropolitan Opera House when it was at Broadway and 39th Street, New York City. CREDIT: *The Granger Collection.*

York within the Park Theatre, which was burned down in 1827, rebuilt, to be burned again in 1848. Opera then moved to the Academy of Music on the north side of Fourteenth Street (not to be confused with the variety house of that name which still stands on the south side). This old Academy was eventually demolished, not for the usual reasons of fire, but because of failure. It had been situated just off Fourteenth Street on Irving Place and was replaced by the Con Ed Building, which used to be called a skyscraper. The new Metropolitan Opera House opened in 1883, its first ballerina Malvina Cavalazzi (1863–1924), former prima ballerina at La Scala.

The new Metropolitan Opera House was situated way uptown, at Thirty-ninth Street and Broadway, north of the proper theatrical district. Its splendid, festive opening marked the end of the Academy of Music, which had been managed by Colonel Mapleson, who had the remarkably bad sense to schedule his season's opening on the opening night of the new, dazzling opera house. Mapleson's theater failed as a result. "You can't beat Wall Street," he was heard muttering. How true!

Very few of the great, old theaters have survived. Most have burned down. The gas and candlelight illumination and the great quantities of canvas, wood and flimsy costumes were spark and tinder together. Only a half-dozen date back to the eighteenth century, among them, the theater in Dröthingholm near Stockholm and the Fenice in Venice and the Palace Theatres built of marble. The Fenice is the only currently operating theater. In the United States we have lost all of the old theaters. Nearly the last great one to go was Ford's Opera House in Baltimore. But this was not lost to fire, this was the victim of demolition and greed. The superb new Metropolitan Opera House, which replaced the Academy of Music in its city functions, fell victim to greed in 1966, when it was wantonly and willfully destroyed by the Metropolitan Opera House Board in order to erect a large business edifice for income. The city lost its finest auditorium and beautiful stage, for the Met, whatever its drawbacks, did have the best and most

beautiful auditorium in America. It got in replacement a somewhat vulgar, very large, rather cold, and in many ways quite unsatisfactory building in Lincoln Center at Sixty-third and Broadway. The new theater is certainly more practical, that cannot be denied, but it lacks the absolute essential of being glamorous, being welcoming, and being conducive to excitement and delight.

Unfortunately, the old Metropolitan Company was established in the period of balletic decline. Its only avowed purpose was to bring great dramatic and vocal music to New York; it had no such intentions about dancing. At that time ballet throughout Europe was in very poor order. Furthermore, unlike all European lyric theaters, the Metropolitan inherited no traditional school to sustain the old ideals. Everything had to be imported, works and performers. In the way of music there was much to import: Mozart, Donizetti, Verdi, Wagner, Puc-

Metropolitan Opera House Opera Ballet corps in rehearsal, 1900. CREDIT: *Byron/Theater Collection of the Museum of the City of New York.*

Rosina Galli, prima ballerina and adored star who later married Julio Gatti Cazazzo, the impresario of the Metropolitan Opera. CREDIT: *Dupont, Theater Magazine/The Agnes de Mille Collection.*

cini, Gounod, Bizet, and Boito. But although the opera dance had by no means kept pace with the opera music, the Metropolitan as a matter of routine included ballet in its plans. The managers, however, had no hopes of anything special in the way of dancing, and in fact they saw no need for it, so the general atmosphere and style remained regrettable. The great dancing days in America had occurred outside this particular opera company. The Metropolitan felt no responsibility comparable to that carried by, for instance, the Paris Opéra, or Le Théatre Royale de Musique et de la Danse. (Please note the equality implied in the title.)

The most famous European dancing stars here went to theaters other than the opera, to the commercial Broadway houses. Nevertheless, ballets of sorts were devised and given at the Metropolitan, and at last a school was established in a half-hearted way. Not that the dancers and teachers were halfhearted; they did their best, but they ranked low in the hierarchy.

It looked as though America had no wish for good dancing. But this was not true. America's own kind of dancing was developing elsewhere, in barrooms, tents, and low-grade theaters, but for one hundred years these innovations made no impression at all on the ballet-minded snobs.

4. POPULAR THEATER BEFORE 1900

OUR talent makes itself known in rebellion against old forms (for we are a country of revolutionaries) and in the development of new and unexpected ones.

It is chiefly from the United States that the new impulses in dancing have come—jazz and the modern dance. Both were discovered, not with pride or ease, but in spite of neglect and ridicule. Both are the products of nonconforming viewpoints and an independent will to survive.

While our ballet enthusiasts were struggling to engraft the court and opera ballet on a semirustic republican community, native dance grew up and took over. Straight off the plantation and into the saloons, dance halls, tent shows, and common theaters went this exuberant, superb, and brilliant entertainment. Whatever place gave foot room to blacks banished from more polite surroundings, there they danced. They didn't think or theorize. They danced. And if they didn't dance pleasingly, not to say astonishingly, they didn't get their supper.

Here, and in the Negro minstrel shows, was the true American pep, creativity, and fun, shut off from all that was refined or honored. This dancing had no pretensions. It was simply ours, and it appealed to everyone. The great Juba (born William Henry Lane, 1825–1852), a black boy of nineteen, became in 1845 the world's champion in a face-to-face knockdown competition with his toughest rival. Charles Dickens, in his *American Notes* (1841–42) described the style.

> Single shuffle, double shuffle, cut and crosscut: snapping his fingers, rolling his eyes, turning in his knees, presenting the backs of his legs in front, spinning about on his toes and heels like nothing but the man's fingers on the tambourine; dancing with two left legs, two right legs, two wooden legs, two wire legs, two spring legs—all sorts of legs and no legs. What is this to him? And in what walk of life, or dance of life does man ever get such stimulating applause as thunders about him, when, having danced his partner off her feet, and himself too, he finishes by leaping gloriously on the barcounter, and calling for something to drink, with the chuckle of a million counterfeit Jim Crows in one inimitable sound?

Juba invented and perfected his own steps and in 1848 took them to London, where he made

The great "Juba" (William Henry Lane), 1841.
CREDIT: *The Harvard Theater Collection.*

an international reputation with his unprecedented skill and his laugh.

All the critics mention his laugh. This was a new sound in the theater. The opera houses did not encourage laughing corps de ballets. It seemed the blacks had thrown away, with other restraints, the dancer's mask.

But this was an illusion. The laughter itself was a mask. A sad black was not tolerated in the theater, nor a light-skinned one; white men performing as them had to black up with soot, and mulattoes and octoroons likewise darkened their skins to coal-black, made themselves into shiny tarboys with enormous grotesque lips and kinky wigs that could be made mechanically to stand on end. It was a real clown getup, and Juba's great laugh, which came from the heart of his genius, was transformed into a trademark. A hundred years were to pass before black artists like Katherine Dunham, Janet Collins, Carmen de Lavallade or Judith Jamison would be permitted to stop laughing and to express sadness, or wistfulness, or despair. Up to that point the black entertainer was tolerated in public only if he was jolly or comic. But Juba and all the people who followed him, together with

The Ethiopian Serenaders. CREDIT: *The Agnes de Mille Collection.*

The Cakewalk, a native dance always extremely popular, belonged to the blacks and to their entertainers. It was universally copied. CREDIT: *Watercolor, © 1980, Albert Meyers/Collection, the Museum of Modern Art, New York.*

Horace Weston, c. 1855. CREDIT: *The Agnes de Mille Collection.*

and Bill "Bojangles" Robinson, Peg Leg Bates, Fred Astaire, Ray Bolger, Gene Kelly, Paul Draper, and Honi Coles. The great stars in this field, as opposed to ballet, have almost all been men. Tapping and jazz are essentially a male form of dancing. Furthermore, the stigma attached to male dancing in the United States has never at any time related to this form.

During waxings and wanings of ballet popularity, through all the phases of two hundred years of theater, the popular entertainments persisted—the clowns, the acrobats, and the cafe and vaudeville dancers. These follow an old tradition. They invent new surprises when they can. But they tend to be cautious. Whatever they think of must be tested right away on an audience that stands no nonsense. There are no endowments for them. Few great works, therefore, come out of this theater, few works that last beyond the lifetime of the performers, but there is always vitality and clarity and presence. And there is never any great bother about making or breaking rules. Here there is one rule: Don't be a bore.

The tradition of the clowns and jesters begins with the ancient totem animal dances, continues through the Greek and Roman theaters (in satyrs, spirits, servants, and common or weak mortals), through the devils of the medieval mysteries, to the great pantomime clowns and improvisations of the Commedia dell' Arte. These people were not dancers proper, but they worked with music and stylized gesture. They worked alongside dancers. They were the link between the high theater, opera and tragedy, and the common people—a sort of leavening. Today they survive in circuses, popular musical theaters, movies, and TV.

They usually wear a grotesque and individual makeup, the mark of their own personality, and they seldom vary it. Costume and painted face become a mask through which they function. This unchanging disguise constitutes, as the critic Walter Kerr once wrote in a *New York Herald Tribune* essay:

> . . . what all honest theater men have been trying to achieve since the wholly rigid mask was formally dropped. They offer us a vision of both the man and the mask in the same, or nearly the

their music, were recognized universally as exponents of our most characteristic theater expression.

Some of their great followers developed an enormous body of technique, a remarkable handling of rhythm and posture, and a kind of surprising humor, an impertinence, and above all a physical exuberance, a hell-for-leather joy, that was deep-down, through-and-through American. "Jim Crow" Rice, whose limp in Rocking de Heel started a vogue; two blackface artists of the seventies, Dan Bryant, who tapped slowly, and George F. More, who invented softshoe; the unknowns who gave us the essence, the sand dance, the buck-and-wing, and the pedestal dance; Harry Bolger, who invented slap-shoe; Eddie Foy, who invented the hand dance; Eddie Horan, who invented the cane dance;

Some famous clowns. CREDIT: *The Agnes de Mille Collection.*

same, instant. The private, personal soul is made visible; but over it and across it like light reflected in a windowpane shimmers the universal grimace, the grimace of common terror or common joy that links so many unique and lonely figures in a vast and universal chain. The one and the many are on top in a single, blinding rush of energy, implying one another, reinforcing one another.

The great clowns of the last hundred and fifty years, mostly men, have been deeply loved by multitudes all over the world. Many of them have become millionaires. They have in time influenced the dancers and musicians in the great opera houses. Many a "stunt," succeessful in the "halls," has become an "effect" in the opera.

This, then, was the state of dancing at the turn of the century—lively fun in the flourishing commercial halls; decadent, repetitious, and withered in the opera houses—until one woman came along to change history.

5.
ISADORA DUNCAN

AT the turn of the century Isadora Duncan (1878–1927), a San Francisco girl who believed that dance was heading up a blind alley, threw off her corsets and her shoes and danced barefoot across Europe. Her effect on contemporaries and successors is incalcuable.

Before Isadora, dancing was not considered important or dignified except to the people who practiced it. After her, it was. This is her major contribution. It seems a simple fact to state, but I suppose, in point of historical significance, no one except Chaucer or Dante worked single-handedly such an astonishing change in the popular reception of an art.

Isadora left only scattered short works. What we inherit is a point of view, an orientation, a tradition of glory in a field long soiled and shabby. For Isadora considered dancing on a par with religion, considered it what it historically is, the mother of the arts; and since she was herself an artist hailed by the greatest of her time, her ideas took on the force of prophecy. The change of status amounted very nearly to a revolution in moral values. She believed herself in touch with the divine when she danced.

She did not, as is popularly supposed, discover a new type of dance or even revive an ancient one. Her style has been called Greek because she chose to wear simple Greek tunics and silk scarves and referred always, when speaking, to classical sources. But her idiom was no more Greek than anything else. It was her own personal form of expression, and for this reason it has not proved lasting, except as an influence. She invented no steps.

She did not evolve her great style entirely without precedent. François Delsarte (1811–1871) had analyzed the gestures and postures of the body for expression just as musicians had analyzed voice and speech; Emile Jacques Dalcroze (1865–1950) had related movement to rhythm scientifically; and a century of pantomime and posturings in imitation of great paintings and statues had preceded her, beginning with Sarah Siddons (1755–1831), and Emma Lady Hamilton (1761–1815), and Henrietta Hendel (1772–1849) and involving very nearly every aesthetically inclined lady at the great nineteenth-century house parties. Duncan went on from there.

Although ballet dancing had become corrupt,

Emma, Lady Hamilton (Emma Hart) was the mistress and favorite model of the great English painter, George Romney. She later married Sir William Hamilton and went with him to Naples, Italy, where she met and fell in love with Admiral Nelson. They had one of the most famous love affairs in history. The length of her hair in these pictures is no exaggeration. CREDIT: *The Agnes de Mille Collection.*

she cleared the theater of the accumulated debris of six hundred years of artificiality. She left it, if unintentionally (she had hoped to destroy it utterly), honest and meaningful. She believed dancing should be harmonious and simple, that is, stripped of all needless ornamentation.

She rediscovered the normal human walk, the run, the easy natural spring and jump, the emotional use of head and arms and hands. Her basic theory was that all movement derives from simple walk-

ing, running, skipping, jumping, and standing. She believed that these movements could be exciting and satisfying in themselves, without distortion, without the turning out of legs and the pointing of toes and the holding of arms in symmetrical, rounded ballet positions. She said all movement should be examined for purity and strength, that to be merely traditional meant nothing. She reminded us that we Americans come from a democratic country with a free point of view and should

bow to nothing but our own ideal of beauty.

She cleared away square miles of painted scenery. Under her championship simple architectural forms, curtains, and lights became important. She swept away all fancy and ornate costumes. Simplicity, which means a choice of what is absolutely essential, returned. Where spectacle had been all-powerful, imagination, evocation, and symbolism, as the Orientals and ancients used them, returned. She got rid of the awful linoleum music that had dragged on ballet for a century— Adam, Minkus, Pugni, Drigo. Isadora danced to Gluck, Beethoven, Schubert, Chopin. Musicians were at first shocked, but she went right on until she convinced them. She got rid of the pastry ballet plots. Hitherto ballet had been about princes with

peculiar relations to their mothers! Or birds! Or dead girls with grudges! Isadora turned to classical Greek mythology for her subjects, not in the spirit of masquerades with the vanity of the French kings, but as believingly and humbly as the ancients did. She scorned the late-nineteenth-century attitude that a dancing career was merely a contest in acrobatic tricks.

She brought the foot once more into contact with the earth—the bare foot. There was more controversy about Isadora's bare feet in 1900 than there was about bare genitals in the 1970s. It was, as a matter of fact, the first naked foot seen on the Western stage in sixteen hundred years. (Eighteenth- and nineteenth-century prints of barefooted actresses and dancers are misleading. The girls

Isadora Duncan. CREDIT: *Theater Magazine/The Agnes de Mille Collection.*

But it is good for us to examine the style of any art from time to time and discard what has grown lifeless. Isadora was like a broom. She worked the briskest theater-sweeping the theater world has ever seen.

There were two unusual characteristics to her dancing—one, her use of time: she allowed enough time for the development of a theme or idea; and two, a total lack of virtuosity. In this she was unique.

Her greatest technical contribution—her personal performance—tends to be forgotten because it cannot be copied. She had the gift of revelation and worked on the audience spontaneously. The technique of improvisation has today all but disappeared, but in the last two centuries it was practiced extensively. Great orators used it. And musical cadenzas were usually left to the discretion of the performer; in fact, when the performer was also the composer, they were frequently invented on the spot (always the case with Beethoven). A substantial part of the training of organists has always been improvisation. But now only a few old vaudevillians and comedians dare perform as the spirit moves them. (What a phrase— "as the spirit moves them"!) Isadora did not usually improvise, but she could and did so on unforgettable occasions.

The lack of modesty and humor in her quoted remarks and in her book, the lack of moderation or humor in her life have elicited from the first an easy sort of ridicule from the unconvinced. Isadora dealt in absolutes. She knew she was beating against congealed prejudice, and any hesitation or diffidence, had she been capable of feeling them, would have been taken as a confession of weakness in the art itself. She admitted no weakness. Dancing to her was a spiritual communication, and before the lift of her head and the summoning of her arms, people, even the prim and the scoffing, little by little fell silent, as before her courageous and vigorous life.

In many ways she was as controversial and arresting a figure as George Sand, but without the balance or intellectual power of that great woman. Her courage was as fierce, however, her spirit as independent, and her voice as clamorous. She spoke out on marriage laws, sex, the rearing of children, prenatal influence, astrology, reincarnation, child-

actually were always in silk tights and usually wore slippers or silk sandals. The one exception was Henrietta Hendel.) Isadora bared the limbs so that we might see, not so much the naked body, but revealed emotion. She rediscovered spontaneity and individual passion. She did to her art what Luther did to the medieval church: she questioned it.

But in throwing away both distortions and formal technique, she dismissed what no art can endure long without. Distortion is a kind of preservative; like the mask, it covers naked sentiment and bare personality and makes emotion communicable and lasting. It is only when it is practiced for its own sake that it cancels emotion.

birth, clothes, diet, government, vaccination, education, and, of course, art in all manifestations. Her pronouncements were an impartial mixture of wisdom and poppycock, all delivered with conviction and all calculated to attract considerable attention. Only a portion of what she said made sense, but due to the range she covered and the violence with which she attempted to prove her beliefs, her influence is felt even today in many fields besides dancing.

Since her time there have been good dancers and bad dancers, but dancing per se has not been considered as it was before, a theatrical entertainment of inferior order, at best frivolous and diverting, at worst an adjunct to prostitution. She made possible the work and the recognition of such originals as Ruth St. Denis, Martha Graham, Mary Wigman, and Doris Humphrey, as well as the ballet renovators Michel Fokine, George Balanchine, and Antony Tudor, and the performers Anna Pavlova, Vaslav Nijinsky, and Tamara Karsavina. After her came the Diaghilev repertoire, Pavlova's *Swan* and *Bacchanal*, and the whole school of Middle European dance. The body of educated,

Isadora Duncan in Schubert's *Unfinished Symphony*. CREDIT: *Arnold Genthe, 1916/The Dance Collection.*

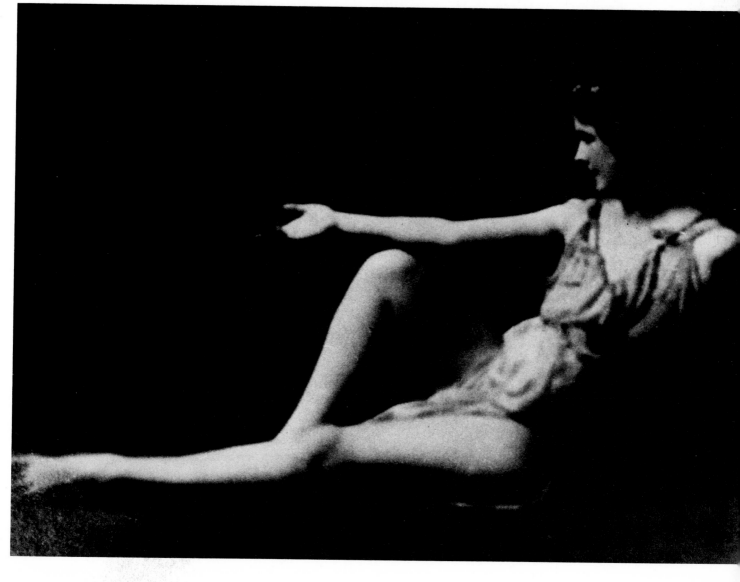

devoted, intelligent choreographers, mainly women, who have given their lives to finding new ways of moving come, not before, but after her.

Isadora opened up the dance to serious artists. Certainly she opened it, in fact, to all women. She believed that dancing was proper for everyone, regardless of class or social standing. Now women of probity and intellect began to join the profession.

Isadora Duncan. CREDIT: *Abraham Walkowitz/The Sid Deutsch Gallery.*

She believed that anyone at all could dance if she or he chose, and that everyone should so choose. What was chiefly wanted, she urged, was a spiritual rather than a physical preparation and no special technique to speak of. Off with the shoes, down with self-criticism, and away to the strains of Schubert. This was artistically a dangerous point of view and one that led to unpleasant excesses—bevies of gamboling young ladies in cheesecloth who were such a nuisance in our grandmothers' day and who did more to confuse Duncan's issues than anything else. A whole generation of men grew up loathing dancing because of their sisters' nonsense. A whole generation of women believed they were artists when they were nothing of the sort. Isadora did not promise that they could readily be the artist that she herself was. In fact, she did not imagine any other dancer could be. Rather she thought the experience of dancing was an emotional tonic and therefore desirable. She appeared at the turn of the century, when there was beginning to be felt a worldwide interest in bettering women's position, in giving them the vote, as Emily Pankhurst urged, in permitting them to hold public office, in opening to them careers in medicine and law, in guaranteeing them legal rights to and control over their children, in permitting them to handle their own money. Isadora talked to a rising tide of interest and conviction. This was the time of the militant suffragettes in England, the time of Shaw and Ibsen and their young, aggressive heroines.

She changed women's clothes. A strong general movement had started in Scandinavia for more sensible dress and physical culture. Duncan rode this bandwagon to international publicity. She cried out against corsets, petticoats, buttonboots, feathered hats, false hair, heavy skirts, and high-heeled shoes. Many women were in similar open protest, including several famous and fashionable dancers like Irene Castle, but Isadora cried the loudest and most publicly. The clothes she advocated made possible modern sports for women, and this meant a great improvement in women's health and childbearing capacity. The sweater girl, free-walking, free-running, naked in bathing, and brown in the sun, is Isadora's bequest.

She preached the basics. Dress sensibly. Move freely. Keep healthy. Consider yourself no one's slave—not even your husband's. Express your emotions deeply and freely in art.

No wonder women were excited by what she said. No wonder they cheered and threw flowers whenever she danced.

She lived a foolhardy, daredevil, bold, and gallant existence. She was an outlaw, a kind of emotional commando. Her way of life took into account no domination—family, friends, loves, or colleagues. She traveled alone, and she questioned every single tradition—artistic, social, religious, and moral—and tested them out for us on her own bleeding spirit.

In the end the wildness, the delirium of her ways, and her loneliness destroyed her. She drank heavily. She was exhausted by melancholy and

The Isadorables—Lisa, Anna, and Irma Duncan, 1916. CREDIT: *Arnold Genthe, 1916/The Dance Collection.*

despair. She made attempts at suicide. She was poor, and she squandered in daft compulsions the money raised by friends.

Her death was just of this pattern. *"Adieu, mes amis,"* she said as she climbed into an automobile on a fine evening in Nice. *"Je vais à la gloire."* Her long scarf caught in one of the wheels, and movement of the car suddenly tautened the silk and broke her neck. It was a questionable jaunt she was off on that evening, with someone nameless she had picked up at a third-rate café. *"Je vais à la gloire."* What a consuming, what a wild, incautious, sacrificial expending of strength and resources!

Like a bacchante, Isadora gave no thought for the morrow but threw herself upon the moment and counted exhaltation return enough. She walked her own high path alone, and the wonder of it burns still with a passion beyond ridicule, beyond censure. She is a great legend, and we live by our legends.

She died a relatively young woman, 48, but she left disciples and pupils all over Europe and America. Her adopted daughters—Anna, Lise, Margot, Erica, Theresa, and Irma—carried on her work, but in fact all the dancers who came after are, in a sense, her children.

6.
EARLY REVOLUTIONARIES

RUTH ST. DENIS (1877–1968), who began a few years after Isadora Duncan, performed reproductions of the religious dances of India. She invented little, but she brought to the West poetic and moving examples of an ancient art. She also reminded people that men had once danced for religious purposes, and moreover that in large sections of the world many still did.

These were the first more or less authentic Eastern dances the West had seen. Before this, Oriental dancing, with the undulating hips, vibrating shoulders, and wiggling arms of partly naked dancers (bare stomach and ribs in the case of women, and often bare feet, bare torso in the case of men), had seemed highly improper to many in the United States. In that era, practitioners who came from Eastern countries were frankly girls of low morals performing in dives for customers who had things other than art on their minds. St. Denis's morals were beyond question; no one in his wildest dreams could have thought her intentions anything but pure.

There had been Oriental ballets previously, such as *La Bayadère* (performed by Taglioni) and *La Péri* (by Grisi), but these had been done in tutus, on point, and from a superficial and theatrical point of view. St. Denis gave us the real thing, without, however, using native music. She danced to Western pieces, romantically composed under Oriental influence and performed on Western instruments. Her chief attributes were her mystic seriousness, her extreme beauty, and her elegance of gesture, which had a finality and completion of quality that was masterly. Her costumes were always exquisite, and her handling of them, the manipulation of draperies and scarves as an integral part of the dance gesture, was unique. She was a sensational success and, of course, like Duncan, she had many imitators and followers.

Again like Duncan, she had her first triumphs in Europe, since America at that time was unreceptive to native talent. Americans simply could not believe that anyone bred here could be "gifted." Only after American artists received the acclaim of Berlin, Vienna, Paris, or London did Americans back home pay attention. This was both tragic for the native artist and pathetic for the native audience, who dared not trust their own instincts and predilections. Many of the artists, including Ruth

St. Denis, actually took foreign names in order to get along.

In 1915 Ruth St. Denis and her husband, Ted Shawn (1891–1972), founded a school in Los Angeles, Denishawn, where dance was studied in conjunction with related arts and philosophies. According to Baird Hastings in his book *The Denishawn Era,* this was "the first serious school of the dance (in the United States) with a curriculum and a standard of achievement."

St. Denis and Shawn attracted great pupils. Boys and girls of education and serious purpose began to study. These were the first American men in this century to interest themselves in any dancing besides tap and ballroom. These were the first girls from "good families" to study professionally.

Denishawn supported itself as a performing company by its school, and this set the pattern for all native companies thereafter, for it was recognized that a dance theater could not pay for maintenance and productions unaided. Anna Pavlova's company, on the strength of her illustrious name alone, and by ceaseless touring, made fortunes, but it was the only company that succeeded in doing this. And Pavlova was, of course, a foreigner. All others have had to find endowment one way or another or form schools with paying pupils.

St. Denis continued to dance until 1966,

Ruth St. Denis as she appeared in her first New York concerts and in her first Viennese performances of *Radha.* St. Denis was double-jointed and remained loose-limbed and supple her whole life. She never at any time put herself through the trouble of doing warm-up exercises. She was incapable of pointe work, but her foot on three-quarter pointe matched any Russian's, even Anna Pavlova's or Ekaterina Maximova's. Adeline Genée, who did not admire Duncan and stated she was not capable of dancing, admired St. Denis. CREDIT: *White Studio/The Agnes de Mille Collection.*

To Ruth St. Denis, Dancing

The success of this young Irish artist who dances barefoot, attired in appropriate costume, the strange esoteric dances of the temple ceremonies of India, has been remarkable. In New York and other cities art enthusiasts have flocked to see her, and now this new priestess of a well nigh forgotten art has gone to London where her vogue will probably be as great.

Is this renunciation, this brown maid
   Swaying within the incense - scented
    cloud,
   Was she that bronzèd idol with head
    bowed
To whom men brought the golden jewels
    and prayed?

Radha, fair spouse of Krishna, hear our
   prayer,
   Throw off thy bondage, teach us to be
    free!
   Enter, great breath of Immortality
Into this spirit's temple, passing fair!

All, I renounce, sweet maid, if this it mean—
   That thy lithe body in that wondrous
    swirl
Of mystic loveliness by us be seen.
   The world's enigma solvèd in a girl!
Dance, Radha, in thy sacred ecstasy
Unveil to mortal eyes divinity.

        —MARGARET NOEL.

White

White

Ruth St. Denis as the Courtesan in *Omika.* CREDIT:
White Studio/The Agnes de Mille Collection.

At the Taj Mahal and other key spots. Oriental tour for St. Denis and Shawn, 1926. CREDIT: *The Agnes de Mille Collection.*

when at the age of 89, a heart condition forced her to restrict her activities. She died in July 1968, less than a month after giving a television interview in Los Angeles.

For thirty years Ted Shawn maintained a school and theater (which still operate) at Jacob's Pillow in Lee, Massachusetts. He and his troupe of male dancers made regular tours, performing so-called ethnic dances, derived from East Indian, American Indian, West Indian, and South American sources, and classic visualizations. He was the first serious artist to use American country forms in concert.

Shawn held annual summer festivals at Jacob's Pillow, except during World War II; and there he gave patronage and exposure to dancers from every country. In bringing to our attention excellent but little-known talent, he performed a service

St. Denis and students at the Denishawn summer school at Mariarden. At the extreme left behind her stands Charles Weidman. In the front row, seated, with her hair braided in coils on her ears, is Martha Graham. Seated third from right in the front row, with fluffy bobbed hair, is Doris Humphrey. Ruth St. Denis' hair went snow white in her late thirties. She was still a relatively young woman when this picture was taken. CREDIT: *The Dance Collection*.

of cross-fertilization that had no counterpart anywhere else in the United States.

St. Denis and Shawn went into vaudeville quite regularly and finally even did a tour with the Ziegfeld Follies. Although this brought their work to the attention of the ordinary public, they were criticized for it. Duncan had always scorned this sort of exploitation and would not stoop to low entertainment houses. But as St. Denis said, "We paid our bills." Duncan notoriously did not.

Another early revolutionary dancer was Maud Allan (1883–1956), who like Isadora Duncan went

Ted Shawn as Adonis. CREDIT: *J. Walter Collinge/ The Agnes de Mille Collection.*

from San Francisco to Vienna to make her fortune. She started as a pianist, but friends dissuaded her from following that highly competitive metier and encouraged her instead to undress as the other California girl had done; to step out to the beauty and delights of nature, to the romantic music of the last century. She was an "interpretive dancer," a term at the time which symbolized an emotion very much in the air—the yearning, compulsive desire for self-expression and freedom and individualism. She made her debut in Budapest a few years before Duncan launched herself in Vienna. Like Isadora, she danced spring dances to Mendelssohn and funeral marches to Chopin and was a great success. Who influenced whom? Which one preceded the other? These are academic points that will never be settled satisfactorily. The dancers came at the same time and they answered the same general need.

Maud Allan in *Salome,* c. 1910. CREDIT: *Otto Bangs/ From the personal collection of William Como.*

Feather of Dawn. Ted Shawn in the Eagle Dance.
CREDIT: © *1980, John Lindquist, all rights reserved.*

Maud Allan in *Salome,* c. 1910. CREDIT: *Apeda/From the personal collection of William Como.*

Roshanara with Ratan Devi, an Englishwoman who married Kumera Swami and who accompanied Roshanara on the tambura and sang raj very beautifully. CREDIT: *Arnold Genthe/From the Museum of the City of New York.*

Duncan was the greater. This fact cannot be argued. Duncan overpowered and conquered, whereas Allan persuaded gently and prettily. Duncan grew with the years to enormous stature, and her influence is perhaps stronger today than it was during her life. Allan faded with age and is forgotten. But while Allan danced, she was known all over Europe. She made famous a dance of Salomé to music by Richard Strauss, which was pseudo-Oriental, pseudo-dramatic, and pseudo-religious (she played with a papier maché head of John the Baptist). It certainly did not have anything of the stylishness and austere fervor of the great mystic, St. Denis, who remained mistress of the religious form for Western audiences.

Roshanara (1894–1926), another exotic performer of the period, was an English girl who made a considerable impression with her more or less authentic dances from India. She was born in Calcutta, the daughter of a British soldier, and studied the native dances with Ghoor Jehan, a noted dancing master. She took for her stage name the Indian name Roshanara, meaning "light-adoring," and went to London, where she studied with Loie Fuller (1862–1928) and was hired by Oscar Asche for his 1911 production of *Kismet.* In England she toured with Anna Pavlova's ballet company, doing native dances. In this she antedated the authentic Indian Uday Shankar, who also toured with Pavlova. In 1913 she came to New

York and gave concerts, and she later toured with Adolph Bolm's Ballet Intime and with her own company. She was often partnered by the musician Ratan Devi, another Englishwoman who was married to an Indian. In 1924 she appeared in the Greenwich Village Follies (as did Martha Graham). She was not a pupil of St. Denis or even a follower, and she was totally uninfluenced by Denishawn, but she had an enormous effect on the audiences that saw her and she was sufficiently authentic and beautiful to serve as a touchstone for comparison. By all contemporary accounts she was a first-class artist and a very fine dancer. She died of appendicitis in London in 1926.

Soon there began to be numerous Duncan and Denishawn imitators in vaudeville—the Marian Morgan Dancers (all women), the Perry Mansfield Dancers, and Evan Burroughs Fontanne. Although these performers were in no sense an approximation of the pioneers they imitated, at least they brought to the attention of the general public a certain amount of free and expressive movement, and they were all successful.

7.
POPULAR THEATER
1900-1930

BETWEEN 1870 and 1920, the popular theater was dominated by the great vaudeville and tap stars and by ballroom dancers. But there was also one exquisite ballet dancer who had a tremendous effect.

In 1908 Adeline Genée (1878–1970), the Danish ballerina, was imported by Florenz Ziegfeld, not for an opera, but for a Broadway revue, *The Soul Kiss*. A dancer of impeccable style and technique, she astonished everyone with her enchanting art and followed up four years of hard work in cheap musicals with a stimulating program of her own—the complete *Coppélia* and a historical review of dancing that included reconstructions of solos by Camargo (1710–1770), Marie Sallé (1707–1756), and Madeline Guimard (1743–1816) and a revival of the entire third act of *Robert le Diable*, which Taglioni had made famous with her father's ballet of dead nuns. (The writers and artists of the first half of the nineteenth century were infatuated with the idea of death and there was a plethora of stories, dramatic scenes, ballets, pictures, poems, and songs about ghosts, revenants, hauntings, graveyards, etc. In this case, *Robert le Diable*, Philippe Taglioni had chosen to use a graveyard in a nunnery with the ghosts of all the dead nuns returning to haunt the leading basso.)

Genée later told of her struggles to revive the full *Coppélia*, which she said audiences of the time were not ready for. Managers acted as though it were the uncut *Hamlet* she was attempting to mount, or *Parsifal*, before an audience of eight-year olds.

Genée tells:

> The management, Oswald Stoll in London, quite frankly fought shy of classical ballet, and anything tragic, like *Giselle*, for example, was dismissed as unsuitable because of its sad story and its graveyard scene. Even *Coppélia* was considered too old and too long.
> When I first suggested this ballet to the board of directors, they said, "Nobody wishes to see an old ballet like that, produced nearly forty years ago." However, eventually I found myself in a position where I could insist . . .
> [Jupiter Recording, Ltd. London, Autumn, 1959]

She also spoke of the dance scene in America during the period she performed here.

Adeline Genée as Camargo. Here Genée is on pointe, which, of course, Camargo knew nothing about and never attempted. Genée prided herself on her perfectly straight line from toe to knee, which was the ideal ballet line for the Danish school. She did not approve of the swelling out of the arch of the foot or the sickling that produced it. (The arch that contributed to Pavlova's great reputation and the excitement of her every step was to Genée a fault and a deformity.) Note also that she maintained the mid-calf ballet skirt in the 19th-century style, and she was complimented on her modesty in adhering to this length of skirt by Lucille Grahn when they met in Bayreuth. The vogue for much shorter skirts was rapidly growing; today they are barely a ripple across the groin. CREDIT: *Mishkin/The Dance Collection.*

Adeline Genée. CREDIT: *Otto Sarony Co., Theater Magazine/The Agnes de Mille Collection.*

Ballet at that time in America was almost non-existent and on my first few visits I had to perform my dances as interludes in musical comedy. I went back to dance in America several seasons, and on the last occasion I gave a few performances at the Metropolitan Opera House when I had my own company on tour. My partner was then the famous Russian dancer, Alexander Volinine, and I and my company crossed America from east to west in a special Pullman car called the *Iolanthe.*

Genée's company was good. Her partner, Volinine, later partner to Anna Pavlova, came from Moscow. This was dancing the likes of which America had not seen in seventy-five years. It made an unforgettable impression on those who witnessed it. She toured her program in America four

Adeline Genée as Sallé, in her own program *La Danse.* CREDIT: *Theater Magazine/The Agnes de Mille Collection.*

times between 1909 and 1914. Once she was told by an old lady that her dancing was reminiscent of Fanny Elssler's and that this resemblance had moved her so greatly that she wept.

Genée still wore the nineteenth-century slippers without stiffening of any sort. Her balance was prodigious, and she could maintain full arabesque *en pointe* for minutes while the curtain closed and opened and closed and opened again. This entailed a foot of extraordinary development (evident in photographs of her), with muscles thickened in the calf and ankle, the real old-fashioned ballet dancer's leg. Genée was one of the last ballerinas to be so endowed.

For the first twenty years of this century there were exhibitions of all kinds of ballroom dancing—in vaudeville, in restaurants, in musical comedies. I discussed Vernon and Irene Castle earlier under popular dancing because of their effect on general social dancing, the Saturday nightly dancing of ordinary people. They were, however, brilliant theatrical innovators as well, and they bred a host of followers: Maurice and Florence Walton, Maurice and Leonora Hughes, Clifton Webb and Mary Hay.

The chorus dancing at the turn of the century was still parades of pretty girls, and pseudo-handsome men who escorted them on and off stage. They could sing just well enough to back-up solo songs. Dancing was not required. The ambition of the girls was to marry wealth. The ambition of the boys would be hard to define. The purpose on stage of both was to show off costumes and provide relief and diversion from the book.

The chorus of Montgomery and Stone's *The Old Town.* CREDIT: *White Studio/The Billy Rose Theater Collection.*

Irene Castle. CREDIT: *Baron de Meyer, Theater Magazine/The Agnes de Mille Collection.*

Florence Walton was known for her exquisite clothes. A new couturier's model arrived weekly from Paris. CREDIT: *Ira Hill, Theater Magazine/The Agnes de Mille Collection.*

"They shall not pass." Irene Castle as France. This was a posed tableau by Ben Alli Hagen, who arranged these patriotic pantomimes and tableaux for charity during World War I. CREDIT: *Charlotte Fairchile, Theater Magazine/The Agnes de Mille Collection.*

Moss and Fontana. CREDIT: *Pach Bros. Photo, Theater Magazine, 1926/The Bettmann Archive.*

But in the twenties choruses of clogging, tapping and soft-shoe dancing began to be popular. These were not in any sense real developments of the tap technique. All effects were achieved by the simple multiplication of the solo dancer. Now many dancers did identical steps in brigade formations. Complex group patterns and rhythms in this promising and lively technique still remain to be attempted.

Later, in the mid-twenties, the Charleston came, the enchanting and lively dance straight off the South Carolina wharves. The variations of this form provided extraordinary displays of virtuosity and invention which through the movies reached the entire world and changed the social dance style of ordinary folk.

There has always been a wide breach between indigenous American theater forms, such as jazz and tap dancing, and our other theater styles. In Europe, a similar divergence does not hold true. Classic ballet developed from the European folk forms and is therefore basically related to them and can incorporate native steps, such as versions of Spanish dances, without any great loss of style. But tap dancing and ballet have no roots in common. This fact has tended to keep them from merging in

Fred and Adele Astaire, a vaudeville team of clever dancers who scored a big hit in *The Passing Show of 1918*, at the Winter Garden. Adele Astaire became the Duchess of Devonshire. CREDIT: *White Studio/ The Billy Rose Theater Collection.*

any way. The divergence is reinforced by the fact that each has an extremely difficult technique. The ballet dancer needs a tight foot and controlled ankle, the tap dancer a relaxed foot and loose ankle. The ballet dancer uses a straight, stiffened knee, the tap dancer a lax knee.

Many of the early Broadway dance routines were by Ned Wayburn (1874–1942) and Seymour Felix (1894–1961) (who set the line routines of *The Hunting Ballet* for Adeline Genée). They were simple arrangements of show-girl chorus lines, mainly marching and kicking like the English Tiller Girls. These routines were replaced in the twenties and thirties by the Albertina Rasch dancers in an expanding of the cygnet variation from *Swan Lake*. Rasch (1891–1967) had been a ballerina at the Metropolitan Opera, and she used her knowledge to put her show girls on point and to augment the original four cygnets to thirty-two strapping beauties. (She did, it is true, an enormous and various amount of routines, but they all turned

The Albertina Rasch girls in *Rio Rita*, a Ziegfeld musical extravaganza. CREDIT: *Alfred Cheney Johnston, Theater Magazine/The Agnes de Mille Collection.*

Maria (Gambi) Gambarelli in the Broadway version of Anna Pavlova's *Swan*. CREDIT: *Courtesy of RKO General Pictures.*

Harriet Hoctor, Ziegfeld star. CREDIT: *The Dance Collection*

Harriet Hoctor, Ziegfeld star. CREDIT: *The Dance Collection*.

out to be a formula.) As rivals there were the Chester Hale girls, the Capital Theatre Ballet, starring Maria "Gamby" Gambarelli, the Florence Rogge ballet girls, and, the most famous of all, the thirty-two Rockettes, schooled by Russell Markert, who did precision high kicks and fairly complex tap and who became as peculiarly a New York attraction as the noise and the high buildings. They were as meticulously drilled as West Point cadets and, choreographically speaking, as subtle. They did not so much dance, as maneuver, but so expertly as to gain worldwide acclaim.

All of these diverting entertainments together, however, could still make no formal claim to dancing as art, because the grand theaters remained exclusive and continued to reject popular native forms.

In the huge, opulent, vulgar movie theaters of this period, the vogue was for dancing and singing prologues before the pictures. Some were line routines, but others were dubbed "atmospheric prologues," especially by Sid Grauman (1879–1950), an enterprising showman of Los Angeles and the West who claimed to have invented them. He certainly made his Chinese and Egyptian theaters known nationally for these prologues, together with famous footprints in the cement and other architectural gimmicks. The prologues may have been atmospheric, but of what it would be hard to say. They rarely had anything to do with the picture. For instance, before Douglas Fairbanks's (1883–1939) *Robin Hood*, a dancing girl dressed in ostrich feathers (one of Denishawn's best, Julanne Johnston, who later played opposite Fairbanks in *The Thief of Bagdad*) proceeded onstage to do a really astonishing Egyptian ostrich dance, which was attention grabbing but certainly not twelfth-century English. These shows did, however, keep employed dancers who otherwise would not have been, and they provided a certain relief from the unavoidable tap routines that climaxed every bill.

The black theater flourished, but never together with nor alongside of the white, with the exception of a very few great stars. The first show to make an exception was *Flying Colors* in 1932, which had a complete black chorus and a complete white chorus. They danced alternately and they danced side by side. They did not mix. The choreography was done by Tamara Geva, Agnes de Mille and Albertina Rasch. It is, however, the latter's name exclusively that appears on the programs. The black theater was segregated to Harlem, to vaudeville, and the black ghettos of other large cities. But confined as it was, it was explosive with vitality and talent.

Russell Markert's Rockettes, c. 1940. The world-famous Rockettes of Radio City Music Hall fame (under the direction of Russell Markert when this photo was taken). CREDIT: *Courtesy of Radio City Music Hall.*

Josephine Baker in Paris in *Bananas*. CREDIT: *Musée des Arts Decoratifs, Paris.*

CETTE PARURE EN BRILLANTS
PORTÉE PAR
JOSÉPHINE BAKER
A ÉTÉ ENTIÈREMENT
EXÉCUTÉE PAR LES
BIJOUX BURMA
6, RUE DE LA PAIX
PARIS

JOSÉPHINE BAKER
DANS LE FINALE DU 2ᵉ ACTE
PHOTO MAURICE TABARD

Josephine Baker. CREDIT: *Musée des Arts Decoratifs, Paris.*

In the twenties, finding New York and America intolerable, several black stars went to Paris. Florence Mills (1901–1927) and Josephine Baker became the toasts of the French music halls and the queens of Paris, Baker (1906–1975) in particular because of her extraordinary physical beauty and long-limbed, lithe, supple body (quite naked in her most famous dance, clad only in a string of bananas). She was a grande vedette in the classic sense and rivaled any of the preceding music-hall stars' reputation, Mistinguette (1875–1956), for instance. They were principally great personalities and charming singers, but they also danced some and what they danced was straight from the Harlem Cotton Club on 125th Street, New York City. They set a very real vogue for Western Europe. They returned to their native shores only for triumphant visits. It was to be four decades before we freely availed ourselves of our enormous black talent.

8.
TWENTIETH-CENTURY BALLET

THE United States had by 1920 produced extraordinary originals—modernists and their pupils who broke with ballet tradition and found ways toward untried patterns and forms. But the grand tradition of opera ballet seemed for a long time to be withering.

Ballet is a costly enterprise and is traditionally attached to a state opera house. But until recently America never had any state-sponsored theater, lyric or dramatic. Nevertheless, throughout the nineteenth century individuals and groups in the United States made private attempts at both. And by the mid-nineteenth century there were opera and ballet companies in New York, Boston, Philadelphia, and Baltimore.

Perhaps because all these companies represented private enterprise and were not supported by state or civic endowments, no first-class new musical works were commissioned for them. Nor were there any guaranteed academies or training schools attached to them.

But there was nevertheless continuous, unbroken activity in the sphere of ballet. Genée came, as I have said, to perform in a Ziegfeld Broadway revue. And in 1909 Anna Pavlova (1881–1931) and Mikhail Mordkin (1881–1944) hired the Metropolitan Opera House to give midnight performances (after a full evening of opera) with their own company. New York was stunned. But the management could take credit for these performances only as landlord.

The prevailing American prejudice against dancing, coupled with the denial of professional respect or civic endowment, were crippling disadvantages for ballet dancers. The Metropolitan developed neither stars nor choreographers. Its ballerinas were foreign like Maria Cavallazzi, its first prima, and only one of them, Rosina Galli, was of any real caliber or recognition, although Albertina Rasch later built herself a lucrative career in Broadway shows and in Hollywood.

In 1912 Gertrude Hoffman (1886–1956) launched a company in New York at the Winter Garden. The repertoire was in effect nothing but a direct piracy of Diaghilev ballets, including *Les Sylphides*, *Cleopatra*, and *Scheherazade*, in which Hoffman herself with her gorgeous red hair, played the role of the favorite slave, Zobeide, Karsavina's great role. For this enterprise she imported really

Anna Pavlova in *Giselle*. CREDIT: *Theater Magazine/The Agnes de Mille Collection.*

splendid Russian dancers, some of whom had worked with Diaghilev and all of whom had been trained either at the Moscow or the St. Petersburg school: Alexander Volinine (who had partnered Adeline Genée and Anna Pavlova), Maria Alexandra Baldina (1886–1927), Theodore Kosloff, and Lydia Lopokova (later Mrs. John Maynard Keynes, now Lady Keynes). They made quite an impression, and so did the pieces they exploited so shamelessly with no thought of giving Fokine either credit or recompense. But the only lasting consequence of Hoffman's venture was that many of the Russians chose to remain in America. In addition,

Anna Pavlova in the dances from *Carmen*. CREDIT: *Theater Magazine/The Agnes de Mille Collection.*

Anna Pavlova in the *Bacchanale*, Fokine's variation of *The Seasons of Glazounov*. CREDIT: *Mishkin, Theater Magazine/The Agnes de Mille Collection.*

Pavlova and Volinin in the *Bacchanale*. In this picture the effect of Isadora Duncan is quite evident. The ballet stance of straight spine and even hips has been abandoned for the uneven hips and undulating torso of the ancient, Oriental, and natural dancer. Fokine, who composed this *pas de deux* for Pavlova, had been studying classic sculpture and was struck with the fact that the weight was often carried on one foot with the hips thrust out. He was in the midst of these studies when Duncan arrived in Russia. Pavlova's passion in this dance, which she first made famous with Mikhail Mordkin and then with Alexandre Volinin, was unmatched and is remembered by anyone who ever saw her flamelike performance. CREDIT: *Theater Magazine/The Agnes de Mille Collection.*

Radha and Krishna, Anna Pavlóva and Uday Shankar. Shankar was studying at Oxford when he became interested in joining Pavlova's company. In 1926 he choreographed for her some betwitchingly lovely Indian pieces, *Radha and Krishna* and *The Hindu Wedding*, which were certainly the most interesting, colorful, and persuasive Indian dances we have ever seen. CREDIT: *White Studio/The Dance Collection.*

Gertrude Hoffman as Zobeide in *Scheherazade.* CREDIT: *Otto Bangs, Theater Magazine/The Agnes de Mille Collection.*

Hoffman had anticipated the arrival of the real Diaghilev company, complete with Nijinsky (1890–1950) by about four years.

News in ballet continued to be made outside of the Metropolitan Opera House. If within, it was always due to lessees of the stage. The startling impression made by Anna Pavlova and Mikhail Mordkin in 1909 was on the public, not, unfortunately, on the opera management. The Russians were mere guests and appeared with their own troupe.

In 1916 the entire Diaghilev Ballet, lacking only its director and its principal female star, Tamara Karsavina (1885–1978), both of whom were afraid of crossing water in wartime, but including Vaslav Nijinsky, Adolph Bolm, Lydia Lopokova, and Flore Revalle, appeared at the Metropolitan and toured the country as far as the Pacific Coast. America was not ready for any such theater, and the enterprise went bankrupt. It was bailed out by

Lydia Lopokova in *Les Sylphides* by Michel Fokine. Lydia Lopokova was a star dancer who, after she had lost considerable weight, became the lead dancer in the Diaghilev ballet in the United States, replacing Karsavina in *Carnival, Spectre de la Rose,* and other charming roles. She danced for years in England and was one of the stars of the Sadler's Wells ballet but retired upon her marriage to Maynard Keynes. CREDIT: *White Studio/The Agnes de Mille Collection.*

the financier and opera patron Otto Kahn, and the Russians returned to Paris, cursing this country as barbaric.

Several stragglers from the Diaghilev troupe remained in America to teach, but there were still no ballet companies. Adolph Bolm (1884–1951) was one of the original Diaghilev dancers who stayed. First he took over as choreographer at the Metropolitan Opera House, then in Chicago, where he initiated his own small ballet troupe, the Ballet Intime, starring himself and Ruth Page, a bonny fifteen-year-old girl who stayed with him for years until finally departing to form her own company. She later became the choreographer of the Chicago Civic Opera, where she remained for decades. Bolm was not a good choreographer and eventually his company died of inanition. He then moved to Hollywood and taught.

Michel Fokine (1880–1942), the creative mainstay of the Diaghilev company, separated from his employer in Paris in 1915 after bitter quarreling, and unable to go back to his home theater in St. Petersburg because of the revolution, tried the New World. He came to New York in 1919, gave a series of concerts with his wife, Vera Fokina (1886–1958), staged a Broadway spectacle or two, and labored for years to establish a full-fledged company of his own. All his effort came to very little financially and artistically, for he had neither the dancers nor the organization to support his grandiose ideas. He did, however, teach, and his pupils included Paul Haakon, Patricia Bowman, and Pauline Koner, who were to become the nuclei of future native companies.

For over fifty years, the precise period in which America was experiencing a dance renaissance, all the Metropolitan choreographers were imported and most were second-rate or old-fashioned. The exception was George Balanchine, who, during his single season (1935–1936), attempted to produce distinguished works, and brought in his own pupils to help. But he found the rehearsal conditions, the board interference, and the public taste intolerable, and left. During his brief tenure he did achieve the creation of a superb ballet for Gluck's *Orpheus* with decor and costumes by Pavel Tchelitchef (1898–1957). It was discarded and never revived.

Since then there have been a large number of choreographers at the Metropolitan. The longest in tenure and the most successful was an American, Zachary Solov, who labored to bring order. His immediate successor, Dame Alicia Markova, soon returned to England.

Each new choreographer undid the work of his predecessor at the Met, and while a noticeable effort was made from time to time to improve conditions, they were never regularized to a point to where good work could be forthcoming.

From 1950 to 1968, when it quite unexpectedly ceased to function, the Met's ballet school was under the expert direction of Margaret Craske and Antony Tudor, both of them British born, but it produced no stars. The leading dancers had still to be borrowed from elsewhere. As long as the old opera house stood and until it was destroyed by its owners—arbitrarily and in the face of protest and popular need—it was rented out to the dazzling companies of the world, which lent to the building an aura of worth and achievement not in any way deserved by the legal owners.

In the season of 1978–1979 the Metropolitan produced *The Bartered Bride*, with direction by John Dexter, a Britisher, scenery by Josef Svoboda, a Czech, and choreography by Pavel Smok, also a Czech. This was an altogether enchanting production, with good acting, beautiful singing, and remarkable, imaginative, inventive staging, a real piece of innovative theater. And the dancers, although perhaps not top-notch by the standards of any of the established ballet companies, still were so much better, so much fresher and more vigorous, than anything that had been seen at the Met for decades that hearts filled with hope to behold them.

For many years, the best European dancers were imported by private impresarios. In 1916 Sol Hurok (1892–1977), a naturalized Russian who brought from his mother country an abiding love of ballet, produced Anna Pavlova at the New York Hippodrome in a version of *Sleeping Beauty* in the Hippodrome's *Big Show*. Hurok began touring her nationally in her own company under his management. She made many cross-country trips until her death in 1929 and through her personal magic hypnotized large sections of the public into an interest in dance. Ballet came to mean Russian ballet; no native ballet stars or companies could draw the public, and no management would risk money on them. Pavlova did much to sow the seeds of great ballet here, and an entire generation of girls, myself among them, owed their initial enthusiasm for dancing to seeing her in local, extraordinary places. She wore herself out touring, but she made a fortune and she was beloved everywhere in America, and indeed around the world, as no dancer ever has

Tamara Toumanova, "The Black Pearl of the *Ballet Russe*." CREDIT: *Maurice Seymour*.

been. Her name in her time was synonymous with very great dancing. No one else's ever has been to quite such a degree.

In 1929 Léonide Massine (1896–1979), the brilliant choreographer of the Diaghilev Ballet, was brought by S. L. "Roxy" Rothafel to his theater on Sixth Avenue, the Roxy, and installed there with the resident ballet company to perform his magic. But he ran afoul of the excessive haste due to the weekly change of program, the interference of the resident ballet master, Florence Rogge, and the producer, Leon Leonidov, and the general lack of maturity in the dancers. He did, however, find in Patricia Bowman, a pupil of Fokine, a most sensitive performer, and he had great faith in her. He grew tired of this stint after a year and went back to Paris, delaying only to stage in 1930 for the League of New York Composers the first American performance of Stravinsky's (1882–1971) *Le Sacre du Printemps*. He worked with a scratch group, but

his choreography was extremely good and effective. In many ways, this version of *Le Sacre*, one of dozens which have subsequently been exposed, is one of the very strongest. His stay at the Roxy is probably forgotten, but he did reproduce fine little ballets there and danced himself, among other things the superb miller's dance from *Le Tricorne*, a masterpiece. It was not locally successful, but many true ballet connoisseurs were grateful to see it.

In 1934 Hurok brought Colonel de Basil's (c.1900–1951) Ballet Russe to New York. This was a company of young dancers, the children of Russian émigrés, born and trained for the most part in Paris. Léonide Massine was artistic director and his works dominated the repertoire. But to large numbers Massine also introduced Fokine's works properly done, and excerpts of the masterpieces of Marius Petipa (seen for the first time in America). Massine attempted gigantic and serious pieces—he was always successful with bold mass movement and

Alexandra Danilova and Leon Danielian in *Danse Concertantes* by George Balanchine. CREDIT: *Maurice Seymour.*

Irina Baronova in *Le Coq d'Or* by Michel Fokine. CREDIT: *Maurice Seymour.*

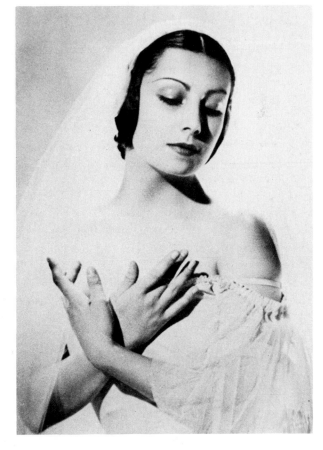

Portrait of Léonide Massine. CREDIT: *Stravinsky-Diaghilev Foundation.*

remarkable sweeping effects—sometimes to entire uncut symphonies, *Les Presages* to the Tchaikovsky Fifth, *Choreartium* to the Brahms Fourth, Beethoven's *Seventh Symphony, Symphonie Fantastique* to Berlioz, *Nobilissima Visione,* a piece about St. Francis of Assisi, to Hindemith (1895–1963). His greater achievements were the lighter *Le Beau Danube, Gaité Parisienne* and *Scuola di Ballo,* with variations of incredible perfection scattered throughout, a brilliant development of the samples of Bronislava Nijinska (1890–1972) and Balanchine, all performed most wonderfully by young, handsome and enthusiastic stars.

Headed by the Diaghilev veterans Léonide Massine and Alexandra Danilova, in the next two years both Russian companies, de Basil's and Sergei Denham's, presented such a roster of stars and

Sono Osato, Vera Zorina, Alexandra Danilova, and David Lichine in *Choreartium* by Léonide Massine. CREDIT: *Maurice Seymour.*

Markova in *The Nutcracker.* CREDIT: *Maurice Seymour.*

soloists as has hardly ever been assembled. There were, first of all, the three "baby ballerinas," all under seventeen—Tamara Toumanova, Irina Baronova, and Tatiana Riabouchinska—then Alicia Markova, who in time achieved absolute supremacy and was called by John Martin of the *New York Times* "the finest ballerina who ever danced." Among the men was that prince of all danseurs, Igor Youskevitch. Principal dancers included Ruthanna Boris, Leon Danielian, André Eglevsky, Frederick Franklin, Roland Guérard, Roman Jasinsky, Casimir Kokic, Nathalie Krassovska, David Lichine, Robert Lindgren, Marc Platoff, Mia Slavenska, Maria Tallchief, Lyubov Tchernichova, Nina Theilade, Gertrude Tyven, Nina Verchinina, Vera Zorina, and George Zoritch. These and their distinguished colleagues established a standard that had never before been matched in this country. Many of them have remained in the United States and are now teachers.

Massine toured the United States for ten years (1934–1944) and did what Fokine himself had not been able to do, and what Pavlova had just begun: he roused America to the beauties and excitement of great ballet.

The first two seasons, however, were unremunerative due to the prevailing apathy with which all dancing (except popular theater types) was generally viewed here. But the third year the enterprise caught on. Thereafter until 1944 the company played everywhere to bonanza business. Hurok is to be commended for his stubborn courage in persisting and for his hardihood in risking money. It is largely due to his efforts that America became aware of ballet, and though not yet quite ready to support its own companies, it was convinced at last that it loved dance—but only as long as it was Russian.

9.
DANCE
IN EARLY
FILMS

DANCE gesture is the last human activity to be successfully filmed with vitality and meaning. This is because dancing has not been considered interesting or important to most makers of films.

There is not an exposed foot of film, for instance, of Isadora Duncan, as far as anyone can ascertain. Scraps of ludicrous footage exist on Loie Fuller (1862–1928) and La Belle Otero (1868–1965) but nothing like entire dances. The great Spanish dancer Argentina (1888–1936), for instance, died long after sound film had been developed, and though she was the mistress of the finest castanets in the world and the glory of her country, she was never recorded, an unforgivable shame, but nobody wished to take the trouble or pay her a decent fee. Even Ruth St. Denis, who lived until well after World War II, was filmed only in some very short news items. She was at the time in her sixties and not at her ablest, and the films are not of entire dances but merely of snatches. Nevertheless, her elegance shines through, but that is about all.

In 1920 Rudolph Valentino (1895–1926) made his sensational appearance in *The Four Horsemen of the Apocalypse* dancing the Argentine tango, and while the camera made no effort whatever to record the dance as such and devoted quite as much time to his facial expressions as to his body and stance, there are indications of an historic and superb presence and the unequaled magnetism of his performance. He was the sex symbol of his age, and part of this was in his manner of moving, in his posture, in his rhythms. The tango, of course, became a success everywhere, and Valentino went on to one of the most meteoric, incandescent careers in the history of the Western theater, unmatched in popularity until Elvis Presley came along.

In 1924 Douglas Fairbanks (1882–1939) and Mary Pickford (1893–1979) thinking that it was a great shame that with the exception of one bad and totally inadequate film, The *Dumb Girl of Portici*, no one had ever filmed Anna Pavlova adequately, turned over their studio to her one Sunday, and there on the set of the *Son of Zorro* she recorded six or seven of her short pieces, all solos. She was filmed by a single camera with an unmoving lens from a set position and, as far is known, without music. But

Rudolph Valentino in *Monsieur Beaucaire*. CREDIT: *The Agnes de Mille Collection*.

The Dying Swan was recorded, at least, and that is a blessing. Pavlova was also filmed out-of-doors at her own home, Ivy House, in London, dancing more or less extemporaneously, moving about in the sunlight under the trees. The film, called *The Immortal Swan* and released in 1953, does show her movement but nothing more. There is one extraordinary sequence of slow-motion film which gives a suggestion of the finish of her gestures.

The regular dances in films were mere incomplete scraps, used for scenic or atmospheric effect.

In 1926 the first musical sound film was shown. The process was not perfected, but it was sufficiently developed to permit commercial use. With it came music and dancing on film. Although film and the stage were quite different media, they were long treated as essentially the same genre. All of the dances for films, for instance, were designed for the stage and photographed as though they were within a proscenium arch. In fact, the films of many of the early dances actually included proscenium, footlights and curtain, and the dances were designed for a live audience, shown applauding and responding as any real audience sitting in a theater would. Refinements and enlargements and trick effects could be achieved through the use of the camera, but the dances themselves were essentially

Rudolph Valentino in the film *Monsieur Beaucaire*. CREDIT: *The Agnes de Mille Collection*.

Anna Pavlova in the 1916 film *The Dumb Girl of Portici*. CREDIT: *Theater Magazine/The Agnes de Mille Collection.*

Agnes de Mille as a nymph in William de Mille's film *The Faun* with Charles duRoche. For this I received five dollars, a day's pay. CREDIT: *The Agnes de Mille Collection.*

Gloria Swanson and Ted Shawn in Cecil B. De Mille's *Don't Change Your Husband*, 1918 (scenario, I regret to say, by my father, William de Mille). Ten hours of burning passion earned Shawn a good day's pay for which, at the time, he was grateful, as were all the dancers in Hollywood. CREDIT: *Film by Cecil B. De Mille, 1918/The Dance Collection.*

John Gilbert as Prince Danilo and Mae Murray as the Countess Sadoja, formerly Sally O'Hara, in a scene from MGM's film *The Merry Widow,* 1925. CREDIT: *The Granger Collection.*

Joan Crawford in the film that made her name, *Our Dancing Daughters.* Her Charleston became famous around the world. CREDIT: © *1928, Metro-Goldwyn-Mayer Distributing Corporation. Renewed 1956, Loew's Incorporated.*

Facing page, "By a Waterfall," one of Busby Berkeley's extravaganzas. CREDIT: © *Warner Bros. Pictures. Renewed 1961, United Artists Associated, Inc. All rights reserved.*

the same as for the stage. Only very much later, decades later, was any attempt made to compose film dances for effects not possible in a live per-formance. In 1933 I said to the director Cecil B. De Mille (1881–1959), my uncle, "I want to design a dance for the camera and not for the naked eye." And he said to me, "What is the difference?" Cecil De Mille was a master photographer and a wizard with the lens, but he did not know what I was talking about.

In early musical films, the young star Joan Crawford (1903–1977) was an extraordinary dancer

of the current popular steps, mainly the Charleston. There is usually as much footage of Crawford's face and expressions in these films as there is of her feet and body, but nevertheless the dances are recorded and one can begin to get a sense of the style of the period.

With the advent of sound and songs, dance numbers appeared on the screen, and soon there was a vogue in tremendous dance displays but always in the style of and with the limitations of stage spectacles, often lavish, semimilitary parades and maneuverings by line choruses of kicking and marching girls. With the help of the camera, the unison dancing could be varied enormously; shots taken from above and below, traveling shots and zooming shots, all lent great visual scope to the routines which of themselves were for the most part stereotyped. Busby Berkeley came into his own as a manipulator of these extraordinary displays. One of the most famous and surprising was a chorus of thirty-two girls at grand pianos, which swung and fanned into view on slowly unfolding platforms, like the petals of a flower. The effect was startling, although it had very little to do with dancing as such, or piano playing either for that matter. Busby Berkeley had no sense whatever of individual dance gesture, emotional communication, rhythm, or line. All he achieved was spectacle. It was, however, extremely inventive thanks to his use of the camera, and he gained millions by it.

Concurrently Albertina Rasch, fresh from her triumphs on Broadway, brought her band of girls

The incomparable Fred Astaire in *Top Hat*, RKO's 1935 musical. CREDIT: *Courtesy of RKO General Pictures/The Penguin Collection.*

Facing page, Fred Astaire in white tie and tails. CREDIT: *The Granger Collection.*

west and placed long lines of kicking cygnets on the screen. In fact, Rasch actually was given the earliest screen credit for dance direction. For a time her routines absolutely dominated moving pictures.

In the thirties the great dance soloists appeared—Fred Astaire, Gene Kelly, the beloved Bill Robinson (1878–1947). And brilliant women stars like Eleanor Powell and Ruby Keeler made their appearance for the first time in the tap medium. A little later the adorable Ginger Rogers

Eleanor Powell and Ray Bolger in MGM's *Rosalie*, 1937. CREDIT: © *1937, Metro-Goldwyn-Mayer Corporation. Renewed 1964, Metro-Goldwyn-Mayer, Inc.*

Frank Sinatra and Gene Kelly in the 1945 MGM film *Anchors Aweigh.* CREDIT: © *1945, Loew's Incorporated. Renewed 1972, Metro-Goldwyn-Mayer, Inc.*

tapped and whirled to international fame in the arms of her wonderful partner Fred Astaire.

Most of Fred Astaire's dances were arranged by Hermes Pan, whose splendid craftsmanship and dazzling technique, rather like that of a goldsmith's, set off the Astaire numbers for the jewels they were.

Bill Robinson with Shirley Temple in the 1935 film *The Littlest Rebel*, directed by David Butler. CREDIT: © *1935, Twentieth Century-Fox Film Corp.*

Bill Robinson doing his famous Step Dance in *Hooray For Love*, RKO 1935, directed by Walter Lang. CREDIT: *Courtesy of RKO General Pictures/The Penguin Collection.*

Gene Kelly in *An American in Paris*. CREDIT: © *1951, Loew's Incorporated. Renewed 1979, Metro-Goldwyn-Mayer, Inc.*

Pan has not been given his proper credit, but he was certainly germane to Astaire's art and should be recognized as one of the most expert workers in the business.

These tapping men and women in their astonishing films became heroes of the entire world, spreading the American cult everywhere. Tap dancing became universally popular. It is hard to exaggerate the enthusiasm for it that seized people. The explorer William Beebe (1877–1962) said that though he sometimes used to barter beads with savages, his ability to tap dance for them was much more efficacious. Rhythm absolutely charmed aborigines in all quarters, he said, and it was an extremely valuable addition to his other paraphernalia for befriending and trading.

All these dances and dance styles were made world-famous by the movies. They originated, however, on the stage and mainly in vaudeville. But because of the movies some of the movie practitioners became the best-loved stars in the world and touched off real crazes. People around the globe did not dance the flamencos the Andalusian gypsies danced, although their dances were perhaps the most provocative of all dances. People danced the way Americans danced in films; they tapped and one-stepped and Charlestoned.

10.
MODERN REVOLU-TIONARIES

THE Americans were not supporting ballet but they were developing and supporting a new form of dance, the foundations of which came from Duncan and St. Denis. The revolution began in the late 1920s.

Martha Graham, the most famous of the Denishawn students, together with her fellow Denishawners, Doris Humphrey and Charles Weidman, and with Hanya Holm, a German and pupil of Mary Wigman, founded the so-called modern dance, which has become a truly American form and has influenced and shaped all our indigenous choreography since 1930. Graham is probably the greatest American choreographer and also stands prominent among the performing theater personalities of our time. In the eyes of some, myself included, she is the most powerful, creative force in the twentieth-century theater. Her annual season on Broadway is the object of pilgrimages from all over the Americas; indeed, from all parts of the world. Her present company, in points of execution, style, and finesse of presentations, places her theater on a par with the great historic companies—with the Diaghilev troupe in its heyday and with the Grand Kabuki of Japan. It is unquestionably the most stylish theater we in America have evolved and it should be taken over by the government and preserved as the basis for an enduring national institution.

She is also a cultural influence in fields beyond her immediate profession, and in her own field she is one of the rare people who have created new styles and techniques of moving. Her invention is prodigious; like Picasso's (1881–1973), her art has changed deeply in style and technique several times during her career. For every new work there was not only a new design in steps, but a new concept in technique and dynamics, a restudying of the basis of movement. No other choreographer has attempted so much.

She unquestionably was influenced at first by St. Denis's Oriental studies and she acknowledges her debt in point of view. But the heritage goes deeper. The use of the ground, the kneeling, squatting, rising, and sinking, which is an essential part of Oriental dancing and is found nowhere in any Western form, she incorporated into her style. She also appropriated the Oriental use of the foot, the shifting and sliding on the earth, the curling in of the toes to act as a hinge.

Pagan Poem, by Martha Graham, with Martha Graham and Charles Weidman. This was one of Irene Lewison's special productions. Lewison used to hire the Shriner's Auditorium on 55th Street (later known as the New York City Center Opera) and bring the Sokolov Cleveland Orchestra complete with conductor from that city to accompany her projects. She would block out the entire parterre floor because she thought the sight angles were bad for dancing and sold only balcony seats. The monetary loss, of course, was gigantic. The professional trade was wonderstruck not so much by the dancing as by Lewison's extravagance. CREDIT: *Nicholas Murry/The Dance Collection.*

Primitive Mysteries, 1935, with Martha Graham and her group. CREDIT: © *1980, Barbara Morgan.*

Martha Graham in one of her first tremendous solos, *Lamentation*, 1935.
CREDIT: © *1980, Barbara Morgan.*

But she is no imitator or adaptor. She is an original, a generic force. There was never anything quite like her before, and everyone who comes after will dance a little differently.

In classic ballet, dance movement had hitherto consisted of moving from position to position, raising or lowering the feet, bending smoothly, going from place to place, always serenely, always lightly. The internal workings of the action, the combustion, so to speak, were carefully hidden, and only the lovely results were shown. Martha Graham exposed the machinery, the effort. Life, she said, is effort. She realized also that the resolution of movement had a cycle; that it flowed to a climax, and ebbed away in relaxation.

She threw aside all the traditional steps and techniques of ballet, the straight long legs, the pointed toe, the quiet, even hips, the flexed foot, the relaxed hand. She stressed continuous unfolding movement from a central core, which is found in

The Graham dancers in *American Document*, 1938. CREDIT: © 1980, *Barbara Morgan.*

American Document (Trio), by Martha Graham, 1938. CREDIT: © 1972, *Barbara Morgan.*

Frontier, 1935. Martha Graham in Noguchi's history-making set. CREDIT: © *1972,*
Barbara Morgan.

Oriental movement, but she added spasm and resistance, which are not characteristic of the East at all.

She incorporated the ground, making the floor a part of gesture in a manner of far greater virtuosity than anything found elsewhere. She invented many beautiful falls and recoveries from the ground. She discovered a whole technique of balancing on bent knees, with her thighs as a hinge and the spine cantilevered and suspended backwards in counterbalance. She invented turns with a changing and swinging body axis.

At first it seemed she was speaking in a language we had not inherited and one quite unintelligible to most of us, but in reality her dance was far closer to natural acting than ballet dancing. It was not a realistic imitation of emotion, as in acting, however; it was an imaginative expansion of acting. Children today who have not been trained in a balletic mold find her style sympathetic and easy to understand.

She began working like Duncan on a bare stage with only costumes and lights, striving to

Martha Graham in her 1943 work, *Deaths and Entrances.* CREDIT: *Cris Alexander.*

Seraphic Dialogue, by Martha Graham, 1955, with Janet Eilber, David Hatch Walker, Takato Asakawa, and Peggy Lyman. CREDIT: *Arlene Avril.*

break all the old romantic molds. Later, she added scenic and costume effects of great imaginative beauty. Her music was contemporary, and much of it was composed to order.

She has always been daring as to subject matter and collaborators, prefiguring many theater vogues and introducing through her works a number of unknowns who became famous, such as composer Aaron Copland and sculptor Isamu Noguchi.

She inaugurated several stage techniques that were taken for granted later: mobile scenery, symbolic props and set pieces, speech with dancing, the chorus of commenting dancers reminiscent of those in the Orient. And she was the first to integrate her group racially by including Asians and blacks.

Her costumes have had a marked influence on dress style, both on and off the stage. The college girl of the thirties and forties, with flat shoes, wide skirt, tight sweater, and leather pouch, was the type established by the Graham dancer. The straight, dark, long-skirted costume and the leotard, replacing the ballet tutu or folk dress, were her invention. The Graham leotard has become the accepted work uniform today for all dancers, ballet and modern. American ballet students wear it with traditional tights and point shoes, and the Europeans are gradually adopting it also. No ballet student anywhere in America works in tutu and bloomers. The leotard has also become ubiquitous in civil life.

Historically speaking, Graham has had as forceful an impact on all branches of the contemporary theater as Duncan. Technically, in terms of invented and added steps and style, hers is the greatest single contribution in the records of dancing. Her dance dramas compare with the work of America's greatest playwrights.

In the words of William Schuman, the composer who was the first president of New York's Lincoln Center for the Performing Arts:

> She has created an original vocabulary of dance movement that has added a new dimension to the expressivity of the choreographic art. She has been gloriously incapable, ever, of being slight, captious, or superficial. Her works—whether tragic or comic—always probe, distill, and

Dances of Women, by Doris Humphrey, 1931, with Katherine Manning, Evelyn Fields, Ernestine Henoch, Rose Yasgour, Dorothy Lathrop. Humphrey is center figure. CREDIT: *Soichi Sunami.*

illuminate. She continues to create with undiminished zeal. Each new work brings the excitement of discovery of previously unexplored facets of her endlessly fertile imagination.

For these reasons she has achieved a position which is not adequately to be described solely as one of pre-eminence in her field. For whether we speak of the world of Dance, of Music, of Literature, or of the Graphic Arts, Martha Graham is one of the greatest artists America has ever produced.

Nothing stops Graham, neither age nor change of country nor condition. She no longer dances, but her stage presence still is oceanic, and each year sees a new work of originality and invention. After a trip to Israel, she returned with *Half Real Half Dream*, a fantasy which seemed to embody large sections of Burton's *Arabian Nights* and which differed from anything she had done previously. Her *Cortege of Eagles* (1967), a study of Hecuba, deals with the acceptance of death and weariness of vio-

The Shakers, by Doris Humphrey, 1938, with Katherine Litz, Beatrice Seckler, Nora Shurman, Doris Humphrey, Peter Hamilton, Charles Weidman, and Lee Sherman (Humphrey-Weidman Group). CREDIT: © *1972, Barbara Morgan.*

lence and speaks for our times as no other contemporary work does. Graham seems to live at the fountainhead, and what she expresses foretells our passion and our intent.

In 1977, at the age of eighty-four, she produced her version of Hawthorne's *The Scarlet Letter,* an extraordinary work of startling symbolism and solid blocks of new, vigorous, astounding group choreography, more effective, fresh, more stimulating than any work of young colleagues fifty years her junior. She is the phoenix, without age.

Her awards and honors are manifold. Among them are the Aspen Award in the Humanities (May 1965), given to honor "the individual anywhere in the world judged to have made the greatest contribution to the advancement of the humanities"; the Honorary Degree of Doctor of Arts from Harvard University (June 1966); the Handel Medallion of New York City (1970); the Medal of Freedom Award, presented by President Gerald Ford (October 14, 1976); and Kennedy Center Honors (February 1, 1980).

Doris Humphrey (1895–1958), also a pupil of Ruth St. Denis and Ted Shawn, and the second of the great contemporary pioneers, revealed the sheer power and delight of pure movement—its diversity, its possibilities, its satisfactions. More than any other choreographer, she worked in form stripped of dramatic content (although she could on occasion deal in storytelling and even comedy), but her major contributions were to focus on mass dynamics as expression, outstripping even Balanchine, the classic abstractionist, because her concepts were grander, larger, and less concerned with details of rhythm and technique. Her major works are historic achievements in the art, *sui generis,* and not to be compared with those of anyone else, even those of her great pupils.

Martha Graham is said to have declared her to be the finest choreographer among the "Modern" American dance composers, and she was so considered by dance leaders around the world. What ballet advocates did not recognize was that her theories of composition were applicable to all forms of technique, whether ballet or modern.

She was always courageous in the use of untried music, and inventive stage design (employing boxes of varying heights to give her levels in order to augment the dance patterns by the added dimension of height. These levels were inspired by Gordon Craig and were currently in use by Mary Wigman, whom, however, Humphrey had never seen). She danced to music of all kinds, classical and modern (she was extremely musical, perhaps the most musical of all the moderns), as well as to poetry and expressive sounds like humming, shouting, and buzzing.

In technique and personal style she herself was the direct product of Denishawn, having worked as assistant and junior choreographer under Ruth St. Denis's careful tutelage. Indeed, her first essays, *The Water Study* (silent) and *The Unfinished Symphony* (Schubert) were done at Denishawn in Los Angeles.

When St. Denis and Shawn went to the Orient with the Denishawn company (1927), they left the home school behind in the care of their pupils and soloists, Doris Humphrey and Charles Weidman. In the ensuing freedom from supervision that the teachers' absence provided, Doris suddenly found her creative strength and began to perfect her music visualizations and her abstract arrangements. She continued in the airy, light, delicate movement based on breath that she had used for Miss Ruth, some of the use of scarves in the St. Denis tradition, and much of the symmetrical design, but there were differences. She added and developed a series of falls and recoils, easy, elastic, seemingly boneless slippings to the ground, turnings and recoveries. And the tentative voice that had begun to express itself in *The Water Study* in 1923 now grew robust. She decided at this point to remain independent and never again to put herself under the supervision of any other artist or any alien judgment. In 1927 she and Charles Weidman founded their own school and were independent and free thereafter.

During the thirties, under the sponsorship of the Works Progress Administration (WPA), which operated as a gigantic charity supporting every kind of project in art, many permanently worthy and some quite remarkable achievements appeared, some very fine dancing among them. It was with government sponsorship that Doris Humphrey was able to mount a monumental work, *With My Red Fires* (1936), in which she played the role of the Matriarch with stunning power. Her grandiose and superb *Passacaglia* (1938), set to music of Bach, and the *New Dance* (1935) were presented at

New Dance, by Doris Humphrey, 1937, with Sybil Shearer (Humphrey-Weidman Group). CREDIT: *Photograph by Bouchard.*

Bennington College, which helped with its own resources. All these compositions required large companies of performers, and although they were splendidly successful they were hard to maintain. When the WPA ceased to function and there was no more government help, Humphrey had perforce to reduce her company with consequent damage to the big works. Later, her projections for the *Orestes* of Milhaud never materialized to the point of stage production for lack of money to pay the necessary singing chorus. This was, unfortunately, before the time of government grants, and videotape did not yet exist. It is therefore forgotten. We have, however, films of nearly all the other big works, some with sound.

The loss to dancing of her recorded complete works would have been tragic, because her ideas were large and the execution very fine. In many

Doris Humphrey in *With My Red Fires*. CREDIT: *Photograph by Bouchard.*

Four Choral Preludes, by Doris Humphrey with Charles Weidman, 1942. CREDIT: *Marcus Blechman/From the Museum of the City of New York.*

ways she would have been unfulfilled to the end of her life, except that she was not defeated by lack of adequate response, as other artists might have been. The very core of her life, the meaning of her achievement, was the endeavor itself and the joy of creation. She cared far less about production, little about recognition, and nothing at all about remuneration. In this, I believe, she was unique, being compelled to create for the joy of the work to the very end of her life.

For eighteen years (1928–1945) she maintained with Charles Weidman a school and performing company which annually gave performances in New York City.

During its final period it was located on West Sixteenth Street and incorporated an enormous practice hall which had a large floor space superbly suited for dancing, and risers for seats, easily accommodating two hundred fifty viewers. Here they initiated most of their new works and made all the studies which they later developed at Bennington College and other places. The studio became the mecca for dance students from around the world and was the focal point for enormous creative experiments. In truth, this spot made history. Her heroic fight to maintain the school, the studio, and her lofty standards of excellence was arduous and prolonged, but the enterprise finally came to an end.

Katherine Litz and Charles Weidman in *Theater Piece,* 1936. CREDIT: *Photograph by Bouchard.*

The company was dissolved, the theater closed, and Weidman and Humphrey separated.

After her theater closed and her school dissolved she put her services at the disposal of her pupil, José Limón, who was starting off on his own, and composed for him several pieces, notably *Lament for Ignacio Sanchez Méjias,* performed to the spoken poems of Garcia Lorca; and a satire, *The Story of Mankind.* Walter Terry wrote in the *New York Herald Tribune* on January 12, 1947: "Doris Humphrey has maintained her position as one of the great choreographers of our day and has contributed immeasurably to the growth of other dance artists. . . . Miss Humphrey's works have exploited heretofore latent attributes of personality and physical virtuosity."

She taught at the Young Men's Hebrew Association and the Juilliard School of Music in New York. She was the only master ever to teach dance composition as a fine art in America, and she wrote one of the five great treatises on the subject, *The Art of Making Dances,* published posthumously in 1959, which at the time of publication was the only book in English on the techniques of choreography. She taught the whole of her adult life, influencing and guiding two generations of professional pupils.

The technique taught in the Humphrey-Weidman school seems in retrospect blurred, even amorphous, and Humphrey's choreographic work on the whole cool, cerebral. But she could on occasion produce works of impassioned grandeur and emotion. Her use of the earth had not the impact or sharply defined dynamics that characterized Graham's technique, nor did her code of technique crystallize into the definite structure that Martha was finally able to give her pupils, that steel-like technique that made for enduring form. The Humphrey-Weidman work and technique may, therefore, not have an equal impact on the general body of dancing. But her choreographic achievement will. She was a power during her life. She remains just that: a strong creative influence, a permanent part of our enduring heritage.

Walter Terry wrote in the *New York Herald Tribune* on January 11, 1959, at the time of her death:

> Her forty years-plus of dancing, choreographing, directing, teaching were immeasurably rich. Her name, of course, is secure in the annals of the theater, in the history of dance, in the memories of those who prospered artistically by her guidance. . . . she found that the materials of dance were born of gravity and that the range of dance lay within the action of fall and recovery, an area she termed "the arc between two deaths," death in vertical rigidity, death in submission to gravity.
>
> On this idea of the "arc," she built the drama of her dances, for not only were there physical daring and virtuosic perils as the body swayed or whirled or dipped away from its safe verticality, but there were, inherently, comparable adventures in emotion, in thought, in drama, in adventures from the safe to the exciting, even to the terrifying. In two of her early solos, *Circular Descent* and *Pointed Ascent,* this technique served to create stirring dances with mainly kinetic meanings, but, in other works, the same technique could reveal the despair, the passion of man himself and project specific conflict and incident and theme.
>
> Later, to this organic action of dance, she added the great vocabulary of human gesture, both inherited and instinctive. . . .

John Martin wrote in the *New York Times* on the same day:

> Nobody has put a deeper or more vital mark upon the dance in America. Ruth St. Denis has written in her notable autobiography, *An Unfinished Life,* that the actual form of what came to be known as the modern dance was first evolved by Doris Humphrey in the old Denishawn days when she gave choreographic body to Miss St. Denis' idea of "music visualization.". . . It is impossible to estimate the number of young artists who owe their awakening, their development, their achievement to the Humphrey influence. . . . Indeed, Doris Humphrey is an enduring part of the dance in America, as the granite under the soil is enduring. We can turn nowhere in the art without finding her.

Humphrey's partner and disciple, Charles Weidman (1901–1975), also a pupil of Denishawn and cofounder of the Humphrey-Weidman company, was a lighter, more humorous artist (as expressed in his choreography for James Thurber's *Fables for Our Time,* his biography *Daddy Was a Fireman,* and kinetic studies which prefigured Twyla Tharp) but capable of innovative, jagged movement and great force as, for instance, in his *Lynch Town.*

José Limón. *Corybantic.* CREDIT: *Photograph by Bouchard.*

José Limón. CREDIT: *Daniel E. Lewis, Courtesy of the Daniel Lewis Dance Repertory.*

The Moor's Pavane, by José Limón, with Dennis Nahat as Iago in American Ballet Theatre's production. CREDIT: © *Max Waldman.*

Charles Weidman had the demon which possessed Martha Graham but which Doris so seldom evinced. He worked through emotion, through inspiration, and he worked through comedic genius. His output is not comparable to Humphrey's, but some of it is very fine indeed and the fine parts were instinctive.

The fourth native name that is always associated with the pioneer modern movement in the United States is that of Helen Tamiris (1905–1966). Tamiris was a handsome, strong-bodied, lithe, agile, and pleasant dancer of enormous gusto but little creative talent, who through sheer energy and a kind of aesthetic chutzpah managed to get herself discussed and recorded as the peer of the great innovators. She was not that, and her works seem paltry beside theirs. Lacking the enormous zest of her presence, they cannot stand up to modern viewing.

Mary Watkins, who was the first dance critic on a daily newspaper in the United States, preceding John Martin by some years, made an evaluation of the modern dancers just before she died at 90. Tamiris was the best technically and in natural ability, she thought, but a very poor choreographer, in fact scarcely a choreographer at all. Doris Humphrey was a bland dancer with great choreographic gifts, probably the best of the lot. Ruth St. Denis diffused and confused her enormous dance skills under veils and incense and general nonsense, but the talent was there. Martha Graham is the most individual, the real revolutionary and the one who made direct contact with the audience and spoke to them with the greatest impact.

Humphrey's pupils have been extraordinarily creative. Alone of all great choreographers, this fine teacher released individuality instead of cramping it and helped develop personal styles that were in no sense rubber-stamp versions of hers.

Mexican born José Limón (1908–1972), one of the most noted dancers and choreographers in the United States, was a member of the Humphrey-Weidman troupe for ten years. After service with the American army in World War II, he formed the José Limón Dance Company, for which he and Miss Humphrey, his artistic director for many years, choreographed a number of important works. These included, in 1949, a masterpiece, *The Moor's*

Pavane, the story of Othello. Limón once said, "I view myself as a disciple and follower of Isadora Duncan and the American impetus as exemplified by Doris Humphrey and Martha Graham. I try to compose works that are involved with man's basic tragedy and the grandeur of his spirit."

In Limón's choreography, the flow of the dancing is marked by the contrasts between lyric and dramatic experiences. Whatever he did is finished in form and has classic structure, order, and formality, but his works are, above all, humanly meaningful. As a young man he felt he was destined to be a painter, and his dance creations always show a predilection for pictorial images.

He tended in his later career to create works demanding large companies and, despite poverty and restricted means, dealt in massive concepts. Although he received small grants from the federal government, the maintenance of a sizable group represented sacrifice on the part of all that is one of the truly noble manifestations of the American theater. His life was an uninterrupted dedication. He lived on what he could earn teaching and spent his substance on rehearsals, keeping nothing for himself.

His ideas were epic, passionate, and heart-stirring. The dances include *There Is a Time* (to music by Norman Dello Joio); *The Moor's Pavane* (Purcell); *A Choreographic Offering* (Bach); *Missa*

Sybil Shearer. CREDIT: © *Helen Balfour Morrison.*

Sybil Shearer in class. CREDIT: © *Helen Balfour Morrison.*

Brevis (Kodaly), and *McComber's Folly* (to electronic music by Jacob Druckman). His pieces were always realized in terms of the most exquisite and original gesture. He made a number of overseas trips for the U.S. Department of State. Limón's travels throughout the world with his troupe brought from *Dance Magazine* the comment: "Not only has he performed in the major cities, but he has also taken his art to remote spots, where the opportunities to see top-flight modern dance are rare, though the interest is high. And whatever the performance, he offers works of substance and maintains the highest standards."

But his largest, grandest works have been seen only in a few places. The *Missa Brevis*, for instance, was performed in the nave of Washington's Episcopal Cathedral with stunning effect. Both church and state took note of what was happening: Limón was reintroducing dance into Christian worship after a separation of nearly a thousand years. In his late work, in fact, Limón established himself to be as great a choreographer as his teacher, Doris Humphrey. Since his death, his work has been kept alive by a group under the leadership of Carla Maxwell.

In the last of the companies directed and choreographed by Humphrey was a former Fokine pupil, Pauline Koner. This distinguished soloist had the courage and perspicacity to put aside her hard-won classic technique and her status as a concert artist and seek fresh means of expression under the great modern teacher. She became a modern dancer of prodigious technical force, with a gamut of gesture possible only to one who has excelled in both schools. She is herself a remarkable teacher, particularly for pupils who start late, and she is a choreographer of poignancy and depth. Under the auspices of the Department of State, Koner has taught extensively in the Far East, and she was on the staff of the North Carolina School of the Arts. Like her teacher, Humphrey, she stressed the development of gesture according to its own internal rhythm, independent of musical phrase and beat. The subject matter of their work is always serious, not necessarily tragic, but thoughtful and searching.

Another Humphrey pupil, Sybil Shearer, withdrew in 1942 to the woods near Winnetka, Illinois, where she teaches and choreographs. But from time to time she appears in university theaters, and rumors of her exquisite performing and composition drift back to remind us of one of the most astonishing virtuosi of our time, and one of the greatest comedians. Her concerts with her own group in Illinois are legendary. But she will not leave home base for long or conform to any of the usual conditions of concertizing. So her influence and force remain circumscribed.

She creates through gestures alone, through a classic impersonality, by means of a sexless, ageless, unrepresentational approach. An architect of movement, she has the gift of building, in empty space, planes and textures and atmospheres. Her mastery of dynamic and spatial variation finds its counterpart only in musical tonality. In dancing, particularly in the Occident, such evocation as hers is very nearly without precedent.

Shearer's muscular technique is superb, particularly in the soft and controlled use of the foot, in the strength of the thighs for suspension and falls, and in her unmatched balance. Like Dalcroze she can maintain three or more rhythms simultaneously and she approaches melody with unexpected associations.

She is by choice kinesthetic, that is, nondramatic, nonstorytelling; her approach is pure dancing—a very rare gift. Her humor is usually based on rhythmic and spatial jokes, but occasionally she enters the realms of zany frivolity. For example, she has done a flamenco zapateado in tennis sneakers, and a Bach courante in a dress that pulls up like a window shade, which, when finally too high for decency, necessitates her finishing the piece in a squat lest the too short skirt appear unseemly.

She composes with a wealth of invention no one else possesses. She waits for the moment of "established contact," of vision. She then frequently creates a whole dance right off, start to finish. Longer dances require many "points of contact" (her term), but seemingly her need for revision and editing is less than other people's. In this superb faculty she resembles Isadora Duncan, who could visualize, we are told, an entire dance and perform it without rehearsal, a dance with form, development, climax, and tension, classic in its economy and singleness of style.

This is a function of genius, this speed and assurance, together with the capacity for being pro-

Trend, by Hanya Holm, 1937. CREDIT: *Photograph by Bouchard.*

lific and varied, and the term genius has been applied to Shearer by José Limón, Doris Humphrey, and many leading writers. Critic John Martin classes her with Isadora Duncan, and Claudia Cassidy of the *Chicago Tribune* states that she is one of the ten immortals (in any performing field) of our time. John Martin once wrote of her (in *Sybil Shearer*, published in 1965 by Helen Morrison):

Obviously she dances herself, yet never *about* herself. What she dances about is everything—trees and people, growth, animals, love, clouds, death, play, and fantasy. She can evolve with humor and tenderness (and perhaps even a saving touch of malice) a whole race of creatures who could not possibly live anywhere except under some stone she has turned over. She can convulse you with erratic nondescripts of action, personal and impersonal, applying to nobody and to everybody. She can give you the lost and the strayed with a simple wisdom and a natural compassion. None of it is remotely realistic, but all of it is touchingly real, some of it spiritually joyous, and much of it as deep as a well. There are no platitudes, no banalities, no morals, no ulterior purposes; there is only the communicative transfer of world experience (perhaps also of other-world experience) by a curiously intuitive, utterly individual, completely fey creature of surpassing innocence.

And Franklin Rosemont wrote in *Cultural Correspondence* in fall 1979:

> She always has been "absolutely modern," in the sense intended by Rimbaud. "Modern," she says, "is the desire and the attempt to reach eternity now." Through her marvelous kinesthetic alchemy, Sybil Shearer has brought a whole world into being—a world of irreducible radiance, warm with the glow of ancient suns, caressed by winds from a wholly desirable future. It is our good fortune that much of her work is currently available on film.

Shearer steadfastly refuses to conform to usual business requirements and remains in her pastoral retreat in Illinois, like a dancing Tolstoi, drawing disciples to her from afar.

Hanya Holm, the German concert dancer, has had far-reaching influence in this country. Originally a pupil and assistant of the great Middle European innnovator Mary Wigman, she emigrated in the 1930s to establish an American branch of the Wigman school in New York City and, because of her ability as a teacher, to spread the Middle European method widely. This proved to be a fruitful and liberating complement to the Graham technique, which at that point had not achieved the broad base and fluid scope it was later to manifest. Holm gave some stunning recitals with her group and for many years appeared annually as a choreographer on Broadway. But it is as a teacher that she has been most effective. Valerie Bettis and Glen Tetley are among her distinguished pupils.

Lester Horton (1906–1953) broke trails on the West Coast in the thirties, establishing an experimental theater based on the style of Martha Graham, at least what he was able to see of it. Horton and his pupils denied all charges of imitation and derivation, claiming that he had never seen the great modern. Maybe not, but her pupils were everywhere, and Horton's initial choice of the basic ground position, the seat on the ground in the open swastika, so unusual, so foreign to Western dancing, as well as the progression from floor exercises to standing and running stints, and the falls, were so intimately related to Graham as to be close kin, and Graham came first. He did, however, diverge.

His performers were voluntary and unpaid and held together by an intense faith in their leader. Their work cannot be compared to that of the great pioneers in New York at the time, Graham and Humphrey, but the school developed some extraordinary personalities, who have gone on to make their own way. These include Alvin Ailey, Bella Lewitsky, Carmen de Lavallade, and James Truitte. These pupils have far surpassed Horton's achievements and prestige, but even though they have become national figures, they maintain an intense allegiance to their teacher.

The five greatest twentieth-century pioneers— Duncan, St. Denis, Wigman, Graham, and Humphrey—founded their own schools and maintained their own companies and traditions. With the exception of Wigman, the German, none of them was, at the time, state-endowed. It is interesting that all five of the greatest rebels against tradition in dance were women, and that four of them were American.

The pupils these artists attracted were mature and came through choice. They were not sent by their parents or indentured to the state when young, as in the European opera ballet companies. They came the way apprentices come to great painters. The new technique, the style, and the compositions were worked out together, master and pupil struggling with the same problems. The performers were rarely paid and had to work for their living at menial jobs, such as waiting on tables in restaurants. They gave their whole time, their strength, and their youth to the formation of these techniques, with no great hope of personal advancement and no guarantee of performing careers; asking merely to serve the art form and their chosen masters. It takes a serious and dedicated human being to do this, and the modern dancer of the 1930s and 1940s was in point of view less like a ballet dancer of the preceding centuries than like an acolyte, or a Renaissance craftsman. These girls and boys and their leaders pulled their profession back into dignity, into the respect of other artists, and into acceptance by the community.

The so-called modern dance has become a truly American form, and it has influenced and shaped all our indigenous choreography for almost fifty years.

Left, *Bear's Track, Sauk.* 1830–1839. Right, *Medicine Man, Performing His Mysteries Over a Dying Man.* 1832. CREDIT: *Paintings by George Catlin, National Collection of Fine Arts, Smithsonian Institution; Gift of Mrs. Sarah Harrison.*

Below left, *White Buffalo, an Aged Medicine Man.* 1832. Below right, *Bull Dance, Part of Mandan Okipa Ceremony.* Not dated. CREDIT: *Paintings by George Catlin, National Collection of Fine Arts, Smithsonian Institution.*

Fanny Elssler portrait by an unknown painter.
CREDIT: *Zachary Solov Collection.*

Kitchen Ball at Sulphur Springs. 1838. This dancing was obviously a direct copy of the white masters' parties. There is no hint of the indigenous Negro dancing.
CREDIT: *Painting by Christian Mayr, North Carolina Museum of Art.*

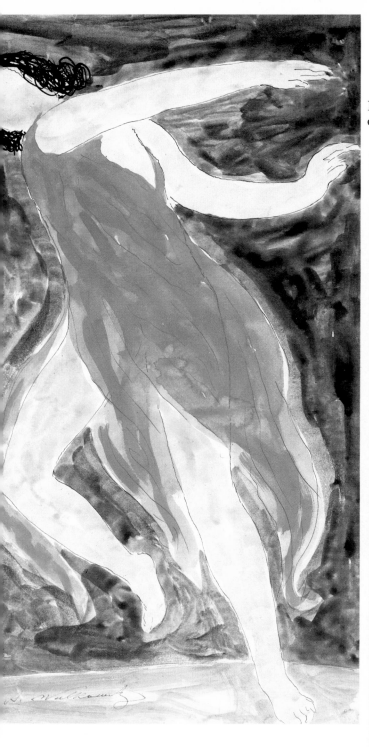

Drawing of Isadora Duncan by Abraham Walkowitz.
CREDIT: *Abraham Walkowitz/The Sid Deutsch Gallery.*

Omika, by Ruth St. Denis, with Ruth St. Denis as the
Poetess. CREDIT: *Arnold Genthe.*

Kristina Sergueyeva and Mark Platt in *Oklahoma*, 1943, by Agnes de Mille. CREDIT: *Gjon Mili, Life magazine,* © *Time, Inc.*

AGNES DE MILLE

Agnes de Mille in *Tally-Ho*, 1944. CREDIT: *Daily News.*

Gwen Verdon in *Redhead*, by Bob Fosse. CREDIT: *Philippe Halsman.*

Jardin aux Lilas, by Antony Tudor, full set. CREDIT: *Jack Mitchell.*

Christine Sarry and David Coll in Eliot Feld's *Intermezzo* (Brahms).
CREDIT: *Arks Smith*.

Judith Jamison in costume for
La Mooche. CREDIT: *Lois
Greenfield/Courtesy of
Capezio Ballet Makers.*

The River, by Alvin Ailey,
choreographed for American
Ballet Theatre. CREDIT: *Arks
Smith.*

Discotheque, Studio 54. CREDIT: ©Robin Platzer.

All That Jazz, by Bob Fosse. CREDIT: *Alan Pappé.*

11. THE MAVERICKS

CERTAIN dancers who have achieved national fame are too individual and independent to be linked with the main stream of either ballet or modern. For the most part, they have founded no lasting schools and have no direct inheritors. Nevertheless, they were influential and should be noted carefully.

Misho Ito (1895–1961) was a pupil of Jacques Dalcroze (1865–1950) and studied with that great man in Switzerland. Like his master he became adept in the manipulation of multiple rhythms and was a remarkable artist in dynamics, achieving a very fine technique and establishing a style which was extremely persuasive and influential. Among his pupils were fine dancers, including Angna Enters, La Meri, Benjamin Zemach, and Geordie Graham, the younger sister of Martha Graham, who was herself of Denishawn.

William Butler Yeats wrote of him "I saw him as a tragic image that stirred my imagination. He was able, as he rose from the floor where he had been sitting cross-legged or as he threw out an arm, to recede from us into some more powerful life."

On present viewing, his dances, which have been reconstructed and exhibited, seem highly sentimental, also repetitious, although they do contain some fresh and very lovely configurations. They are strongly influenced by Duncan, while lacking the stern, almost sparse skeletal structure and form which Isadora's work always maintained, nor any of her wealth and depth of feeling.

The great pantomimist, Angna Enters, belonged to no school, had no pupils and left no followers, but she was a remarkable artist and one of the finest actresses of our time. Her *Compositions in Dance Form* will not be forgotten by anyone who saw them.

She was born and educated in Milwaukee. She took ballet lessons in early childhood but, as a teenager, studied art in New York and became interested in movement and composition, although she never gave up drawing and designing. In fact she has exhibited her own paintings and sculpture both here and in Europe. Her first professional dance experience was with Misho Ito, who invited her to join his company and to be his partner, an opportunity she declined. In 1924 she gave her first program of compositions in dance form, solo, character vignettes of remarkable force. She has performed in England

and contemporary students) and people in dancing situations, using my ability to encapsulate the style and spirit of a dance genre in a few movements and find the pithy, telling gestures that would outline a character as Daumier outlined a face, but with humor that was warm and gentle and in many instances pathetic. John Martin paid me the great tribute of comparing me to Charlie Chaplin. During my time as a concert dancer, I developed a keen sense of dramatic structure. Oscar Hammerstein once said that some of these short dance pieces were as well formed as good one-act plays. This skill stood me in fine stead later, as I shall relate. As a dancer and choreographer, I was, before all else, a gifted storyteller.

Carmelita Maracci, a Californian trained in Spain, was an important but little-known artist of the late thirties. She baffles criticism because her technique fell into two categories: ballet, which, although impeccably correct (entrechat huit, five pirouettes on point), was not classically orthodox in style; and Spanish, which although virtuoso (she handled castanets like Argentina), was also highly unorthodox in form and flavor. She had no wish to perpetuate aesthetic tradition and used only those stock gestures so deeply imbued with emotion as to become under her manipulation original. Working in the spirit of the great caricaturists, she was more of a grotesque than a satirist and played with cruelty in a manner suggesting Goya or Toulouse-Lautrec. Her best solos were the most passionate and powerfully devised of any I have ever seen. Although she performed infrequently and was seen by few, no one who saw her ever forgot her. She left a very real legend behind her. I quote notes I made in January 1936 after watching her in her dance studio in Hollywood:

Pavane, with Angna Enters. CREDIT: *Frances Brunnaire/The Agnes de Mille Collection.*

and Paris and been the recipient of several Guggenheim grants. For a time in the forties, she was a very successful screenwriter. Her books include *First Person Plural*, *Silly Girl*, *Artist's Life*.

As for myself, I was a trained ballet dancer with, according to the critics, a remarkable flair for acting. In fact, many of them considered me the best comedienne in the field. I made a repertory of solo and double dances which were character studies of dancers (Degas girls, chorus girls, ballet

Last night my jaw dropped. I am trying to remember exactly how it was. I sat in a studio where we had done a daily practice for six months, where we had had parties, where Carmie and I had improvised, kidded. The place smelled of wood and floorwax. The trumpet vines tapped at the windows. Carmie walked on incredibly high heels to the center of the room and sat down on a kitchen chair. She said to the pianist in her plain dancing-class voice, "I'm ready, I guess."

And it began, the great experience. Not in Covent Garden, during a Ballet Russe gala, when Kschessinska, Sokolova and Danilova stood on

Ballet Class (after Degas), 1939, with Agnes de Mille. CREDIT: *Soichi Sunami.*

Left, Agnes de Mille in concert in *Scherzo* (Beethoven). CREDIT: *Henry Waxman/ The Agnes de Mille Collection.* Center, Agnes de Mille in *Elizabethan Suite.* CREDIT: *Angus McBean photograph/The Harvard Theatre Collection.* Right, *'49.* This was my first dance and my first essay into Americana. CREDIT: *Doris Ullman/The Agnes de Mille Collection.*

the same stage, not in Pavlova's presence, not in Graham's concerts or in the most dazzling opera houses of the world have I experienced more. The girl worked with thunder. The dance she showed me was her *Canto Hondo,* or "Deep Song." She began sitting. She sits before she stands. Her head is snapped forward on her breast; her arms hang like ropes to the ground. In the maw of her spread knees her torso waits, ready, until a shudder of energy twitches through her feet, jerking her knees and lifting spasmodically her head. She is ready. The ground becomes vital under her heels. The ground takes possession of her. Her insteps quiver, the heels ring out nervously. Long shudders pass up her body. The head rolls on its supporting shoulders. She rocks on her hams, the weight of her head, of her emotion carried on arms thrust square against her knees. Braced, square, of a piece, resisting, she waits. Then suddenly, like the splitting of wood, the earth anger erects her and throws her out on space. She wrecks herself against the surface of the world. Her knees double up, jackknife fashion. She spikes at the ground with her heels. Her head rears back. Her chest lifts taut as she drills and drums. Oh, a merry hard tune, a tattoo

such as I never heard. Doubling and straightening, wrapping and slapping, she flays the air in naughty punishment. See the clavicles close and open under the taut skin. The cage of her little ribs works like a bellows. Her fingers poke and stick. Flecks of foam are dashed from her teeth. Her sturdy legs trot and strike like the hooves of a pony. She can kick up the ground alright! She can slap the air! Again and again! She can lash out at the sky! Olé, Carmalita!

This is the rage of the dust, the very wrath of the grave. Against the dirt of eternity she thrusts her pounding heart. The weakening pulse shudders through her body. Her eyes roll back. The fear becomes audible. "Ay!" she cries, and her teeth cannot hold the quivering lips. "Ay!"

She feels an anger in her bones, in her tight young sinews. She rages at the stones and the dirt, the waste of the dead. It is done. "Ay!"

"The terrain I traveled," says Maracci, "was not the studio floor, for my world led me into Goya's land of terror and blood-soaked pits. . . . The life I lived could not make me a dancer of fine dreams and graveyard décor . . . so I danced hard about what I saw and lived." And again, "I think that a technique should be subordinate

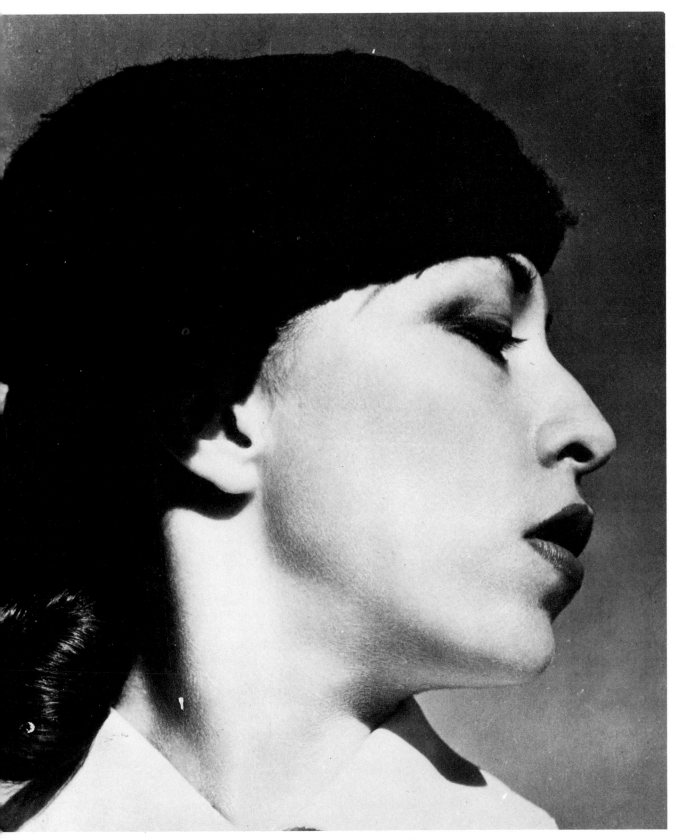

Carmelita Maracci, *Viva tu Madre*. CREDIT: *Edward Weston*.

Carmelita Maracci. CREDIT: *The Dance Collection.*

to the idea, and, of late, the opposite is true. . . . I don't want to see a well-trained dancing army in government hire who leap without question."

She is a famous teacher and holds regular classes. Janet Collins was one of her pupils. Another is Cynthia Gregory, who was lifted to star status by the American Ballet Theatre and now ranks behind only Nureyev, Baryshnikov, and Makarova in box-office draw. So although Maracci's tremendous career was cut tragically short by illness, her influence is still intense, and she has left a mark on the lives of those who ever knew her.

Janet Collins was a pupil of Carmelita Maracci and was therefore a mistress of point work and impeccable ballet style. She had Maracci's beautiful foot, the small bones, and compact body, and in many ways was like her, but in a miniature and gentler version. She also studied modern dance with Lester Horton and was a choreographer of real cre-

ativity. She gave splendid concerts in New York, did a stint on Broadway playing Night in *Out of This World*, and then became, under the direction of Zachary Solov, the prima ballerina of the Metropolitan Opera House.

We Americans have no heritage group and no national company dedicated to our indigenous and historic dance forms, and in this lack we are very nearly unique. Only two people have attempted to fill the gap in this field, Katherine Dunham and, much later, I myself with the Heritage Dance Theater. Both of us have been inactive for years because of financial exigencies. Both of us wait for an opportunity to resurrect and function.

Katherine Dunham was the first person to organize a black troupe of concert caliber and explore the rich folklore of her race. In studies of the American urban forms, the Caribbean types (Cuban, Haitian, and Jamaican), and certain African derivations, she proved herself not only a consummate theater artist but an anthropologist of note.

When Dunham started in the late thirties, there were only a half-dozen black dancers in New York. There were tap dancers, it is true, there were eccentric dancers, and there were the lively members of the Cotton Club line, but they were all in the commercial media, and the black commercial dances did not include any modern, any ballet, any ethnic or folk, not one. There were no black students of dance either, for since there were absolutely no opportunities, there was accordingly no hope. Out of such material, misfits mostly, Dunham made her first group with patient, antlike industry. Day by day by day. It is hard enough to compose dances with ready-trained students. Dunham had to do all the training as well, and she produced results that were astonishing. She asked of her group nothing they could not do, and do right away, without months of study (although she did set them studying and practicing hard daily). She was able with the most simple and direct means to produce a sense of spontaneity and exuberance. This requires the highest skill. She simply set them dancing, and they seemed just to be having a good time, because what she asked of them was natural. They were thus able to enjoy immediate results, and this was probably the main reason she was able to hold these tatterdemalion gypsies together.

Veracruzana, by Katherine Dunham, 1950, with Katherine Dunham in the "Danzon" section.
CREDIT: *Courtesy of Katherine Dunham.*

Katherine Dunham in her work *Bal Negre*.
CREDIT: *Vandamm Studio/The Billy Rose Theater Collection.*

Dunham and her husband, John Pratt, the designer, gave us a theater that for stylishness and joyous observation had no superior, yet could be understood by everybody and loved and participated in by everybody. It was her tragedy that she was the first, because at the time her concerts were introduced to the American public, black audiences were alien to the white theater environment. They were accustomed to tap dancing and nightclub routines in the theaters they frequented and that's all they were accustomed to. Dunham's sophisticated studies of fine folk materials were new to them, and moreover they had not formed the habit of going to downtown Broadway theaters and mixing with white audiences. That came about very slowly, in the North as well as in the South. So for years Dunham had to plow ahead with largely white audiences, which she conquered completely.

She conquered London, was the toast of Paris, quite literally, returned here a *grande vedette*, was a smash in New York, Chicago, and Los Angeles, and then took on South America, top to bottom, and afterwards the Caribbean islands. Everywhere she was an adored success.

She had a very simple body technique. What she gave was her personality, and that was nothing short of magic, for she had a most unusual combination of qualities: seductiveness—very real and very sweet—and humor. She never attempted what she could not do, and whatever she did she did with great finish and deftness. Moreover, Dunham combined all of this with the viewpoint of a scholar and a scientist. In this I think she was unique.

And always she seemed simple, natural; indeed, her large scenes seemed spontaneous—both totally deceptive impressions. Her large scenes were works

"Mantis" from *Imago* by Alwin Nikolais. CREDIT: *Photo: Robert Sosenko; Nikolais/Louis Foundation for Dance, Inc., Archives.*

of art and were organized with enormous skill.

Not only is she a great teacher but she is a pioneer, very really and truly. She had to train her company, of course. Many do. She had also to care for them, shield them, protect them, and, in a sense, maintain them, often to the point of renting houses to bed them down on the floor, but they were clean houses which otherwise they would not have had. She had no money, but still she saw that her people were housed and fed. Hers is an historic achievement. Now, God be thanked, people can forget, but in the thirties and early forties it was terrible for her, particularly on tour.

Her Broadway shows included *Le Jazz Hot From Haiti to Harlem* (1940), *Tropical Revue* (1943), *Carib Song* (1945), and *Bal Nègre* (1946), which were seen not only on Broadway but throughout the world.

Several of Dunham's pupils have become distinguished choreographers: Talley Beatty, Asadata Dafora, and Pearl Primus. Among the dancers she taught and starred in her company for years were Archie Savage, Eartha Kitt, and Lavinia Williams, whose daughter, Sara Yarborough, became one of the shining stars of the Alvin Ailey Company.

At present Dunham is teaching at the University of Illinois in East St. Louis, a bleak spot with not a friendly tree or a friendly bush, in a neighborhood of decaying houses and obsolete businesses and cracked pavement, a neighborhood of sinister aspect like a dream, sinister to enter, dangerous to stay in. Indeed, her lead dancer was murdered for the few dollars he had withdrawn from a bank to visit his mother. It seems friendless and hopeless. But there Dunham is established with her drums and her tape equipment and her many assistants and helpers and believers. And there she teaches. And the young men and women come to her by the dozens. She was quoted in an article in the *New York Times* in January 1979:

> Our people came from the streets. I wanted to offer a rational alternative. If they didn't want to learn dance, we taught them karate and judo and percussion. I taught the War Lords, a street gang, for a while. They must have thought I was kind of crazy. But, I can say for sure that we were responsible for breaking up a drug district called The Corner. We used to recruit down there. We were rehearsing on a nearby high school stage, so we could offer at least a warm

Loie Fuller. CREDIT: *The Dance Collection.*

evening. They got interested in drama. They made up their own scenes. They did cantata-form musicals about their own folk heroes, the people from their own streets.

She is making the desert bloom.

In 1979 she won the Albert Schweitzer Fellowship Music award.

Probably our finest scholar of African dances is Pearl Primus, who has made a lifetime study of native forms and practiced them for years. She had her own troupe and now does excellent ballets for such companies as the Alvin Ailey troupe. She herself was a spectacular dancer who specialized in jumps and a robust percussive style of fierce energy.

Lotte Goslar is a German who made her career on the Continent. She is a comedienne, or rather a clown, a true clown in the European sense, and her performances were distinctive and unmatched. America has few, if any, clowns; comedians, yes, but clowns, no. This seems to be a European form of expression. Goslar came here in the thirties and repeated her German success. She now has her own small and distinguished company.

Alwin Nikolais, of Russian and German ancestry, also stands apart from all other modern trends and schools. He is a true artist in the fusion of sound, color, light, and dance. He approaches the stage as a painter and sculptor. His is a special form of dance theater in which lights, stage properties, and sound (frequently electronic and composed by him) are equally as important as the dancers, who become, in effect, shapes in motion—instruments for the formation of ever-shifting patterns.

In 1963, he originated a suite of dances with a sound score seemingly derived from the noise of heavy industry. In *Sanctum* the dancers are encased in material which leaves their bodies free but holds their heads and feet. *Somniloquy*, a 1967 production, features backdrops and paths of colored lights that are invisible until someone steps into them. In *Galaxy* he uses fluorescent lighting to create triumphant flights from reality into the realm of theatrical magic, setting in motion things that are not supposed to move, materializing dancers out of emptiness, then blotting them out again. Four of the dances are performed to the accompaniment of brief lectures on armadillos, bacteria, astronomy, and aviaries.

He was once a puppeteer and this is perhaps a clue to his mysterious and lovely work, for he regards human beings as puppets or things. "My work looks 'far out,' " says the choreographer, "but I think of it as classical."

It would be hard to guess his artistic antecedents: the circus, the Oriental theater, certainly the music and variety halls, displays of fireworks, mechanical signs, animated drawings, kaleidoscopes. But above all he is the direct inheritor of the nineteenth-century music hall star Loie Fuller, whom he far surpasses.

At the turn of the century Loie Fuller (1862–1928), an American girl, introduced in Paris music halls a popular and spectacular act of skirt dancing. She wore dresses a hundred yards around and manipulated them with sticks under the play of colored lights. In a way she set a trap, which a whole school of scarf-waving, cloth-swishing, veil-tossing performers who came after her fell into, many of whom should have known better.

Fuller, who remained in Paris during her whole career, was the first person to experiment with

Alwin "Nick" Nikolais with dancers (and prop mannequin) in *Guignol*. CREDIT: © 1977, *Lois Greenfield.*

Noumenon, by Alwin Nikolais. CREDIT: © *Max Waldman.*

moving lights. She was able to do this owing to the invention in her day of the first safe lighting in the theater. Candle and gas footlights had caused many a death in the past. But with electricity, light could safely be turned on and off, or moved or varied in intensity. Electric light affected dance style to an enormous degree, for with it scenery and costumes could be made simple and suggestive, as well as more mobile. This dance technique seeks to establish goals not as a set of patterned actions. Its object, Nikolais says, is "to get the body to respond to any kind of dynamic that the mind dictates." His dancers thus seen able to accomplish all sorts of technical feats, and they have developed an acute sense of space.

Nikolais is today perhaps the finest theater electrician in the United States, and light plays a dynamic part in his compositions. The kind of effects he achieves have been hinted at hitherto in revues and pageants, such as those of New York's Radio City Music Hall, but his taste lies far beyond the gross or obvious. His invention seems endless, for his themes are always abstract, his dancers impersonalized objects never brought into any dramatic relationship or confrontation. Nothing is ever aligned, nothing is resolved, there is no catharsis, and so, while the imagination is teased and delighted, the emotions are never purged. It is as impossible to identify with the Nikolais dancers as it would be to identify with molecules under a microscope or flotsam on water. And yet the effects are endlessly suggestive. One watches in hypnotized surprise. There is often an air of poetic mystery or eerie wistfulness in Nikolais' work. It is a new technique and someday it will find its dramatist. In the meantime, Nikolais is spading up enormous tracts of new territory. He is a genuine pioneer, *sui generis,* unlike anyone else.

Nikolais's former star dancer, Murray Louis, is a splendid technician in the modern style and a sound and effective deviser of compositions just a step nearer humanity than those of his former master. Louis choreographs for several groups, including the Alvin Ailey.

12. THE INHERITORS OF THE BALLET

THE history of ballet dancing and ballet companies in the United States has been interrupted and broken due to the fact that there were no endowed institutions, no great state companies of any kind. This was unfortunate in some ways for the performers but most fortunate for the art as a whole, because it forced the performers to find their own method of expression and style, a situation not pertaining in any other country, and it called upon the great ingenuity of all our creative young people. The remarkable aspect of the situation is that those dancers who loved the ballet tradition went on practicing all through the sad hiatus, very strenuously and faithfully, and they were able to work in the twentieth century under good masters. The Russian Revolution scattered many of the imperial dancers over this continent, and they brought their great tradition and knowledge with them. We had the Theodore Kosloff School in Los Angeles, Adolph Bolm in Chicago, and Fokine and Mordkin in New York—three Diaghilev dancers and one superb choreographer. Their pupils worked under them without surcease for years, so when companies finally formed in New York during the forties, there was a body of dancers to choose from who were all ready, and there were choreographic talents of real strength to call on. There had been no indication that there would be endowed theaters, none—and there certainly was no promise or sign for another twenty years that there would be any federal or state support. But the dancers continued on faith alone and stood ready and primed when they were needed.

In Philadelphia Catherine Littlefield (1905–1951) and her sister Dorothy founded with their own money the Philadelphia Ballet Company, with Catherine as the choreographer. The works were not good, but the technique was excellent because she was a remarkable teacher. She trained a generation of girls who later became very well known, including Karen Conrad (1919–1976), Joan McCracken (1923–1961), and Dania Krupska. The company made one European tour but ceased to exist after Littlefield's untimely death.

The Mordkin Ballet (1937) was founded around the great Russian, Mikhail Mordkin, with Lucia Chase, Patricia Bowman, Karen Conrad and

Voices of Spring, by Mikhail Mordkin, 1939, with Patricia Bowman and Mikhail Mordkin. CREDIT: *The Dance Collection.*

Nina Stroganova as stars. It furnished a repertory of almost exclusively old Russian pieces in a re-casting and reduction so that these ballets could be toured easily. The company did tour extensively. Its value lay in preparing artists and taste for the great renaissance that was to come a few years later.

The New York City Ballet was founded in 1933 as the American Ballet by Lincoln Kirstein, a young Bostonian of private means with access to great wealth. While at Harvard he had made a reputation with his quarterly magazine *Hound and Horn*. On graduating he embarked on a distinguished literary career. He published books, pamphlets, and articles, at first mainly on contemporary art, then gravitating quickly toward the dance. He became one of the chief literary spokesmen of the dance and has published a large number of extremely important works in the field. He was also the impulse and guiding intelligence behind Romola Nijinska's life of her husband, Vaslav, and has written very fine treatments of Pavel Tchilechew and Elie Nedleman.

But his chief role has been that of patron, artistic director, business genius, and promoter and apologist for George Balanchine, whose School of the American Ballet has become one of the greatest schools in the world, and whose company, the New York City Ballet, is now one of the ranking companies. He served the New York City Ballet as Lucia Chase served the American Ballet Theatre, wholeheartedly, with energy, with time, with attention, with money, with acumen—literally with everything he had. Without him it would be hard to think Balanchine could have made the success he has made in the ballet world, though he was a great success on Broadway and could always be counted on to make himself tidy sums in the commercial media. The dance world proper is a very tough one artistically and financially, and there were not institutions or organizations to support choreographers when Lincoln Kirstein stepped into the wilderness and decided to establish them. The initial venture had to recess for long years because of financial stress, but when he reorganized the company and reconvened his artists, he was prepared for a long haul. The company now occupies the State Theater, where they flourish unchallenged and have biannual seasons in New York with resounding success. Balanchine is undoubtedly a genius and behind him has stood Kirstein, stalwart and faithful and astute.

He imported George Balanchine to New York in 1933 with the avowed purpose of establishing a truly American school and company in the best Russian tradition. The choreographer was, of course, Russian-Parisian, and the point of view and style were wholly European, as was the entire teaching staff (with the exception of Muriel Stuart, an English girl trained by Anna Pavlova). But the performing personnel were local, and it was hoped that

Lucia Chase in *Les Sylphides* by Fokine. CREDIT: *Maurice Seymour.*

under the direction of the master, native choreographers and teachers would in time develop.

Balanchine had been an orthodox product of the Imperial Ballet in St. Petersburg until he unexpectedly widened his technique in vaudeville. Owing to the generally reduced and chaotic economic situation following the Russian Revolution, the young dancer and his first wife, Tamara Geva, were forced out of Russia in 1924. He sought employment in the popular music halls of Western Europe and was there exposed to types of work his elders had been protected from and which, under continuing Imperial conditions, he might never have seen.

At that time the variety and music halls in Europe and America were exploiting a kind of stunt dancing called acrobatic adage, or adagio. The first famous practitioners were a French team, Mitti and Tillio. They were soon copied by troupes of boys and girls who climbed, tossed, hurled, slid, and threw one another all over the stage.

But even when the tricks worked, and notwithstanding the fact that they were always performed to music, the adage remained pure circus acrobatics. However, these remarkable lifts and holds, never dreamed of in classic ballet, invented with great audacity, even hardihood, proved useful to the young and hungry choreographer. For it was in the music halls that Balanchine learned the acrobatic stunts he later incorporated into the classic technique, and through his genius, the tossing, carrying, wrapping, and writhing found their way into meaningful design. He introduced these tricks first under the enterprising and open-minded sponsorship of Diaghilev in Paris, where the young choreographer's great initial style was formed. In my very first article published in *Theater·Guild Magazine* in 1930 and entitled "Acrobatics in the New Choreography," I wrote:

> It remained for Diaghilev, canny impresario, who barred from his stage nothing however grotesque until he had tried it, to see in commercial adagio technique the elements of new dance expression. Patterned on the relation of bodies to one another and not on the relation of bodies to rhythm and space, it presented the means for intense emotional symbolism. . . . Hitherto the female part of the design had been treated as a 95-pound weight handy for displaying the combined skill of the dancer. . . . Now for the first time, the ballet dancer finds herself a vertebrate. She has come to have substance, contour, emotions, and the customary means of expressing them. . . . What magnificent possibilities this new

Michael Kidd in Loring's *Yankee Clipper* for the Ballet Caravan, 1937, with Lew Christensen, Harold Christensen (rear), Fred Danieli, Eugene Loring, and Michael Kidd. CREDIT: *George Platt Lynes/The Dance Collection.*

John Kriza in the American Ballet Theatre's production of Eugene Loring's *Billy the Kid*, 1942. CREDIT: *The Dance Collection.*

point of attack opens to every branch ·of the theater.

Since the first experiments and largely because of Balanchine, the average *corps de ballet* dancer has achieved turns and *batterie* (beaten jumps), split leaps, and lifts barely within the compass of a ballerina in the pre-Diaghilev period. Technical virtuosity has come to be taken for granted. The Bolshoi of Moscow uses many of these acrobatic lifts, throwings, and tossings with hair-raising effect, but with far less imagination than Balanchine.

Balanchine was the last great choreographer to be developed by Diaghilev, and it was under Diaghilev's aegis that he choreographed his early masterworks, *Apollo* (Stravinsky) and *The Prodigal Son* (Prokofiev). These were revolutionary works, influential and dramatic in nature. But he derives chiefly from Petipa, and he has a veneration for the master's works and an endless enthusiasm whenever there has been an opportunity to renovate them.

Balanchine continued to work in Europe with

The *pas de quatre*. A resetting of the famous dance performed by Taglioni, Grahn, Cerrito, and Grisi before Queen Victoria, reset by Anton Dolin with Alicia Markova as Taglioni, Nora Kaye, Rosella Hightower, Annabelle Lyon. CREDIT: *Dwight Godwin/The Agnes de Mille Collection.*

Diaghilev, de Basil and Charles Cochran (1872–1951) of London until he was brought here by Lincoln Kirstein in 1933. The American company he came here to found was drawn from various schools and from all parts of the country, but was always under the sole supervision of Balanchine, who also established his own school.

After an initial season of two weeks in 1935, the company was suspended for nearly fourteen years. During the interim the school continued with growing strength and influence.

In the long hiatus Lincoln Kirstein gathered a few of the students of the school together and formed in 1936 a splinter group, which he called the Ballet Caravan. This traveling troupe gypsied around on a very modest budget and even toured South America. It produced several splendid dancers and one outstanding choreographer, Eugene Loring, whose *Billie the Kid* (1939) is one

Dark Elegies, by Antony Tudor, with Cynthia Gregory and Gayle Young. CREDIT: © *Arks Smith*.

of the staples of American Ballet Theatre. This is a splendid work, the first genuine American masterpiece, to a wonderful score by Aaron Copland, a remarkably unified synthesis of scenery, music, and choreography. Loring's invention is brilliant, and the synopsis of the ballet is sound and strong. *Billie* preceded by four years my own ballet *Rodeo*, but although the style of the two works is in some ways similar, they were evolved far apart, if concurrently, my work in England, his work here, providing an interesting example of two artists working on similar subjects at the same time with similar responses. Loring's last ballet for the Caravan, *City Portrait*, came close to being equally good, but it was given only a few performances because the company disbanded shortly after the work was introduced.

The Caravan was responsible for developing Lew Christensen, who later took over the San Francisco Ballet; Marie-Jeanne, a brilliant prima ballerina; William Dollar; Michael Kidd; Ruthanna Boris, the choreographer of *Cakewalk*; and Eric Hawkins, who later partnered Martha Graham and then became a choreographer-soloist on his own. The Caravan disbanded in 1941. Loring then joined Ballet Theatre as a charter member but a year and a half later formed his own company which was short-lived. He went to Hollywood and there he has stayed. The home school continued as the American Ballet School, a recognized power in the dance world.

Ballet Theatre, formed originally by Richard Pleasant and Lucia Chase in 1939 out of a nucleus of the Mordkin Ballet, boasted a staff headed by Michel Fokine.

A partial list of the stars and soloists of the American Ballet Theater:

Adams, Diana	Carter, William
Alonso, Alicia	Caton, Edward
Babilé, Jean	Chase, Lucia
Baronova, Irina	Conrad, Karen
Baryshnikov, Mikhail	Danielian, Leon
Baylis, Meredith	d'Antuono, Eleanora
Bentley, Muriel	Dokoudovsky, Vladimir
Bolender, Todd	Dolin, Anton
Bolm, Adolph	Dollar, William
Bowman, Patricia	Douglas, Scott
Bruhn, Erik	Eglevsky, Andre
Bujones, Fernando	Feld, Elliott

Antony Tudor, Nora Kaye, and Hugh Laing in *Dark Elegies*, 1943, American Ballet Theatre. CREDIT: *Carl Van Vechten/The Dance Collection.*

Fracci, Carla
Glassman, William
Golden, Miriam
Gollnar, Nana
Gregory, Cynthia
Hayden, Melissa
Hightower, Rosella
Hobi, Frank
Howard, André
Karnilova, Maria
Kaye, Nora
Kidd, Michael
Kirkland, Gelsey
Kivett, Ted
Koesun, Ruth Ann
Kriza, John
Laing, Hugh
Lander, Toni
Lang, Harold
Lazovsky, Yura
Lichine, David

Loring, Eugene
Lyon, Annabelle
Makarova, Natalia
Markova, Alicia
Marks, Bruce
Maule, Michael
de Mille, Agnes
Nagy, Ivan
Nahat, Dennis
Nureyev, Rudolf
Osato, Sono
Petit, Roland
Reed, Janet
Riabouchinska, Tatiana
Robbins, Jerome
Romanoff, Dimitri
Ross, Herbert
Sergava, Katherine
Serrano, Lupe
Shabalevski, Yurek
Skibine, George

Stroganova, Nina
Sutherland, Paul
Tallchief, Maria
Toumanova, Tamara
Tudor, Antony
Van Hamel, Martine

Varcas, Leon
Wilson, Sallie
Workman, Jenny
Youskevitch, Igor
Young, Gayle
Zorina, Vera

Over the years American Ballet Theatre has employed the services of nearly every distinguished choreographer alive.

The achievement of American Ballet Theatre as well as its survival is due to the passion, the unremitting concern, and the generosity of one patron, Lucia Chase, whose gift in terms of money equals, or possibly surpasses, that of any single patron to a cultural institution in the United States, and in terms of energy and dedication is unmatched. For over forty years she has given all her time, all day and night, summer and winter, as well as all her faculties, all her will, all her steady patience and endurance and sanity. What she has

Pillar of Fire, by Antony Tudor, 1941, with Annabelle Lyon, Lucia Chase, Nora Kaye, and Antony Tudor (center). CREDIT: *Maurice Seymour.*

built is the longest-lasting ballet theater in this nation and one of high excellence. America owes her a great debt.

Beside her, as codirector has stood Oliver Smith, the distinguished scene designer, a man of impeccable taste and judicious skill. The two have weathered every possible kind of storm with gallantry and vision.

Lucia Chase and Oliver Smith were presented with the Handel Medallion of New York City by Mayor Lindsay.

American Ballet Theatre developed more talents than any other theater in the United States. One of the foremost is an Englishman. Antony Tudor studied with and choreographed for the Ballet Rambert in London but failed to find real recognition in his home city. At the invitation of Lucia Chase, he came to America in 1939 and reproduced four works for her company. In two years he became choreographer-in-chief and artistic director.

He is perhaps the most individual and lyric choreographer of our time. He is a true romantic: his ballets are deeply felt and personally expressed through dramatic movement that is subtle and evocative. No other choreographer has so fused feeling and movement, nor composed scenes with such insight and delicacy. He has been called a psychological choreographer because he deals with human emotion truthfully and examines thoroughly each situation and character. He uses no dancing for merely decorative purposes; each gesture must serve the situation; dance and acting being indistinguishable. His work, therefore, although lyric, demands acting of the most sophisticated and subtle kind.

Indeed he has developed the storytelling quality of his choreography to such a degree that each gesture, formed out of the emotional components of the moment, is almost as explicit as though the dancers spoke. The new choreographer does not arrange old steps into new patterns; the emotion evolves steps, gestures, and rhythms.

And for this reason, the line between dancing and acting is no longer clearly marked—though by acting I do not mean realistic imitation. Consider the role of Hagar in *Pillar of Fire* (created by Nora Kaye)—a frustrated woman who gives herself to a man she does not love through fear of spinster-

hood. Her turns are an agony of spirit, her repeated balances and falls a bewilderment and frustration, her leaps a striving for release. A sailor beside me in the audience, seeing her throw herself into the arms of a man she did not love, groaned aloud. He had, as it happened, just witnessed a passage of technical virtuosity very nearly beyond the scope of any other living dancer. But he was not aware of this and did not clap. He did not cheer. He groaned. He could recognize trouble when he saw it.

Pillar of Fire (1941) is one of the theatrical landmarks of our era. It widened the idiom of dancing for all time, and has had a profound influence on all contemporary theater. Nora Kaye and Hugh Laing were the stars of most of his ballets and the greatest exponents of his style.

Within a span of nine years, Tudor gave Ballet Theatre eight masterpieces: *Lilac Garden, Judgement of Paris, Dark Elegies,* and *Gala Performance,*

Diana Adams as a Lover in Experience in Tudor's *Pillar of Fire,* 1941. CREDIT: *Alfredo Valente.*

Sono Osato as Rosalind in Antony Tudor's
Romeo and Juliet, 1944. CREDIT: *Walter E.
Owen/The Dance Collection.*

created in England; and choreographed here *Pillar of Fire, Romeo and Juliet, Undertow,* and *Dim Lustre.* These ballets changed the history of dancing. They are quite different, one from the other, and timeless. They introduced a style of lyric-dramatic gesture, explicit but nonrealistic, revealing and evocative, that has influenced everyone except the die-hard classicists, the descendants of Petipa, notably Balanchine, who nevertheless admires the younger man. Tudor produced a style of continuous action in dramatic form unbroken by set pieces, comparable in its effect on ballet to that of the Wagnerian music drama on the then contemporary opera.

Tudor has choreographed in Toronto, Stockholm, Tokyo. His ballets are in repertories around the world. In 1967 he returned home to London to produce his first work for the Royal Ballet, *Shadowplay.* He came back to American Ballet Theatre to mount his *Echoing of Trumpets* (first produced by the Royal Swedish Ballet). His recent work, *The Leaves Are Fading,* is a lovely piece of nostalgia in his most lyric vein.

He is now reviving all his old works, one by one. They remain the jewels in American Ballet Theatre's crown.

I was a charter member of the troupe. I had developed my skill in storytelling and character delineation in my concerts, and I now brought this to the ballet world, adding, I hope, a new sort of lyricism. The critics said that this combination sometimes achieved brilliant comedy and sometimes seemed a break in style, but out of this divergence I was able to develop my own style. Sybil Shearer called me a romantic. Technically, my work is eclectic, a mixture of classical and modern, which makes special demands on the performers.

I built a whole technique out of riding and roping movements and added them to traditional authentic cowboy steps. The mechanics of these movements are adaptations of techniques used in American sports such as tennis and baseball. I introduced them first in *Rodeo,* and, since then they have generally permeated the American folk style.

Muriel Bentley and Nora Kaye in *Dim Lustre*, by Antony Tudor, 1947. CREDIT: *Walter E. Owen/The Dance Collection.*

Judgement of Paris, by Antony Tudor, with Agnes de Mille as Venus. CREDIT: *Carl Van Vechten/The Dance Collection.*

Sallie Wilson and Marcos Paredes in Antony Tudor's *Pillar of Fire*, 1966. CREDIT: *Jack Mitchell.*

Tally-Ho, by Agnes de Mille, with Harold Laing, Anton Dolin, Miriam Golden, Muriel Bentley, Shirley Eckel, and John Kriza. CREDIT: *Louis Melancon.*

Cynthia Gregory in Antony Tudor's *Jardin aux Lilas*, 1972. CREDIT: © *Bil Leidersdorf.*

In *Rodeo* I also employed virtuoso tap dancing for the first time in the ballet. This was paralleled by my incorporation of realistic comedy into formal dance pattern. My best-known works are *Rodeo* (for the Ballet Russe de Monte Carlo), *Fall River Legend*, *Tally-Ho*, *Wind in the Mountains*, *The Four Marys*, *The Bitter Weird* (for the Royal Winnipeg Ballet), and *A Bridegroom Called Death* (for the Joffrey Ballet).

Elizabeth Kendal wrote, at the time of the 1979 revival of *Oklahoma!*:

> Agnes de Mille is the only American choreographer who approaches Fokine in her musicality, a musicality which can be seen in her phrasing . . . and in her use of the corps de ballet as plastic material to animate the whole stage.

In 1976 I was presented with the Handel Medallion by Mayor Beame of New York City.

Antony Tudor at rehearsal. CREDIT: *Arks Smith.*

Three Virgins and a Devil, by Agnes de Mille, with Muriel Bentley, Lucia Chase, Agnes de Mille. CREDIT: *Carl Van Vechten/The Dance Collection.*

Agnes de Mille in *Rodeo*. My husband carried this portrait with him through the war. CREDIT: *Louis Melancon.*

Fall River Legend, by Agnes de Mille. Oliver Smith's history-making set. The house could be taken apart in sections and even reversed to change scenes. The gallows fits in as a roof tree. The original cast included Patty Barker, Alicia Alonso, Peter Gladkey, and Muriel Bentley. CREDIT: *Louis Melancon.*

Four Marys, by Agnes de Mille. (Left to right) Judith Lerner, Paul Sutherland, Cleo Quitman, Judith Jamison (her first part with a big company and her first appearance in New York), Glory Van Scott, Carmen de Lavallade. CREDIT: *Jack Mitchell.*

Sallie Wilson in *Fall River Legend,* by Agnes de Mille. CREDIT: *Jack Mitchell.*

Jerome Robbins, a brilliant soloist, appeared in many works with American Ballet Theatre and studied the choreographic methods of Fokine, Massine, Balanchine, Tudor and myself. Most of his contemporaries regard him as the greatest stylist in American ballet today. He works in both classic and modern dance, makes frank use of jazz idioms, and, like me, employs natural gesture instead of the

Oliver Smith's set for Agnes de Mille's *Fall River Legend*. CREDIT: *Friedman-Engler photographers.*

stylization of traditional ballet, or he has in the past, but now he has begun modifying toward the old works because, for all of his unorthodoxies, he is a classicist and prides himself on his strong sense of form. His influence on the younger generation of artists both here and abroad is unmatched.

His subject matter at first tended to be bitter, nervous, and warped, in spite of the fact that his great contribution was humor, possibly the most incisive in the dance world, on a level with the best American humor in any field, particularly that of the great comedians of the early motion pictures. As far as is known, there has never been in dancing anything like his capacity for making audiences laugh. His humor is not warm. It is zany and satiric. It involves a degree of exaggeration and tremendous physical technique. The timing of his jokes can serve as a model for actors the world over.

He has expanded physical technique to the totality of action, as in sports. He has also incorporated jazz (he was deeply influenced by Jack Cole [1913–1974], the jazz choreographer) and loosened the rigid Balanchine back and neck, liberating arms and legs, in every sense freeing

Fall River Legend, by Agnes de Mille, 1965. Original cast—Alicia Alonso as Lizzie Borden, and John Kriza. CREDIT: *Louis Melancon.*

Fancy Free, Jerome Robbins' history-making ballet which launched his great career in 1944, with Paula Lloyd, Muriel Bentley, Jerome Robbins, John Kriza, and Michael Kidd. CREDIT: *The Granger Collection.*

movement. He, Balanchine, and Tudor work in the classical idiom, but their styles now differ widely, and Robbins's is the most experimental.

After two initial hits for Ballet Theatre, *Fancy Free* and *Interplay,* he left for a long interval in the Broadway theater. When he returned to ballet, it was to the New York City Ballet, where he danced in a number of George Balanchine's works, including *The Prodigal Son.* For that company he produced a dozen or so successes, *The Cage, Afternoon of a Faun* and *The Concert* among them, and eventually became joint director of the organization.

In 1965 he returned to Ballet Theatre to create his great work *Les Noces* (Stravinsky), a reworking of a ballet by Bronislava Nijinska that had first been performed by the Diaghilev company in Paris in 1923.

Robbins then returned to the New York City Ballet to create the masterpiece *Dances at a Gathering,* first presented in 1969. It is performed by ten

Los Caprichos, by Herbert Ross, with Alicia Alonso, Eric Braun, and Kelly Brown. CREDIT: *The Dance Collection.*

Les Noces, by Jerome Robbins, with the company of the American Ballet Theatre. Photo taken at the première performance at the New York State Theater, March 30, 1965. Featured (left to right) are William Glassman, Bruce Marks, Ted Kivitt, and Erin Martin (as the bride). CREDIT: *Jack Mitchell.*

Other Dances, by Jerome Robbins, with Mikhail Baryshnikov and Natalia Makarova.
CREDIT: *Beverley Gallegos.*

Other Dances, by Jerome Robbins, with Natalia Makarova. The extreme suppleness of spine, pliancy of neck, and free arms are characteristic of the current Soviet style. They would not have been possible for a dancer 100 years ago—for one thing, the ladies wore corsets. CREDIT: © *Max Waldman.*

dancers in conventional dress on a virtually empty stage to a solitary piano playing Chopin. The humor is delicate and absorbed into the dance gesture, leaving only the barest trace of pantomime. The mood is joyous but courteous, noble even, and haloed with a kind of earth simplicity, earth love. One feels the work to be a gesture of gratitude.

For all its seeming classicism, *Dances at a Gathering* is highly revolutionary, and Robbins's handling of the Chopin music is extraordinary. It is, of course, impossible to achieve visual results by the same patterns and devices upon which audible ones are built, and yet musical imitation has been the history of theatrical choreography for

a century. Where, for instance, the musical pattern is symmetrical, the dance will follow, becoming often wearisome or trivial and failing precisely through fidelity. Robbins has a gift for asymmetry and a magical sense of translation, which free the gesture from musical ground rules, yet never betray or controvert them. After one sees the mazurkas in *Dances,* I do not think one will ever again hear the music without remembering the ballet. In truth, a dimension has been added, not of interpretation, but of collaboration. With these pieces, Robbins proved himself one of the subtlest musicians working. Next came his monumental *Goldberg Variations* and the mysterious and exquisite *Water Mill* to a Japanese

Alicia Alonso and her superb Cavalier, Igor Youskevitch, in their matchless *Nutcracker pas de deux* by Lev Ivanov. CREDIT: *Gjon Mili, Life magazine,* © *Time, Inc.*

score. These, together with his many pieces to Ravel and Stravinsky, fill out a repertory that is formidable, the richest and most complete of any native choreographer. *Dances at a Gathering* is as important as early Tudor, early Graham, early Balanchine. It is a watershed in the theater.

Jerome Robbins received the Handel Medallion in 1976 and was awarded the rank of Chevalier de l'Ordre des Arts et Lettres by the French government in 1964.

Michael Kidd is a veteran of Lincoln Kirstein's Ballet Caravan. He was a sturdy, excellent character dancer who proved himself the worthy heir to Robbins in many of his parts: such as his sailor in *Fancy Free*. While in Ballet Theatre he launched a choreographic career and had a genuine success with his first work, *On Stage,* in which he himself danced a Chaplinesque role very delightfully.

Herbert Ross, a student of Caird Leslie, started as a modern dancer but shifted his interest to ballet when the American Ballet mounted splendidly and brilliantly his *Caprichos* (based on Goya's etchings of that name). The ballet is a miniature, but extremely fine, and has always been most impressive. He followed it in 1957 with *The Maids* (music by Bartok), a work of savage irony and sadness that is given few performances because of its difficult requirements for the performers and because of its bleaching and withering effect. It is,

Alicia Alonso and Igor Youskevitch in *Giselle,* by Jules Perrot, restaged by Anton Dolin. CREDIT: *Maurice Seymour.*

however, stunning and is in the repertory of several large companies.

The pioneering native choreographers (Robbins, Kidd, and I) have translated into ballet style some of the dynamics and techniques of the modern, or Martha Graham, school and many authentic colloquial folk steps, both country and urban, such as buck-and-wing, tap dancing, cowboy struts, jive, jitterbug, rock 'n' roll—in short, the whole popular vocabulary. The ballet dancer now on occasion droops and convulses, falls to the floor, spins on a nonvertical or changing spinal axis, beats and jumps off beat.

Ballet gesture before had always been based on the classic technique, even in quoted folk styles, and whatever deviated from this occurred only in comedy caricatures. The style throughout, the body stance, the walk, the run, the dynamic attack, the tensions and controls, were all balletic even when national folk dances were incorporated into the choreography, and the great solos could be interchanged with no break in idiom from one ballet to another.

Miss Julie, by Birgit Cullberg, with Violette Verdy. CREDIT: *Maurice Seymour.*

Erik Bruhn. CREDIT: *Jack Mitchell.*

Melissa Hayden and John Kriza in *Le Combat*, by William Dollar. CREDIT: *Maurice Seymour*.

Paquita, with Nora Kaye and Erik Bruhn. CREDIT: *Maurice Seymour*.

Les Sylphides, by Michel Fokine, with Natalia Makarova, Ivan Nagy, and Karena Brock. CREDIT: *Louis Péres*.

The younger choreographers, on the other hand, believed that every gesture must be proper to a particular character under particular circumstances. In this way, we Americans have tried to diversify the root impulse and, just as Gershwin impressed on the main line of musical development characteristics natural to his own unclassical environment, we added gestures and rhythms we had grown up with, using them seriously and for the first time without condescension. This is not a triviality; it is the seed and base of the whole choreographic organization, for if dance gesture means anything, it means the life behind the movement. To the classic base we have accordingly added colloquialism. We have come down to earth; we have put our feet on the ground. Above all, pantomime is not as arbitrary

Sargasso, by Glen Tetley, with Sallie Wilson, American Ballet Theatre, March 1965. CREDIT: *Jack Mitchell*.

Romeo and Juliet pas de deux, by Kenneth MacMillan, with Gelsey Kirkland and
Ivan Nagy. CREDIT: © *1976, Max Waldman.*

or formal as in the older ballets. All this came
about inevitably as ballet began to take contemporary subjects for themes. The king's stance and
bow, his formal acting, were suitable to monarchs,
birds, and ghosts; they are not suitable to us.

In our native American ballet the acting is

natural and incorporated into the dance; the ballerina behaves like a human woman. *The Swan
Queen* permitted no liberties, emotional or physical;
the prince might touch only her hand or her waist,
and then only circumspectly. The girl you now see
in a Tudor, Robbins, Ross, or de Mille ballet knows

Apollo, by George Balanchine, with Lew Christensen.
CREDIT: *George Platt Lynes/The Dance Collection.*

Prodigal Son, by George Balanchine, with Maria Tallchief and Jerome Robbins. CREDIT: *George Platt Lynes/The Dance Collection.*

American Ballet Theatre Gala, 1972. First row, Lucia Chase, Eleanor D'Antuono, Agnes de Mille, Margot Fonteyn, Carla Fracci, Melissa Hayden, Judith Jamison, Maria Karnilova, Gelsey Kirkland, and Natalia Makarova. Second row, Merce Cunningham, Leon Danielian, Anton Dolin, John Kriza, Lawrence Rhodes, Helgi Tomasson. Bonwit Teller presented each female soloist with a bouquet of four dozen carnations which ranged in color from dark red through salmon to pale pink. The stage looked like a bower. CREDIT: *Fred Fehl.*

no such restraint. She has all the normal inclinations, and her young man is more than happy to oblige.

Over the last decades, the personnel of Ballet Theatre has gradually changed its character. The emphasis today is on classical dancing and neo-classical works. There have been only two new Tudor ballets in the last ten years, no new Robbins, and only one of my own, which was very short-lived. The bulk of the recent choreography is by Glen Tetley and dance stars Mikhail Baryshnikov and Natalia Makarova. The last two, not primarily choreograpers, have restaged a number of seventy-five-year-old Russian classics—*La Bayadère*, *Don Quixote*, *Sleeping Beauty*, and *The Nutcracker*.

The advent from Russia of these superb stars and their unmatched popularity has profoundly changed the tone of the company, because of late it has been the object to serve them first, which is in some ways the best box office. They were trained in the classic style and literature, and naturally they want the vehicles for their superb talents. But the name of Ballet Theatre was made on another kind of dancing and another kind of composition; not necessarily American, although it was in large effect just that, but certainly contemporary, deeply felt, and meticulously thought through. This gave Ballet Theatre its stamp and made it different from every other company in the world. It is still a ranking, first-class company, but it is now like the

Prodigal Son, by George Balanchine, with Edward Villella. CREDIT: *Martha Swope.*

Royal Ballet, like the Canadian National Ballet, and somewhat like the Stuttgart; that is, it is beginning to lose its definite profile. Those of us who loved it as it was mourn this fact.

In 1979, the appointment of Mikhail Baryshnikov to replace Lucia Chase as head of the company was announced.

Although Balanchine's company was dormant for nearly fourteen years while Balanchine worked on Broadway and in Hollywood, the School of the American Ballet, still under his supervision, never closed its doors. It trained generations of able dancers. In 1947 Kirstein revived the performing company under the title of the Ballet Society, with

Cynthia Gregory and Terry Orr warming up for a Doris Hering lecture demonstration, 1973. CREDIT: *Harold Glaser.*

The Cage, by Jerome Robbins, with Nora Kaye. CREDIT: *George Platt Lynes/The Dance Collection.*

Afternoon of a Faun, by Jerome Robbins, with Peter Martins and Suzanne Farrell. CREDIT: *Beverley Gallegos.*

Balanchine again in charge. It performed first at the Needle Trade School, for no theaters were then regularly available for dance companies. In 1948 it moved to the New York City Center Theater and took the name of the New York City Ballet. In the following decade, it became one of the leading ballet companies in the world and toured everywhere. The addition of Jerome Robbins in 1949 as codirector somewhat broadened but did not alter its approach.

Balanchine is almost incredibly prolific, having completed* 152 ballets outside of his Broadway and motion picture work in America and, at least 25 works in Leningrad before 1924. His influence on the younger generation in the United States and other countries is profound.

More than any of their contemporaries, he and Martha Graham have influenced theater dance. Because of his pristine sense of design and his

* As of 1979.

Serenade, by George Balanchine, with Susan Hendl (in arch), Susan Pilarre (in air), and *corps de ballet*. CREDIT: © 1980, Paul Kolnik.

Concerto Barocco, by George Balanchine, with Suzanne Farrell, Sean Lavery, Kyra Nichols, and *corps de ballet.* CREDIT: © *1980, Paul Kolnik.*

illuminating grasp of music, he has imbued all ballet with an approach toward pure form, rhythmic and spatial, and he has eliminated frivolity, fussiness, and trivial decoration. He has brought ballet back to the essentials but with a wealth of technique and sophistication. He has rid the stages of the world of false romanticism and the leftover claptrap of the nineteenth-century operatic displays. His imitators are innumerable, and although many of them are paltry, what he has taught them to strive for is the basic architecture of pure dance. None of them, however, can approach his own wizardry in relating simple abstract forms to musical pattern. In this he is supreme. Guided by a special genius for the classic form and for pure ballet, he holds that neither story nor decor nor costumes should be allowed to distract from the main point—the dance. His impulses and ideas come from the music, and he conveys them to his dancers with a simple twist of a hand, a quick movement of feet. "We communicate like whales in water, or like birds," he has said.

In the interest of purity his demands on the dancers are mainly for physical precision, rarely for musicianship, never for comic or dramatic skill. Indeed, he tries to suppress all realistic show of emotion, even to the extent of erasing personality. Mime is reduced to a bare indication, and the performer is urged to strive for anonymity and absence of personality. Balanchine is interested in the dancers as tools, much in the way a composer is interested in instruments, relying for effect on composition and dynamics. Nevertheless, his ballets are often deeply moving and exciting, and he can, by means of rhythm and pattern alone, produce effects of great wit, as in *Agon* (Stravinsky), while his *Liebeslieder Walzer* (Brahms) are perhaps the most exquisitely poignant lyric pieces of the century, excepting Fokine's *Les Sylphides* and Robbins's *Dances at a Gathering.*

While keeping the style and shape of his pieces formal, Balanchine borrows colloquially the laced interweaving of American square dances and the acrobatics, stunts, and syncopations of our popular theater steps. He has in many ways taken on the coloring of his new background, but his so-called

American pieces, *Western Symphony* (Hershy Kay), *Square Dance* (Vivaldi) and *Stars and Stripes* (Sousa-Kay), are European spoofs of popular American forms. They are highly amusing to people who know the forms intimately, but they are neither authentic nor sympathetic treatments of authentic material. On the contrary, they are deeply Russian, imperial and balletic. Despite his avowals, he remains abstract, and an apologist for the great imperial tradition. He has re-adapted three of the Petipa classics and Fokine's *Firebird* in his own style, and because of his genius, the changes spell

Symphony in C, by George Balanchine, with Tanaquil LeClercq. CREDIT: *George Platt Lynes/The Dance Collection.*

Firebird, Balanchine's version, with Maria Tallchief, Francisco Moncion. CREDIT: *George Platt Lynes/The Dance Collection.*

no deterioration. In his current repertory are his two great Diaghilev triumphs, *Apollo* and *The Prodigal Son,* the glory of the last Diaghilev season, and after fifty years they seem in no way outmoded. Unique among ballet choreographers, Balanchine has shown no falling off. He has good years and bad years, turning out five or six full-scale works a season, some trivial, some arresting and revolutionary. There is perceptible, however, a steady growth, a deepening in emotional values.

At his best Balanchine has achieved dances as fine as the greatest musical compositions. In his less fortunate moments, he tends to be bloodless and cerebral. But the impact of the body of his work on his time has been to lift dancing into parity with other fine arts, in structure, intent, subtlety, and discipline. He is a true master and will go down in history as such. The organization of his schools and protégé companies ensures the preservation of his

George Balanchine rehearses Patricia McBride in *Tchaikovsky Pas de Deux* for taping of *Dance in America*, Nashville, Tennessee. CREDIT: *Costas*.

Agon, by George Balanchine, with Suzanne Farrell and Peter Martins. CREDIT: © *1980, Paul Kolnik*.

Above left, *Liebeslieder Walzer* (Brahms) by George Balanchine, with Violette Verdy, Nicholas Magallanes, Jonathan Watts, Melissa Hayden, and Diana Adams. CREDIT: *Fred Fehl*.

work as no other man's has been, excepting only Fokine, who achieved the same degree of immortality through the simple device of being universally pirated. But with Balanchine, dissemination is a plan of propaganda and faith.

George Balanchine has been offered every prize and award which America has to give. He declines most but he has accepted a few of the very best, including the Handel Medallion in 1973 and in 1978 the first Kennedy Award in Washington, given to him at the White House by President Carter.

The company has acquired one of the largest, most faithful, most intelligent, and most enthusiastic

Chaconne, by George Balanchine, with Suzanne Farrell and Peter Martins.
CREDIT: © *Max Waldman.*

audiences in America. In 1963 the Ford Foundation gave Balanchine and his pupils a grant of more than seven million dollars, which lifted them into a position of financial independence unique among American theater institutions. Their permanent home is now the State Theater at Lincoln Center, New York City, their summer home is Saratoga Springs, New York. They have made tours abroad for the Department of State. Because of their endowment they have been able to produce works comparable to European ballet in opulence. They also give scholarships and to this end have set up a network of interlocking endowments across the country and generously donate teachers, stars, and repertory from the Balanchine treasure as they find deserving followers and opportunities. It is a job of proselytizing and education such as the United States has never before seen. And the quality of choreography and dancing everywhere has risen

Natalia Makarova and Anthony Dowell in rehearsal for the Glen Tetley ballet, *Contredance*, March 26, 1979. CREDIT: *Jack Mitchell.*

Watermill, by Jerome Robbins, with Edward Villella. CREDIT: *Martha Swope.*

perceptibly as a result. The resulting danger involved is the stultifying effect of a company so powerful exerting a single pervasive influence or artistic monopoly. But America is too large and diverse to fall victim to any such limitation.

The American Ballet, Ballet Caravan, and the New York City Ballet featured the following among its stars.

American Ballet and Ballet Caravan:

Asquith, Ruby	Christensen, Harold,
Boris, Ruthana	Lew, William
Caccialanza, Gisella	Danieli, Fred
Heater, Mary	Hobi, Frank
Kavan, Albia	Kidd, Michael
Marie, Jeanne	Laskey, Charles
Reiman, Elise	

New York City Ballet from 1948 on:

Adams, Diana	Tyven, Sonja
Farrell, Suzanne	Verdy, Violette
Govrin, Gloria	Watts, Heather
Hayden, Melissa	Wilde, Patricia
Jillana	d'Amboise, Jacques
Kai, Una	Baryshnikov, Mikhail
Kaye, Nora	Bliss, Herbert
Kent, Allegra	Bolender, Todd
Kirkland, Gelsey	Bonnefous, Jean-Pierre
LeClerq, Tanaquil	Carter, William
McBride, Patricia	Dollar, William
Mazzo, Kay	Eglevsky, Andre
Mounsey, Yvonne	(guest artist)
Neary, Colleen	Laing, Hugh
Paul, Mimi	Lindgren, Robert
Reed, Janet	Lland, Michael
Schorer, Suki	Magallanes, Nicholas
Sidimus, Joysanne	Martins, Peter
Sobotka, Ruth	Mitchell, Arthur
Tallchief, Maria	Moncion, Francisco

Prinz, John	Tomasson, Helgi
Robbins, Jerome	Villella, Edward
Thomas, Richard	Watts, Jonathan
Tobias, Roy	Wislow, William

Its fine choreographers have been limited to Balanchine and Robbins, and in its narrow concentration on these two individual talents it has differed radically from Ballet Theatre, which is probably the most catholic in taste of any company.

Todd Bolender, one of their choreographers, is influenced by Robbins, but deriving from and trained by Balanchine. He choreographed several good works for the New York City Ballet but did not find his real strength until he took over the ballet at the Cologne Opera in Germany and later the Frankfurt Ballet.

One must mention Rebekah Harkness, although her ballet adventures were short-lived. For a time, she backed Jerome Robbins's small company, Ballet Export U.S.A. and then the first Robert Joffrey Company. Breaking connections with both choreographers, she put her troupe into the care of the Canadian Brian MacDonald, and later replaced him with Benjamin Harkarvy. It was a fine company numbering Larry Rhodes and Elisabeth Carrol among its stars. After buying and renovating the Walter Hampton Theater on upper Broadway she suddenly closed down the company forever. She had spent a fortune on new works and new experiments, but after a short time the theater, old and venerable, with a distinguished history, was pulled down.

The opulent school on East 75th Street is still open for classes and rents out its beautiful practice rooms.

13.
THE NEW MODERNS

THE Revolutionary moderns and in turn their pupils were bred into a tradition of independence. They all formed their own groups and maintained their own schools, in which they taught their personal variants of the Graham, Humphrey, Holm, and Wigman techniques and in which—and this is important—they developed their own individual choreography with no borrowing back and forth of repertory. The results have been a great refertilization of the art of dance. While much of the composed work is ineffectual, some of it is good and some of it is remarkable.

Ballet dancers do not, probably cannot, form their own companies, and we would not have had any new companies in the old tight-webbed system which produced very few young choreographers. Therefore our new fine ballet choreographers are for the most part drawn surprisingly from the ranks of the moderns—José Limón, Glen Tetley, Anna Sokolow, John Butler, Alvin Ailey. Russia does not have this seedbed of independents, and as a result Russia does not have fresh choreography. But in America a large percentage of our dancers are continually risking on their own, trying, composing, ceaselessly, without leave.

Graham's pupils, like her audiences, are drawn from all over the world and they are, like the Denishawn pupils, educated people. Many have become teachers in American universities. Several have become good choreographers; the most outstanding to date being Anna Sokolow, John Butler, Paul Taylor, Pearl Lang, and Merce Cunningham.

Anna Sokolow was a member of Graham's great charter group and participated in the creation of the early masterpieces, *Primitive Mysteries, American Primitives,* and *American Document.* She left Graham to become a choreographer in her own right and for ten years resided in Mexico City, where she and José Limón did much to awaken the people to sources underlying and diverging from their European heritage. She has worked also with great effect in Israel with Sara Levi-Tanai and her famed Inbal troupe.

On returning to New York she found her true voice, and now furnishes ballets to companies all over the United States and Europe.

Her idiom is personal and American, but as she makes no special technical demands on performers, once the dancers grasp her approach to dynamics

159

they can readily reproduce her style, an advantage not shared by other modern choreographers. Her themes are somber, and the mood of many of her pieces is frightening and obsessive. And as her means are simple and direct, the impact can be, and often is, brutal. Melancholy and an absorption with terror have always been among the American characteristics and, like Edgar Allan Poe, who had such a dominant influence on our art in the past century, Sokolow deals with the dark side of the mind. Her dances are concerned predominantly with people caught in recognizable and remem-

bered dilemmas, most of them traumatic. But they are truthful and emotionally moving, and while they tend to be macabre, they are shot through with the choreographer's sardonic wit, her fresh invention, and her killing perception. She is a master of rhythm, and the concentrated force one of her groups attains just by standing still and moving their heads or one shoulder is memorable. She is also a master of choreographic and structural development.

Merce Cunningham, a Graham pupil, has made a tremendous name with his unorthodox and

Steps of Silence, by Anna Sokolow, with members of the Contemporary Dance System, including Teri Weckler, Laura Glen, and Hannah Kahn. CREDIT: © *1975, Lois Greenfield.*

Exchange, by Merce Cunningham, with Merce Cunningham and dancers (in rehearsal). CREDIT: © *1977, Lois Greenfield.*

always experimental style. He is the subject of lively interest on the part of students, but his devotion to the difficult, atonal music of John Cage and his inexplicable stage effects, such as shining spotlights directly into the audience's eyes, or maintaining rigid lack of motion throughout the entire length of a piece, or confusing the dance patterns with floating sofa pillows, ensure him a limited audience. He is an enthusiastic and aggressively provocative and always unorthodox speaker. He preaches choreography by accident, by happenstance. He has made the statement that any movement can effectively follow any other. Many critics approve of these ideas, and his fol-

lowers are avid, almost fanatical.

Sophie Maslow and Jane Dudley, pupils of Graham, and William Bales, a pupil of Humphrey and Weidman, formed a trio called the New Dance Group. For years they performed beautifully wrought concert pieces. They went everywhere in the United States and brought works of skill and taste to colleges and schools. This was an achievement of real proselytizing, for they spread the word that enjoyable art did not depend on the expenditure of large sums. They were good, they were charming, and they were effective. Jane Dudley now teaches in Israel, Sophie Maslow teaches in New York, and William Bales for years headed the

Department of Dance at the Purchase campus of the State University of New York.

John Butler's work is patently derivative from that of his great teacher, Martha Graham. He has borrowed her technique, combining it with ballet, her use of symbolic props, her economy of dance personnel, and her general approach to thematic material, which tends to be allegorical or mythical even in story pieces, the characters remaining types rather than individuals. Yet his style is markedly his own, for his gift for movement is outstanding. He can produce long stretches of lyric motion that are nothing short of rapturously lovely, and his pas de deux rank with the best in contemporary choreography. His *Sebastian, After Eden,* and *Season in Hell,* done for the Harkness Ballet, are powerful

After Eden, by John Butler, with Alba Calzada and Lawrence Rhodes. CREDIT: © *Max Waldman.*

Carmina Burana, by John Butler, with Judith Jamison and Sara Yarborough. Alvin Ailey American Dance Theater, 1974. CREDIT: *Jack Mitchell.*

dramatic pieces exploring with penetrating clarity dark and terrifying relationships. His *Carmina Burana* and *Catulli Carmina,* although naked studies of sexual passion, remain exquisite because his discretion throughout is elegant and seemly; the connotation never vitiates or weakens the beauty and decorum of the style. The invention, rhythm, and architecture of dynamics are masterly. The stage is filled with moving beauty for fifty straight minutes. The ballets have become staples of a half-dozen companies.

Butler studied dance first in Mississippi. Then he won scholarships to study with Muriel Stuart at the School of American Ballet in New York and with Eugene Loring, whose Dance Players were at

that time based in Bucks County, Pennsylvania. When I chose him for the lead in my *Oklahoma!* ballet, he used part of his salary for lessons with Martha Graham, whom he subsequently partnered. Intensive work in television provided the funds for experimentation with his own company. He was the first choreographer to make use of contemporary jazz musicians. His John Butler Dance Theater functioned from 1955 through 1961, appearing abroad as well as in the United States. Members of that troupe included Carmen De Lavallade, Glen Tetley, Buzz Miller, Mary Hinkson, and Scott Douglas. Butler has made many experimental programs for television in the 1950s and 1960s and may have been at that time the only serious choreog-

Carmina Burana, by John Butler, with the Alvin Ailey American Dance Theater, 1973. Heads of (left to right) Sara Yarborough, John Parks, Michikiko Oka, and Judith Jamison. CREDIT: *Jack Mitchell.*

Paul Taylor in his *Option*, March 1962. CREDIT: *Jack Mitchell*.

Carmina Burana, by John Butler, with Carmen de Lavallade. CREDIT: *Zachary Freyman*.

rapher to work consistently in this medium in the United States. His real success came first, however, in opera companies. *Amahl and the Night Visitors, Catulli Carmina*, and *Carmina Burana* were done by the New York City Opera Company and *Jeanne au Boucher* by the Santa Fe Opera Company of New Mexico, *Bluebeard's Castle* (Bartok) for Sarah Caldwell in Boston.

He has won success in ballet, modern dance, grand opera and light opera; on the musical comedy stage, the motion picture screen, and the television tube—even in ice-skating extravaganzas. He is adept in both modern and classic ballet techniques, and both are components of his style. His works are now performed around the world, possibly more frequently than those of any other contemporary choreographer with the exception of George Balanchine.

Paul Taylor, another former member of Martha Graham's company, broke away to do individual and memorable work. His scherzo movements are unmatched (except by Gerald Arpino in his very best inventions). The dynamics are seemingly new and the technique is fresh and astonishing. He has taken the Jack Cole use of slides and explored them, not only on the knees but with the whole body and on the arms. And he has expanded Martha Graham's falls, certainly not emotionally but in physical range and variety. His dancers skim, plunge, glide. They have made friends with gravity. They tease gravity. The solid terra is no longer firma, it is transparent. It is beyond depth. They penetrate the earth, go through it. In the *Aureole* of Handel, in the finale of the *Esplanade* (Bach), there is an entirely new range of vocabulary, quite astounding and vigorous inven-

Pearl Lang in her work *The Possessed*. CREDIT: © *1975, Lois Greenfield.*

tion. As in all his compositions, and there is some-times a conceit of great charm and effectiveness. The last movement of *Airs* (Haydn) in which a pas de quatre, brilliantly quick, is, for instance, followed by a slow-motion exploration of the details by one couple is beautiful, revealing, and charm-ing. His story ballets or satires tend to be hazy, but there is always a point of view that is piquant and at times achieves high fantasy.

Taylor's group is of high excellence and his

tours, particularly the college tours, are successful, although like all modern dancers—in fact like all ballet companies—he has a constant struggle against poverty and this curtails his efforts.

His troubles, however, are not only financial. Because he is something of a pioneer, he encounters indifference, often hostility, from the unknowing. When Taylor and his company played Russia, the popular response was enthusiastic and spontaneous, but the ballet hierarchy was very disapproving, calling them gymnasts and not countenancing anything that broke their rules, which were laid down in the late nineteenth century.

Pearl Lang is a performer of great personal beauty and a rich, creamy elegance of gesture that has stood her choreographers in good stead. She created many of the outstanding roles in the Graham repertory (Polly in *Punch and the Judy,* a Child in *Deaths and Entrances,* the Red Girl in *Diversion of Angels*) and since the retirement of her great master, Martha Graham, has taken over with real power and distinction the star roles in *Letter to the World* and *Clytemnestra.* She now also has her own company. It is one of choice and exquisite dancers, and her works are thoughful and moving, notably *The Dybbuk.*

In recent years the company of Alvin Ailey, Lester Horton's pupil, has taken a dominating place

Dancer-choreographer Pearl Lang, 1971. CREDIT: *Jack Mitchell.*

Revelations, by Alvin Ailey, with Sara Yarborough. CREDIT: *Susan Cook.*

in popular dance attractions. It is by all odds the most successful of all our dance export groups and plays to sell-out audiences throughout our own country. Almost entirely black (there are only three or four whites), its repertory is composed largely of Ailey's own works, which show the influence of Lester Horton and Jack Cole but which also have a personal theatricality that is extremely telling. When Ailey utilizes spirituals (without, however, employing historic steps; he is strictly a modern dancer) or popular music like Duke Ellington's (1899–1974), his pieces are irresistible and make an overwhelming effect on any audience. He has also created a fine and successful ballet for American Ballet Theatre, *The River,* with a score by Duke Ellington.

His company also performs pieces by Donald McKayle, an able and inventive choreographer, John Butler, Katherine Dunham, and Pearl Primus.

The shining particular star of Ailey's troupe is Judith Jamison, who is surely one of the greatest dancers of our time. But all of the soloists have passion and a bright commitment.

Ailey has worked a true miracle: he has reached the black audience and converted them to serious dancing, an audience hitherto impervious, since the dance audience was white and the blacks did not (with cause) feel welcome. Now they do.

Bella Lewitsky, another Horton pupil and his partner and star throughout the latter part of his career, is a composer of an entirely different stamp. She is thoroughly nondramatic and abstract, and a

Night Creature, by Alvin Ailey. CREDIT: *Susan Cook.*

Blues Suite, by Alvin Ailey, with Sara Yarborough, Estelle Spurlock, and Donna Wood. CREDIT: *Susan Cook.*

Judith Jamison, for whom Alvin Ailey's *Cry* was composed. CREDIT: © *Max Waldman.*

stern and beautiful disciplinarian. Her own technique is possibly the strongest among all the modern dancers performing in the seventies, and she combines intense feeling with lovely lyricism. Her movement invention is seemingly endless. She pulls movement like taffy into permutations, developments, transfigurations all of a piece, unbroken but changing constantly and without repetition. Her patterns are therefore never banal and for choreographers they provide a mine of suggestion.

In Iris Pell she has a dancer of star caliber who focuses and furthers her work in masterly fashion. Her headquarters are in Los Angeles, and she works thence for all her tours and guest performances. She is the pivot stone of the West.

Bella Lewitsky in her *Greening*, set to an Aaron Copeland score. CREDIT: *Marion Valentine*.

Twyla Tharp has made a phenomenal success in a very few years and is one of the most sought-after concertizers in the business. Her style is very much her own, seemingly spontaneous and improvised with a kind of loose formless nonpattern that is at first very engaging but which can become in time slightly tedious and wearing. Her dances, of course, are not spontaneous but subtly patterned and highly disciplined. The effect, however, is one of careless off-the-cuff happenstance, quite unlike any other choreographer's.

Like Merce Cunningham, Tharp deals in broken patterns, but her design is usually a little easier to follow than his although it is scattered over the whole stage and the effect sometimes is like pattern on pattern. She claims to fragment gesture, to shred it to its component parts, reassemble them, and study them. One is put in mind of the early kinesthetic studies of Charles Weidman, who did just that—reassembling, reorganizing, and redesigning with comic, often witty, results.

In her work to a marked degree, but in her contemporaries' work also, is the strange phenomenon of nonrelationship. Her dancers do not seem to touch one another; although they lift each other and spin each other around and carry each other, they do it all with total impersonality. If a man lifts a woman, he then turns around and lifts another, or lifts a man, or jumps by himself. This can be wryly comic. It is also sardonic and teasing, if it does not become restlessly uneasy. These are uprooted, unattached people, who never at any point, even at the end, come to a conclusion or form a relationship. They have adhesions, one might say, but no connections. Also, in Tharp's choreography, the movement is broken with inconsequentials, with nervousness, with abrupt changes of direction and pace. Designed? Certainly. Humorous? Often. But in the long run tiresomely neurotic. Many of the dance phrases slide over the musical phrases and at the finish of the pieces continue their own life and their own way of moving in compulsive fashion

Push Comes to Shove, composed for American Ballet Theatre by Twyla Tharp, with Elaine Kudo and Mikhail Baryshnikov. CREDIT: *Beverley Gallegos*.

like animal jerkings after death. The audience laughs, but I am sure they sometimes wonder what they are laughing at. In conjunction with the formal, classical music she uses, this dichotomy becomes markedly apparent. The contrast is merry and silly but fundamentally macabre. I personally am a classicist, so to me this is unnerving. I come to the conclusion that any music, or none, would serve.

I hasten to add that she has the flexibility to compose not only for her own excellent troupe but for standard ballet companies. She has furnished hit works for Robert Joffrey and for the American Ballet Theatre. In fact, her work for the latter, *Push Comes to Shove*, starring Mikhail Baryshnikov,

Untitled, by Pilobolus Dance Theater. CREDIT: © *1980, Tim Matson.*

proved to be that great star's best essay into the modern genre and displayed his subtle comedic gifts to their full.

Pilobolus Dance Theater takes its name from a genus of phototropic fungi. It was founded in the summer of 1971 in Lyndonville, Vermont, by Moses Pendleton and Jonathan Wolken, undergraduates in science at Dartmouth College. They were soon joined by Lee Harrison and Robbie Barnett and in another year by Allison Chase and Martha Clarke. All but one of the members had college degrees, only one, Mrs. Chase, in dancing, the others in philosophy, psychology and literature. Within a year of its founding Pilobolus had evolved into a completely self-sufficient organization, its programs choreo-graphed, danced, managed and publicized by the four men and two women. It is unique in that its creative work is done communally and the dances evolved are apparently the work of joint conference.

The members of the troupe are superlative gymnasts without using the exercises and display pieces of the usual gymnast's repertory, and although it is possible that they could do as well as the best on the bars and horses, they try none of these tricks and have scrupulously avoided any over-development of muscles. They are more provocative and surprising than any other new group. Air now is also the dancer's medium, the manipulation of aerial lifting and levitation, suspension and tum-bling. Many ideas of bodily configurations are seem-

Monkshood's Farewell, by Pilobolus. CREDIT: © *1978, Tim Matson.*

ingly endless, avoiding all references to sexuality or indeed to humanity and the performers become, as with Nikolais, absolutely impersonal things, pieces of pattern, a limitation which does not hurt their dazzling technique. Occasionally, as in their long piece, *Untitled,* they reach a level and touch a sphere of imagination that promises a truly new kind of theater. It is evocative, Proustian, atmospheric and haunting. This could open the doors.

They are, in essence, dancers, although the critic Clive Barnes claims they are not, and while unorthodox in the extreme, their work is dance material and cannot be considered as anything else. Whatever they are they are extraordinarily effective and frequently moving and have grown to be in a short time extremely popular, appealing to all kinds of audiences over a range of countries.

Like so many of the moderns they have discarded all traditional music, in which I include even the most modern, and rely solely on electronic effects. Pilobolus, together with other contemporaries, in electing to do without the structural help of auditory pattern take the risk of finding their own formats, and this is a hard risk. There have been many dancers, it is true, who have yearned for the freedom to create without music. Ruth St. Denis was one, together with Doris Humphrey. Marie Rambert another. Soundless dance has succeeded very seldom. Certain native dances like Uday Shankar's, using only the rubbing and beating of his feet and bells, managed to set up their own rhythms and satisfy the senses without any auditory stimulation. The French clown, Marcel Marceau, never uses sound, and his work is extremely rhythmic and completely satisfying, but he is unique. Even a great mime like Charlie Chaplin found that sound was a help. The electronic scores that are used by the contemporaries today are very nearly formless, or so it seems to me, and the dances which are set have a strange linear appearance. Without the uses so deeply ingrained in our nature of rhythm and harmony, or apparent rhythmic patterns, even simple ones as those of a drum beat, we enter a new free world with enormous possibilities, it is true, but at the same time with grave aesthetic dangers.

One is always tempted to speculate on the function of the unions with their prohibitive monetary demands as a cause for the gradual preference of electronic to musical scores. Contemporary composers are abandoning the classic instruments and their players for the simple reason that they simply cannot afford to pay them. A machine costs far less and can be duplicated free, and has, as of this stage of writing, not been unionized.

And what do these uncommitted neuters wear? What do they use for decor? Nothing for decor except lights, and as a rule they wear the minimal, men and women alike—bare sex coverings which, of course, of necessity are somewhat different.

It would be interesting to speculate how much of these theatrical symptoms are dictated by plain theatrical economics: leotards cost a lot, it is true, but nothing comparable to a cotton skirt, and as for a silk shirt or fitted trousers—out of the question.

There are a few, however, who indulge themselves in elaborate structural fabrications of enormous complexity and of such weight and size as to virtually obstruct movement. They too call themselves avant-garde, but in fact they are about three hundred and fifty years out of date. This parading around of costumes goes back to the French and Italian courts of the seventeenth century and the Royal Ballet troupes of the period. Anyone so garbed could not possibly move very much and the royal participants did not, confining themselves to mere strutting and prancing. The modern dancer does the same; in fact, reduces himself to the role of showgirl. This strange and invidious custom was reestablished by Picasso in the 1922 ballet, *Parade,* in which he had two mannequins cross the stage in outfits that were miracles of Postimpressionist construction but that obviated, of course, any of the skills and art of the dancer. Such paraphernalia is used appropriately in religious dances, with primitive symbols and totems by our Indians and the islanders of the South Pacific, but there is no religious symbolism in the modern getups. Although intriguing in design, such gimmicks are anti-dancing.

There are several choreographers, among them a few extremely well-known, even nationally famous, ones, who have made their careers on being just this—avant-garde (whatever they mean by that), and who deal in abstract subjects and abstract techniques that are on the whole mystifying to the general public and bewildering even to the experienced professionals. These performers have made a cult of being shocking or disturbing or

Pilobolus, by Pilobolus. CREDIT: © *1980, Tim Matson.*

titillating, of doing anything they can to catch attention, without ever being clear or definitive in any aspect of dance. They deal in the splintered pattern and the illogical idea, and they profess to believing that this is more significant to our times than any logical or readily understandable statement. It is almost impossible for them not to jump to the next assumption, that if any gesture follows any other gesture, as one of the leaders has stated, then why not the insane gesture, the demented action? Perhaps because we have built up our entire aesthetic on signs and indications that are partly understood and only partly exploratory and suggestive, we cannot accept what is wholly unintelligible. The avant-garde do not mind in the least being unintelligible; they prefer it, in fact, and probably wisely, but the rest of us come to the inevitable conclusion that somehow in these strange and alien patterns there is a major hoax being perpetrated and that we are being confronted with another case of the emperor's new clothes. The general public, of course, will not accept this strange, pretentious, opaque art, but the specialists rave. The specialists, however, cannot support the practitioners, so there must always be gifts and outside help. The remarkable fact is that in the 1970s there seemed to be an abundance of such gifts.

The outstanding common characteristic of all the aforementioned styles—Eric Hawkins, Paul Taylor, Twyla Tharp, Louis Falco, Paul Sanasardo, Meredith Monk, Margot Sappington, Stuart Hodes, Pilobolus and their successors, various and divergent as they may be, popular or specialized—is without question their dehumanization. If grief or joy can be separated from the human who feels in a reversal of the pathetic fallacy, what the moderns might call the unpathetic truth, distilled like color, like form in nonobjective painting or sculpture, certainly like sound and music, then this is pure grief, pure joy.

But is it? How can there be joy without a human heart, delight without a human body? And these have histories of their own and particularities. And up to now in our race they also have sex. But now we are given over to machines. The language shows it: "hang-ups," "groovy," "turn on," "turn off," to physics, to chemistry (the test tube in place of the phallus).

Is this impersonal dancing then the real voice

Paul Sanasardo in his work *The Path*, with Joan Lombardi, Douglas Nielsen, and Marianne Folin.
CREDIT: © *Max Waldman.*

of our age? Here we are being enticed into the footling entrapments of aesthetics, of brain teasings with no results. The fact is, the dancers of Paul Taylor, Alwin Nikolais, Twyla Tharp, Merce Cunningham, Pilobolus are indeed without sex, the performers varying only in musculature and, therefore, to a very slight degree, in function. (Even Balanchine, a profoundly abstract artist, uses sex in a pronounced and respectful way.) The moderns celebrate the unisex striven for on our discotheque floors and embraced by all the young. At the same time, paradoxically, they certainly symbolize the impersonality against which an entire generation now is openly rebelling.

In conclusion, I am brought up inevitably against the fact that none of these avant-gardists seem to have an argument, a point of view, an emotional statement to make. They tease. They titillate, they delight. They very seldom move. This is a lack, without which the form cannot progress.

Nevertheless, under the guidance of the really gifted, and several are truly that, the whole scope of dance broadens. In the case of Nikolais, by means of sound, light, visual effect, and scenic devices. In the case of Pilobolus, by means of new movement, for they have added the entire vocabulary of the gymnast to the dancer's training.

These companies have a tremendous popular following. People go and go again, ordinary people. They are fine artists besides, but more, they are timely. They speak to us.

All this activity spells the most astonishing furor about dancing that the Western theater has ever known. There are four major ballet companies in New York City playing lengthy annual seasons, sometimes simultaneously. The major stars are beginning to attract audiences as fervent and widespread as those of baseball stars. The companies that play at the colleges are manifold and they do very well and the audiences are good, and in all the cities, particularly New York, but also in San Francisco, Dallas, Washington, there is an enormous amount of solo or small groups. In the season of 1978–79 in New York City there were small companies playing one or two nights or short week seasons. These dancers, of course, lose money and have no guaranteed audiences. They are, for the most part, unknown outside of the aficionados of their trade, but they spring into view and make themselves known for a night or two, and they provide new ideas, some banal, some useless, some moribund, some very good and fresh, and that means that there is always a carpet of sustaining life renewing itself under the feet of the veteran performers.

14.
THE NEW BALLET COMPANIES

THE remarkable and surprising aspect of the contemporary scene is that although our ballet schools and companies are excellent, as good as any except the Russian (which are state-endowed and run like seminaries), and although they are producing dancers and technicans as good as any (except the Russians), they are not producing choreographers (the Russians do not produce choreographers either, excepting the nonballetic arrangers of folk forms, notably Igor Moiseyev). The creators of these come mostly from the moderns.

All young ballet choreographers inherit tremendous technique and weighty traditions, but these can be inhibiting. Tradition can confound free imaginations. The moderns, however, are still inventing their technique. They are up to their elbows in the machinery. In fact, they're making their machinery, they have to, and the effort, the sheer necessity, calls upon all their ingenuity and daily skill. Of necessity these faculties are exercised in full, and the tradition is not yet set and it is by no means august. So most of the fresh ideas come from the moderns. Unfortunately modern work doesn't pay, because the audience is by nature lazy, being used to the classics or to derivations and developments of the classics. Only a small part of the paying public would prefer to stretch its attention. So, in short, the moderns do the new thinking, but it is the traditionalists who must exploit and utilize it. Adapting the alien style to ballet is a matter of mere translation.

There are, however, a few young ballet directors and choreographers who are creating excellent and attractive companies.

Robert Joffrey, the artistic director of the Joffrey Ballet, founded in 1956, is a classicist. He produces works of delicate and refined invention which miraculously escape the traps usually encountered when working in an antique form. Son of an Afghan father and an Italian mother, both immigrants to America, Robert Joffrey was born Abdullah Jaffa Anver Bey Khan in Seattle, Washington, in 1930, and began his career in dance at age nine. An outstanding solo performer in earlier years, he is now a company director, teacher, and choreographer. His Joffrey Ballet, official resident ballet company of the New York City Center, has toured the United States repeatedly and has been acclaimed on visits to countries around the world.

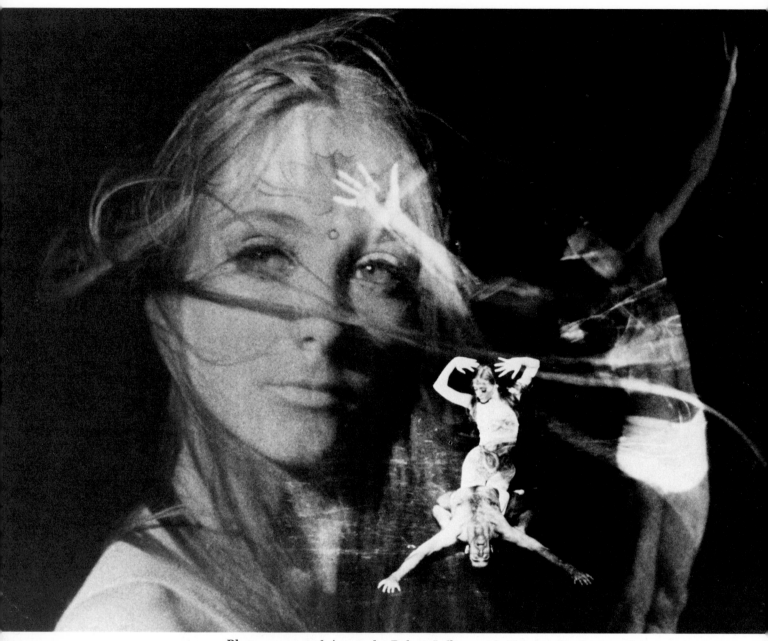

Photo montage of *Astarte*, by Robert Joffrey, with Trinette Singleton and Maximilian Zamosa. CREDIT: *Herbert Migdoll.*

He is a superb drillmaster and his young company dances impeccably. They have not yet had time to develop star personalities, but it is almost inevitable that they will. Joffrey's program of inviting in veteran choreographers assures this. He is building a repertory that is distinctly his and nationally needed, not the large Russian operatic classics but smaller pieces, equally good—ballets by Frederick Ashton, Kurt Jooss, Massine, Brian Macdonald, Alvin Ailey, Twyla Tharp, and me.

Dance critic Anna Kisselgoff wrote in the *New York Times* in May 1979:

Its guiding intelligence has been its director's taste. The record has been more than good. The company has had its moments of greatness. Unique in its exuberance of style, a repository of masterpieces rescued from oblivion, and for many, an introduction to ballet, the Joffrey has played a vital role in the development of dance in the United States.

Joffrey's chief resident choreographer is a young artist of outstanding merit, Gerald Arpino. Many of his themes, like Anna Sokolow's, are macabre, and like hers, they are haunting. His is a nightmare world, but it is truly felt, and he never avails himself of hackneyed symbols or easy devices. He plunges into the entrails of emotional disturbance and brings forth figures that are atavistic and enduring. He is capable also of fine formal composition in the classic manner, and his *Viva Vivaldi!*, a study in joyous abstractions, is sheer delight. His recent suite to a piano concerto of Saint-Saëns is straight bravura dancing and bravura choreography. Watching is like standing in a flight of meteors.

Among the leading dancers in the Joffrey are:

1956–1963:

Arpino, Gerald
Consoer, Diana
Grandy, Maria
Jorgensen, Nels
Martinet, Francoise

Rhodes, Lawrence
Ruiz, Brunilda
Sutherland, Paul
Tetley, Glen
Tomasson, Helgi

Tompkins, Beatrice
Watts, Jonathan
Wilson, John

1965–1980:

Arthur, Charthel
Blankshine, Robert
Bradley, Lisa
Corcle, Francesca
Chryst, Gary
Danias, Starr

DeAngelo, Ann Marie
Fuente, Luis
Holder, Christian
Huffman, Gregory
Jackson, Denise
Rodriguez, Beatriz
Singleton, Trinette
Sultzbach, Russell
Taylor, Burton
Wright, Rebecca
Zamosa, Maxiliano

The Joffrey maintains an excellent second company of apprentices, the Joffrey II, which travels modestly and inexpensively around the country. They use taped music and they keep the dance personnel down to twelve. They are training fine technical dancers, who step up regularly into the major company with complete aplomb and readiness. They are also producing choreographers, and their 1979 season saw the premieres of two fine and sensitive works, *Kani No Yama*, by Saeko Ichinohe, a Japa-

Kettentanz, by Gerald Arpino, with Joffrey Ballet Company. CREDIT: *Herbert Migdoll.*

nese national, and *Momentum*, by Choo San Goh, a native of the People's Republic of China.

The most interesting new talent to emerge in the late sixties was Eliot Feld. A member of Ballet Theatre and a protégé of Jerome Robbins, he revealed himself in his first ballet, *Harbinger* (for Ballet Theatre to music by Prokofiev), as a lyric choreographer of the first magnitude. Since Feld had been a member of Jerome Robbins's company and a true disciple, the work was understandably derivative in certain aspects. But it had vitality, a freshness of gesture, a grasp of form, and above all, poetic

A Footstep of Air, by Eliot Feld, with Edmund LaFosse. CREDIT: © *1978, Lois Greenfield.*

Eliot Feld in rehearsal. CREDIT: *Tom Victor.*

content. It also had compassion, even nobility. The humor was never coy, as sometimes happens, or used to happen, with Robbins; it was direct and stringent and altogether male, and the relation between men and women was poignantly felt. Feld never descended to what was precious or pedantic or trivial. This initial work was followed in 1967 by the equally effective *At Midnight* (Mahler) and in 1968 by *Meadowlark* (Haydn) for the Royal Winnipeg Ballet.

Later Feld created for his own company *Early Songs* (Strauss), *Consort* (Elizabethan composers, arranged by Christopher Keane), and *Intermezzo* (Brahms). The Brahms pieces rival anything in this

genre, including the loveliest works of Balanchine or Ashton. They are full of exquisite fantasy and invention and are superbly musical. Indeed Feld's musicality is without blemish, his style ravishing and quite unmatched for one so young. (All these works were composed before he reached thirty.) His youth, however, shows in his point of view, and on occasion the emotional or philosophic content can become jejune, even banal, as in his *Soldier's Tale*. He tends also to be repetitious in theme, too frequently dealing with the loneliness of the individual set against the activities of the crowd. In effect, his vocabulary tends to be way beyond his messages. His works are played in ballet companies around Europe and America. In the States he has his own small troupe of excellent performers, and he himself is a first-class dancer.

Glen Tetley, a pupil of Hanya Holm, later studied with Graham and joined her group. Then he made a striking success choreographing on his own in Holland and England, and although basically a modern he followed John Cranko (1927–1973), on the latter's untimely and tragic death, in the directorship of the Stuttgart Ballet. His work is now internationally known, and he has ballets in the repertory of the American Ballet Theatre, the Pennsylvania Ballet, and the Royal Ballet of Great Britain. His *Sacre du Printemps* starred Mikhail

Christine Sarry in *Intermezzo and Waltzes* (Brahms), by Eliot Feld. CREDIT: © 1980, Lois Greenfield.

Baryshnikov when it was performed by the American Ballet Theatre.

John Neumeier comes from Milwaukee and was a pupil and member of the troupe of Sybil Shearer, whose influence he claims was the strongest on his work. "When I began choreography, I found layers of Sybil." He went from her small group to the Royal Ballet School in London and from there to Stuttgart to join John Cranko's company and study under that master. He began to choreograph there and in other German cities and was an outstanding and instant success. He has done several brilliant and original ballets for the Royal Winnipeg Ballet, notably his version of *The Nutcracker*, which is completely unorthodox. He also created a new version of *Baiser de le Fée* for American Ballet Theatre. He is now (1980) tenured with the Ballet of Hamburg in Germany and exerts a strong influence in the dance world of central Europe.

The Boston Ballet was founded by E. Virginia Williams in 1954 and later aided with a Ford Foundation grant. Indeed, Williams is one of the very few people to obtain a large Ford grant who was not a pupil of Balanchine. An excellent teacher, she maintains strict discipline in her school and troupe. She also recruits fine dancers and the best choreographers she can obtain in order to have a truly catholic repertory. Among her faithful and able soloists are Anamarie Sarazin, Woytek Lowski, David Brown, Elaine Bauer, and Laura Young. One of her pupils, Bonnie Wyckoff, an exquisite dancer with a real flare for drama and comedy, became a lead with the Royal Winnipeg and the Joffrey Ballet.

Since its creation, the Boston Ballet has expanded and flourished. Its major limitation is that it does not tour far afield and therefore can keep its dancers working only during seasons in and around Boston.

The Boston Ballet has initiated an annual competition for young choreographers of promise. In 1980 seven out of two hundred applicants were chosen to have their works mounted, the winner among them to get a five-thousand-dollar cash prize, all seven to get their expenses paid from wherever they came (and some of them came from Germany) and two hundred dollars pocket money. But they had the golden opportunity of seeing their work produced by a first-class company and of getting it reviewed by the international press. It is an incomparable chance and they are all most eager to avail themselves of it. The Boston Ballet is the only company to sponsor such an event.

The Pennsylvania Ballet was founded in 1964 with a grant from the Ford Foundation. Under the direction of Barbara Weisberger (George Balanchine's protégé), it worked its way up from a local school and semiprofessional troupe to a company of national standing. In the classics and works by Balanchine or Limón, its corps work is extraordinarily fine, but the repertoire is uneven and the company has been guilty of including light pieces of no value whatever. As of 1979 it was under the direction of Benjamin Harkarvy.

Arthur Mitchell, a pupil of Balanchine and long a brilliant black star of the New York City Ballet, has, with an endowment from the Ford Foundation, produced a remarkable ballet company entirely of black students called the Dance Theater of Harlem. So far they have performed mainly classic works along with several Balanchine pieces. Their work is not only winning and stylish but also socially important, because the entire enterprise—workrooms, studios, offices, and wardrobes—involve parents and children, adolescents and apprentices, all participating on a professional basis, constituting a settlement project of far-reaching dimensions. The company has traveled to Mexico, Europe (with a command performance before the Queen of England), and all the states. The youngsters know they have a future and glory in the idea. They are very proud and they should be. Every participant has a new and dignified image of himself. They are, however, in desperate need of creative leadership and choreographers.

Dennis Nahat, who has studied and performed with all the great ballet choreographers of the contemporary theater, now has his own troupe in Cleveland. He is an able choreographer in the classic, lyric, nondramatic style and has composed several good pieces for American Ballet Theatre. His company is very young but thriving. He is himself a remarkable technician, a dashing performer, and a skilled comedian.

There are also ballet companies in Pittsburgh, San Francisco, Akron, Dallas, Houston, Atlanta, Washington, Salt Lake City, and a number of other

Arthur Mitchell teaching a class at the Dance Theater of Harlem. CREDIT: © *Lois Greenfield.*

places. For the most part they carry on the classic tradition in a very tidy style and rely for modern inspiration mostly on the old Balanchine repertory, which is readily obtainable and free, Balanchine charging no royalties for his works. They all train fine dancers and endeavor to establish individual and strong repertoires while employing their own local choreographers, none of whom has had national impact. Where there is no creative force of real power and worth to build on, local groups cannot sustain themselves for long, certainly not with distinction.

The best of the lot is undoubtedly the San Francisco Ballet, which had a rather weak start under Lew Christensen but which has pulled itself together and improved vastly under Michael Smuin. It now has the support of the city, financial guarantees, and a standard of genuine excellence in its performance quality. Its classics, like *The Nutcracker* and *Swan Lake*, are very good without being extraordinary. But it lacks, as do all of these companies, true inspiration, and needs the leadership of some greatly gifted original.

The sad fact is that our best and most creative talents are either in the three big companies in New York or have followed the example of John Neumeier, Glen Tetley, and dancer Richard Cragun and gone to Europe to work. But as young choreog-

Songs of Mahler, by Michael Smuin of the San Francisco Ballet Company, with Betsy Erickson and Gary Wahl, 1978 season. CREDIT: *James Armstrong/A San Francisco Ballet Production.*

raphers develop, or proven ones are invited to function around the country, the standard of production and performance in these companies will inevitably rise.

In 1973 I went to North Carolina to start, with the North Carolina School of the Arts at Winston-Salem, the Agnes de Mille Heritage Dance Theater, devoted to works based on folk tradition and historical forms of dance in the United States. This was in no way a museum collection of reproductions, but creative works by Anna Sokolow, Katherine Dunham, and me, all built in the tradition of our native forms. The body of dancers was made up largely of students trained by the school faculty, headed by Robert Lindgren, Pauline Koner, and

Duncan Noble. The soloists were imported from New York. It was a mixed company of blacks and whites, and it had large plans for the future. After three big tours it was forced to shut down due to my illness. But it is an excellent idea and cries out to be renovated. America is the only country that has no folk theater, no place to preserve and keep its marvelous dance forms, after the manner of, say, Igor Moiseyev in Russia.

One of the most conspicuous developments of the past ten years has been the proliferation of regional ballet companies with state and federal help. As of June 1978, there were more than two hundred sixty. These are amateur in the sense that the performers are not paid, but they have professional teachers and directors. The standards vary, but in general the directors try to maintain correct ballet technique and teach the big nineteenth-century classics. The local companies perform publicly once or twice a year, often with the assistance of local symphony orchestras. For these galas, nationally known stars are usually imported. In return, talented teenagers are recruited from these groups to enter the ranks of the big companies (American Ballet Theatre, the New York City Ballet, the Joffrey Ballet, and the Dance Theater of Harlem) on scholarships. In this way the regional companies serve the great national companies the way the minor leagues service the big-league baseball teams—by preparing recruits and covering the talent throughout the country. Their weakness is that they cannot afford yet to hire good choreographers and must make do with threadbare classics like *The Nutcracker* as remembered by some onetime performer.

But the sad prospect of talent wasting for lack of proper opportunity and training is a thing of the past. Geography is no longer the insurmountable hurdle to the young that it was thirty years ago. There are hundreds of scholarships in the good schools, and a respectable, if not inspired, showcase is now open to all gifted young children.

THE SCHOOLS

There have been hundreds of good schools and it is not the scope of this book to list or analyze them. One of the greatest of the twentieth-century ballet schools was undoubtedly Michel Fokine's, but that ceased to exist with the master's death. I shall, however, record a few of the outstanding ones that have lasted into the seventies.

The Metropolitan Opera House School was not founded officially until 1909 with Malvina Cavalazzi as the first director and main teacher, although such fine dancers as Maria Bonfanti coached its dancers. Cavalazzi was followed in 1913 by Margaret Curtis, who stayed at the head for decades until the ballet training was taken over by Margaret Craske and Antony Tudor, both English. Its training was orthodox and fine but without inspiration because it led to no good goal, i.e., to no interesting company but merely to the dead end of the Metropolitan Opera residence company. It was soon

The 1964 Regional Ballet Festival in Houston, Texas. Robert Joffrey teaching a class. CREDIT: *Jack Mitchell.*

dwarfed by powerful rivals. The term, "member of the Metropolitan Opera House Ballet" or "graduate of the Opera House School" means virtually nothing. The school closed down June 23, 1968.

The School of the American Ballet was founded in 1933 by Lincoln Kirstein and George Balanchine in an attempt to build a company and to assemble a body of students with which Balanchine could work. It has maintained its standards ever since and become one of the most respected schools in the world. Its staff is largely Russian but it does have the distinguished presence of Muriel Stuart, who was a member of Anna Pavlova's English company, and there are several Americans working on the faculty now. It has turned out literally hundreds of soloists for its own companies and for companies around the world. The right to state that one has studied for five years at this school is a guarantee of excellence. It maintains a generous scholarship program, auditions students annually and accepts pupils from ages nine to fourteen.

American Ballet Theatre School was founded in 1951 after Ballet Theatre had established itself in a permanent residence in New York. It also is excellent and somewhat different from the School of the American Ballet because of the catholicity of styles and because its staff of teachers is not limited to the Balanchine point of view in technique and aesthetics. There is now a scholarship class of forty or more in the summer for six weeks. Between twenty and twenty-six are retained for the winter season from September till June. The ages range from fourteen to eighteen.

Robert Joffrey's Ballet School (American Ballet Center) is first-class. It was founded in 1952. Joffrey himself is a splendid teacher and often teaches in the school as well as adjudicating and demonstrating at congresses, meetings and conferences around the world.

Ballet Arts was maintained for decades by Virginia Lee in Carnegie Hall with a distinguished teaching staff headed by Yeichi Nimura and numbering, among others, Vera Nemtchinova, Nina Stroganova, Edward Caton and myself. It was found to be an excellent place for professionals to drop in for their daily practice and for visiting artists to be coached, and this has proved of enormous stimulation to the young students working alongside at the bar.

Barbara Fallis and Richard Thomas, onetime soloists with Ballet Theatre, have opened a very fine small school for ballet students, the New York School of Ballet. Their training is strict and orthodox and taught with splendid taste. Many of the great stars practice there.

Ruth Page and Bently Stone maintained for decades a school in Chicago, perhaps the focal point for all ballet training in the Midwest. It produced brilliant students, many of whom distinguished themselves internationally in the big companies.

Martha Graham has maintained a school since 1924, first in Rochester, New York, in connection with the Eastman School, and then in New York City. She was forbidden to teach any of the Denishawn technique and exercises so she invented her own perforce, and this was the beginning of the Graham technique. It is taught still and the school is the fountainhead of her style. It maintains its caliber without blemish. Most of the Graham company members have taught in the school and a great many of them have left to form splinter groups and schools of their own or to teach in colleges, but, at basis, it is the Graham technique they teach, which is so strong that it can withstand all permutations and personal adaptations.

The North Carolina School of the Arts was authorized on recommendation of Governor Terry Sanford in 1963 and is unusual in that it has a dance department which embraces both modern work and ballet, both administered by experts. Robert Lindgren, once of the Ballet Russe de Monte Carlo and then the New York City Ballet is the head, and under him work expert ballet teachers Duncan Noble, Sonia Tyven, Maria Eglevsky, and Salvator Ajello; for the modern wing, Pauline Koner, Nelle Fisher and Robert Crutch of the Graham Group. This school is unique in that it takes boarding pupils as young as ten years old and educates them right through upper grade school and college, and in that it teaches music, drama, scene design and dance with equal emphasis so that every student is brought into contact with the other performing arts. It is funded by the state of North Carolina and by private gifts. It has a generous program of scholarships open not only to the citizens of the state, but to foreign students as well.

The Juilliard School, founded at the instigation of President William Schuman, sought to establish the teaching of dance on a par with the teaching of music, and to house both arts in the same building. It has both ballet and modern wings of the highest excellence. In ballet it had Margaret Craske and Antony Tudor. For modern it had Doris Humphrey, José Limón and Anna Sokolow; for pantomime, me; for composition, Louis Horst. The faculty, in fact, was probably the finest of any in New York City and the most broad-minded and cultured. The leading guide is Martha Hill.

A startling but gratifying phenomenon of the nineteen-sixties and seventies has been the inclusion on very nearly every college and university campus of dance courses. These are frequently taught by name performers of national importance, maintain standards of recognized excellence, and are offered in ballet technique as well as modern dancing for college credits. They are administered not always in the physical education department, but quite frequently in the fine arts division. Among the outstanding dancers who have gone into academic work are Igor Youskevitch at the University of Texas at Austin, Eugene Loring and Antony Tudor at the University of California at Irvine, Tudor at the University of California at Los Angeles, Mark Ryder at the University of Maryland, Carmen De Lavallade at Yale, Gemze De Lappe at Smith, Ruthana Boris at the University of Washington in Seattle, Bella Lewitsky at the University of Southern California in Los Angeles.

15.
BROADWAY

URING the early thirties Albertina Rasch was the czarina of Broadway. She had the choice of every show offered as well as numerous opportunities in Hollywood.

During the Rasch regime, other choreographers tried for a foothold. Doris Humphrey and Charles Weidman choreographed several shows with more or less happy results, notably *Lysistrata* (1930), which Humphrey choreographed brilliantly for a large cast, achieving effects far beyond the usual Broadway standards. But their work and their style of technique and composition did not find many adherents and they set no vogue. Accordingly in the commercial world, their day was brief.

Martha Graham never went near Broadway except to stage the dances and general movement for several Katharine Cornell plays, *Rape of Lucretia* and *Romeo and Juliet*. The Broadway demands and ambience were not for her, she learned, and thereafter she very wisely avoided all contact.

Jack Cole (1913–1974) was the first commercial choreographer to put a lasting stamp on the national style. A pupil of Denishawn, he developed jazz versions of East Indian and South American dances. Although his pieces were seen mainly in nightclubs and on Broadway (the notable exception being his *Requiem for Jimmy Dean*, done by the Harkness Ballet), he influenced many serious choreographers by his astonishing and vital handling of rhythm. His *Magdalina* to music by Villa-Lobos, although short-lived, included dances that had an enduring impact. His nightclub acts and movies were unforgettable as well. From him stems the idiom of Broadway ballet, a vernacular style that requires enormous technique, in that it involves considerable classic training plus acrobatic falls and many kinds of knee slides. This dance idiom is called ballet-jazz, and is taught as a separate technique in many New York schools. It has gone into the vocabulary of later choreographers—Robbins first, then Bob Fosse, Michael Kidd, Herbert Ross, Gower Champion, Donald McKayle, and Peter Gennaro.

With the collapse of the American Ballet in 1935, George Balanchine was enticed to Broadway, and he took with him his extraordinary ballet dancers, young, fresh, brilliant, and superbly trained. He also took his talents, which were beyond anything Broadway had ever experienced. Every-

Jack Cole. CREDIT: *Maurice Seymour.*

thing he touched seemed to turn to box-office money. Among his hits were *I Married an Angel*, starring his then wife Vera Zorina, once of the Ballet Russe de Monte Carlo, and *On Your Toes*, starring Ray Bolger and featuring Tamara Geva, his first wife. He then departed for Hollywood, taking his entire ballet company with him, and made the *Goldwyn Follies* for Sam Goldwyn. But he did not stay there very long. He returned to Broadway and continued his triumph. None of the success, however, or the money he made altered his feeling that this work was ignominious and to be scorned. He did not respect it, he did not like it. He has since utterly repudiated it and as soon as the funds were accumulated to reconstitute his ballet company, now called The New York City Ballet Company, he abandoned commercial work, seemingly forever.

In 1943 *Oklahoma!*, with music by Richard Rodgers, book and lyrics by Oscar Hammerstein, hit Broadway and changed history. It opened on April 1 to a success that has not been equaled in the twentieth century. The show has played without stop around the world for over thirty-seven years since, and at no time and in no production has any at-tempt been made to change or omit the big dances I created for it.

The success of this show depended on two things—the remarkable and happy amalgamation of music, text, lyrics, action, scenery, and costumes, which had never been approached in a light musical form before in this country, and the fact that it was essentially native in texture and appeal, because America was at war. From the first night there was a triple row of uniformed men and women standing at the back of the theater, moved often to the point of tears although the show was a happy one and full of jokes. The show appealed to their love of country and home; many of these men and women were in the greatest staging area of America and shipping out for life-and-death duty overseas.

The story is roughly about a girl's choice of partner for a picnic supper, not, one would think, an extraordinary crisis on which to base an entire evening. The ballet, however, showed what was going on in her mind and heart, her terrors, her fears, her hopes; so in fact the happiness of her life, her life itself, depended on the choice. And the first act, which normally would have ended with a bland and ordinary musical comedy finale, ended starkly with the murder of the hero. The audience was caught on the suspense of the girl's terror. This was brand-new in the musical comedy theater, and it was so effective it became the first of a kind.

The dances were innovative in that I linked them tightly to the drama. I was aware very sensitively of the play, its style and its needs, and the dances I designed were neither blocks to the action nor ornaments. Rather, they augmented the characters and they complemented the text and lyrics. They were an added comment, so to speak, an added dimension, and whereas the dialogue was folksy and realistic and the decor and action were, in a sense, frivolous and lighthearted, the ballet was in some sense tragic, even foreboding, and it gave to the piece an additional aura of otherworldliness, poignancy, and haunting nostalgia. In short, it brought an added quality such as only dance can bring, or music, or great color. I had always shown an observing eye for character in my work, and my gestures here, though economic, were revealing. The characters were continued from the ballets into the shorter, lighter dances and became characters in the cast. They always appeared in the same

Gemze de Lappe and Robert Pagent in the ballet
from Agnes de Mille's *Carousel*. CREDIT: *Photo-
Atelier Philippi/The Agnes de Mille Collection.*

Agnes de Mille during rehearsal of *Brigadoon.*
(Left to right) Trude Rittman, Virginia Boslar,
Agnes de Mille, and James Mitchell. CREDIT:
C. A. Tripp.

James Mitchell as Harry Beaton in Agnes de Mille's
Brigadoon. Ziegfeld Theater, 1947. CREDIT:
Vandamm/The Billy Rose Theater Collection.

plausible characterization. They were part of the
people. In this manner a lighthearted and bucolic
piece proved a genuine section of folklore with enduring qualities. The score was unmatched as were
the lyrics, and the whole made for what approaches
a true work of art.

This play had an astonishing success, went
all over the world as soon as the cessation of hostili-
ties permitted, was played in every language, and
continues to this day. The ballets were copied
everywhere.

Since *Oklahoma!* I have done eighteen more
shows of which ten were hits and nine broke new
trails for dancing in commercial ventures. For one
thing, I tried to introduce a new excellence into the
standard of performing, using experts of all techniques and demanding acting quality and musicality.

My greatest social accomplishment, not to be
forgotten, I feel, was breaking open the market for
dancers in the trade so that the basic wage rose
from $45 a week in 1943 to $85 in 1953 and $355
in 1979, and this was of major importance. This
was terribly important. The dancers began to live

like human beings. They lived as they liked. They could take lessons, they could save, they could house themselves decently and dress nicely. They had never been able to do these things before. The dancer as a member of a brothel ceased to exist on Broadway.

I directed the book of several shows and was the first choreographer to do so. The first was *Allegro* by Rodgers and Hammerstein. This highly experimental show contained some lovely writing, but the book as a whole was faulty, the score was weak, and some of the dancing was strained. I was not given freedom of choice in many matters which I should have had as director, and the venture, al-

though it was a pioneer one, could not be said to be a success.

My successes were *Oklahoma!*, *One Touch of Venus*, *Bloomer Girl*, *Carousel*, *Gentlemen Prefer Blondes*, *Brigadoon*, *Paint Your Wagon*, and *110 in the Shade*. I consider my best dances to have been in *Paint Your Wagon*.

Jerome Robbins began his Broadway career in 1944 with the musical *On the Town*, which was memorable because it exploited the talents of three extraordinary twenty-five-year-old men—Robbins, stage designer Oliver Smith, and composer and conductor Leonard Bernstein. It made all three famous. Robbins's second important show was

Jerome Robbins with dancers in the rumble sequence of *West Side Story*. George Marcy, Thomas Hasson, and Larry Wert. CREDIT: *Fred Fehl.*

Gemze de Lappe and James Mitchell in *Paint Your Wagon*, by Agnes de Mille, 1952. CREDIT: *Will Rapport/The Harvard Theatre Collection.*

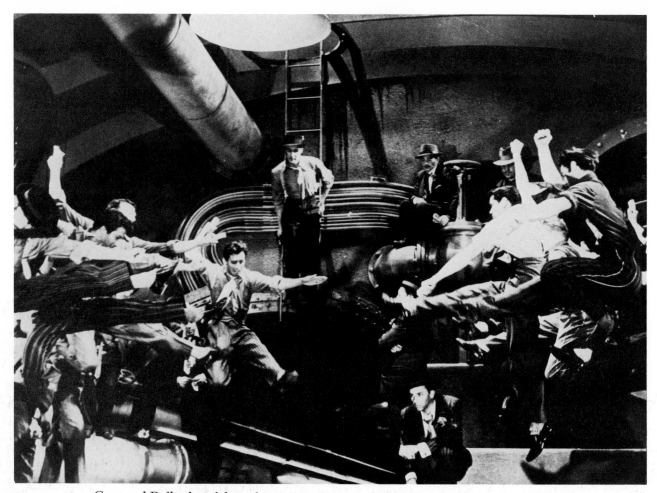

Guys and Dolls, the celebrated crap game by Michael Kidd. CREDIT: *Maurice Seymour*.

High Button Shoes, for which he did his unforgettable Mack Sennett Ballet in 1947. This was followed by a semibiographical piece, *Look, Ma, I'm Dancin'!*. His Siamese dances for *The King and I* were miracles of good taste and invention.

He fused dancing and drama into what was virtually a new balletic form in *West Side Story,* a story-ballet with dialogue and songs in which much of the action is nonrealistic dance pantomime. Because this work was, like mine, directed by the choreographer, he clarified and realized the potentialities of an effort that I began in *Allegro*. It was a landmark production, which united once again the golden talents of Robbins, Bernstein, and Smith. It was *ballet d'action* with dialogue. But the most arresting thing about it was its success. It played on Broadway for nearly three years and became a smash hit in London. Then it showed all over the world in both the theater and the moving picture versions.

Robbins's later successes included *Gypsy; Oh Dad, Poor Dad, Mama's Hung You in the Closet and I'm Feeling So Sad; A Funny Thing Happened on the Way to the Forum;* and *Fiddler on the Roof,* all of which he directed. Hitherto there had been scant opportunity for tragedy and lyricism in musical comedy. Robbins is the master of both. He is the best-known American choreographer in the international musical theater.

Michael Kidd gained fame as a Broadway choreographer with *Finian's Rainbow, Guys and Dolls,* and *Can-Can.* His dances are lively fun and of extraordinary brilliance and speed. He took his gifts to Hollywood for a while, but returned to Broadway to find his real and best field in directing and shaping musicals. He is a past master at this very difficult craft and is much sought after. His name stands among the very best.

In the forties and fifties, Helen Tamiris and Hanya Holm were popular choreographers for musicals and achieved considerable success, Tamiris with *Annie Get Your Gun* and *Inside U.S.A.*; Holm with *Kiss Me, Kate, My Fair Lady,* and *Camelot.* Holm's best work, however, was reserved for the *Ballet Ballads* and for *The Golden Apple* by John Latouche and Jerome Moross. This choreography was really choice and memorable.

After the initial three, Robbins, Kidd, and me,

the two choreographers to make the biggest impact on the Broadway scene have been Robert Fosse and Gower Champion. Both men learned their craft in show business, and although neither has created a ballet, they know the technique of dance construction thoroughly. They have produced brilliant, inventive, and spectacular pieces that are invariable showstoppers and that have become the dazzling ornaments of our commercial theater, setting new standards for this field. They are directors as well and, like Robbins, can establish the tone and pace

All That Jazz, by Bob Fosse. (Left to right) Kathryn Doby, Ben Vereen, Roy Scheider, and Ann Reinking in "Bye Bye Life" number. CREDIT: *Alan Pappé.*

of an entire musical so that the dances are of a piece with the texture. Their lists of successes are famous the world over—for Champion, *Bye-Bye, Birdie, Carnival, Lend an Ear,* and *Hello, Dolly!*; for Fosse, *The Pajama Game* (dances only), *Damn Yankees, Sweet Charity,* and *Red Head.*

Both were fortunate in having wives who were skilled artists as well as women of taste and perception. Marge Champion partnered her husband for years in vaudeville. Gwen Verdon Fosse is one of the most enchantingly irresistible stars of our musical theater. Verdon made a name for herself first with Jack Cole, then with Robert Fosse, whom she married. Her fame is lasting, and Fosse gave her a framework and support that set her off like the bright jewel she is.

In 1978 Fosse directed the all-dancing revue *Dancin',* a dazzling display of showstoppers, pitched at breakneck speed and heartbreak intensity, staged stylishly and slickly, and performed by brilliant young virtuosi. This was something new, a dance evening for the general public, playing eight times a week and entirely composed by one man; a tour de force.

In the sixties Herbert Ross, with two brilliant ballets to his credit and a number of TV commercial shows, began to choreograph for Broadway. He was in no sense an innovator and could not possibly compete with the leaders in the field, but he was to make his mark elsewhere and to make it with glory.

Peter Gennaro, who collaborated with Robbins on *West Side Story,* has done charming, lively work, notably in *The Unsinkable Molly Brown, Fiorello,* and *Annie.* He is, however, somewhat derivative.

Danny Daniels is a brilliant tap dancer who performed in Jerome Robbins's *Ballets U.S.A.* and on Broadway with *Flora, the Red Menace.* He has several fine choreographic jobs to his credit, including *All American, Walking Happy,* and a revival of *Annie Get Your Gun.* He would certainly have had a continuing career, but he suddenly pulled up stakes and went to Hollywood with his family. There he now runs a school.

Pat Birch in rehearsal for *Over Here,* with Ann Reinking and John Mineo. CREDIT: © 1974, Lois Greenfield.

Scene from *Ballroom,* by Michael Bennett, 1979. CREDIT: *Herbert Migdoll.*

Onna White and Patricia Birch have also made excellent contributions to the Broadway scene, White in *The Music Man, Irma la Douce,* and *Oliver*; and Birch in *A Little Night Music, You're a Good Man, Charlie Brown,* and *Grease.* Birch has been a soloist for Graham and me and is the impeccable mistress of several styles. It is this versatility that makes it possible for her to do dances in the current vernacular with sensitivity. Her biggest opportunities to display her choreographic imagination to date have been in *Music Is* and *Pacific Overtures.* Her greatest asset is her rare understanding of plot and the overall proportion of the disparate factors in a musical play. She shows fine theatrical discretion.

Donald McKayle has done very little compared to the others, but he has done it well and movingly. He is a fine director and his *Raisin* is a landmark.

Michael Bennett has achieved a remarkable feat in creating the biggest money-maker in the history of Broadway, *Chorus Line.* His dances are lively, fast-paced, but old-fashioned, reminiscent of the tap routines of the thirties. They are, however, an unprecedented success because there is a hunger, obviously, for just such nostalgia. Audiences adore it and come from the world around,

quite literally in the millions, to see it.

In 1978 Bennett introduced in *Ballroom* an evening of ballroom dancing. The dances were limited to what went on in a dance hall with a dance club of people who were there as amateurs, for the love of the exercise and their own entertainment, and it reflected all the styles of the forties and fifties, performed by a cast of extraordinarily able veterans from the best ballet companies and the finest schools. Stylistically it was impeccable, and the variety of pattern derived from couples performing independently and then in unison at climactic points was extremely fine and suggested the use of pattern on pattern that is the stock in trade of Twyla Tharp. The tact of keeping the patterns clear and introducing unison movement at climactic moments, like brass into an orchestral piece, was of a very high order. It would be nice if these dances could be preserved as a compendium of ballroom style.

Bennett's chief achievement is very probably his wonderful sense of executive organization. He has an arrangement with his dancers whereby they share in a profit-making scheme in which they become, in fact, partners of the business structure. They rehearse for long periods of time, much longer than any other group in existence, under union minimum pay, but when they share in a success, and they did in *Chorus Line,* they become the richest line dancers in the history of the business.

In the sixties and seventies the dancing on Broadway, with the exception of those contributions made by choreographer-directors, unhappily has not been as interesting as that of the middle forties and fifties. That is because most of the playwrights have turned away from lyric or dramatic movement to short, unattached, frivolous set dances, decorative in purpose and mainly gymnastic in nature. The apparent dearth of choreographic talent is, therefore, due probably to lack of opportunity. The best choreographers have been diverted to directing as more profitable and now do both choreographing and directing. Several take on the responsibilities of writing and producing as well.

Lee Theodore, an erstwhile member of Jerome Robbins's company and one of his star soloists ("Anybody" in *West Side Story*), organized in 1976 a small company called the Dance Machine with the avowed purpose of remounting and saving the fine works which had been done in Broadway musicals. This was an extremely ambitious project and one fraught with difficulties, but she has overcome many of them and the extreme doubts of the choreographers. Her first performances were at the Ford Theater in Washington where she played for weeks. This was followed by six months at the Century Theater in New York and then fourteen weeks in Tokyo. She has been asked to give a state performance at the White House for a formal dinner honoring the premier of Thailand. The company represents a very neat package of fine dancers, modest but inventive costumes, a small music ensemble of two pianos and timpani, and expert direction. It has mounted thirty-eight dance numbers and represents nineteen choreographers, including all the leading dance directors of the American stage with the one exception of Jerome Robbins.

The drawback is the limitation of funds. The American musical comedy dancer is the best in the world for what he does and the leading soloists are genuine stars and often, as in the case of Gwen Verdon, transfer to genuine solar stardom. They cannot be replaced by talented youngsters no matter how gifted. A star brings something of

experience, power, personality and forcefulness to the stage, which has no counterpart, and this is the very stuff of the Broadway scene. The dances therefore are lacking in an essential dimension and the dancers trained by Lee Theodore, although fine, cannot be held together when there is a call out for a big show. She loses her personnel repeatedly. There is one cure for this, one thing needed for this excellent troupe without which it cannot survive and with which it can go on to what it purports to be, a national storehouse for our treasure, one thing: money.

With the overwhelming success of the Broadway ballets, the economic condition of the ballet and the modern dancer in the United States has changed from starvation and despair to possible security. As a result, many more men are training than ever before. Hitherto, a dancer entering the popular theater in our country learned to do only tap or acrobatic stunts. The line dancer, the chorus boy or girl, and the "specialty," or one stunt, performer have been replaced by experts skilled in several styles, who can as a rule act very well too and even sing a little.

The sheer caliber of the modern performer and his serious attitude are gradually changing what was long unfortunately the attitude in the United States. Dancing as a profession is now permitted in America, still less to men than to women, but permitted. Wherever dancing is part of the religious and communal life, it is accepted as an art quite normally; where it is not, it is reserved for the outcasts and misfits. Where it is not economically viable, it is of course not practical or desirable.

All the stage dancing in this book had to pay for itself or receive private gifts. The life of every company, both ballet and commercial, was precarious, and the careers of the performers hazardous. Dancing was a career for gypsies, as all theater artists found, a career to be avoided and scorned. This was not true in other countries, where there were established theaters and where dancers could be taken in as youngsters and trained in state schools, then accepted as government employees with status, respectability, and remuneration, and retired on good pensions and often with teaching jobs. In America there were no guarantees, and an aging dancer was in great peril. But dancing is now viable.

16. DANCE IN FILMS AFTER 1950

THE Soviets have made many films of their ballets, gradually getting better over the years. There have also been a few British films devoted to dancing, notably *The Red Shoes* in 1948. But real film techniques for the dance are only just now beginning to be found.

With the complete renovation of the musical comedies on Broadway following *Oklahoma!,* there was a landslide of new ballets. There was also a great deal of talk about transferring these ballets to films. Nothing, however, of any great note happened before 1950. Jack Cole made some excellent dances that were filmed with great intelligence, chiefly because he himself designed the camera work and supervised it setup by setup. And Michael Kidd did some excellent pieces. But on the whole, dance work in film lagged behind that on the stage.

Then in 1954, *Oklahoma!* finally reached Hollywood, and I was able to bring the "Dream Ballet" in good order to the screen with the help of the director, Fred Zinnemann. This was followed shortly by Jerome Robbins's film work in *The King and I* and *West Side Story.* He was given a hand in directing great sequences of the latter, and he was largely instrumental in bringing the dances to the point where they actually projected the vitality and emotional force of live movement. In this picture Robbins "broke the sound barrier," so to speak, and filmed motion for the first time.

It remained, however, for Herbert Ross in *The Turning Point* to give us dancing, pure dancing, with all its vitality and strength and beauty and persuasiveness.

Herbert Ross abandoned Broadway for Hollywood, and with the help of his wife, onetime ballerina Nora Kaye, has established himself as one of film's most successful directors. He staged the dances for a number of Marilyn Monroe and Barbra Streisand films and then began directing pictures himself, some of which employed dancing, but by no means all. Ross had served a long apprenticeship in television and had learned a great deal about the techniques of camera, and while the television camera is very different from the moving picture camera (mainly in the amounts and kinds of distortion involved), there are many aspects that are identical. Ross now knows how to use both with mastery.

Romeo and Juliet, by Agnes de Mille, with Norma Shearer. CREDIT: © *1936,
MGM Corp. Renewed 1963, MGM, Inc.*

There are many reasons why movement is very difficult to catch significantly in a camera. The director must accomplish the almost impossible feat of making dancing interesting and vital while at the same time overcoming the lack of physical presence and dimension. This is purely a matter of technique and cutting and it involves high skill. The human eye is a remarkable instrument. It can see and recognize details and whole patterns at the same instant. It can focus on any part of a pattern while keeping in view that part's relationship ·to the whole. It can judge distances. It can judge speeds. Cameras cannot do these things as easily or as quickly. There is a loss of three-dimensional perception so closely linked to presence. The camera can focus on a detail or a grand pattern, but not on both simultaneously. These lacks have to be compensated for with great skill. They have been recognized in the photography of sports, particularly for television, and they have been coped with magically, but that is because people wanted to photograph sports and because the audience clamored to see them. Now a tennis game can be shown as it is played, not only with accuracy, but with the immediacy and impact of living presence. That is a real achievement, an art in itself. There has been no such clamoring for dancing, or so the producers assumed.

The Court Dancers from *Romeo and Juliet*, by Agnes de Mille, 1936, with Bella Lewitsky second from left and Warren Leonard second from right in front. CREDIT: © *1936, MGM Corp. Renewed 1963, MGM, Inc.*

Oklahoma! in its Todd-AO version. "The Cowman and the Farmman" with Evelyn Taylor, Mark Platt, Gene Nelson, and Kelly Brown. CREDIT: *Schuyler Crail/The Agnes de Mille Collection.*

Mikhail Baryshnikov and Leslie Browne in Herbert Ross' *The Turning Point*. CREDIT: © *1977, Twentieth Century-Fox Film Corp.*

In 1978 in *The Turning Point*, a film about ballet dancing, Ross drew a large proportion of the cast from the American Ballet Theatre and used their studios and workrooms for much of the locale.

It was his most successful picture to date and has been an enormous help in establishing dancing in the mind of the public as a legitimate line of work and an interesting and entertaining way of life. The dance sequences in it are masterpieces of photographic skill and project not only the movement but the personalities of the performers. The film also made a nationally known star of Mikhail Baryshnikov.

The actual dances in The *Turning Point* may not be very great (there is one sequence by Sir Frederick Ashton that is enchantingly lovely) but they are moving and they do display the great mastery of the balletic style of Baryshnikov.

It is curious that the picture deals almost entirely with quotations from the classic Russian repertory and with none of the modern work by Tudor, Robbins, and me, which Nora Kaye spent her career in interpreting.

In January of 1980 Robert Fosse released his film *All That Jazz,* a most extraordinary treatment in parable and metaphor of the current dilemma of the successful stage personality. Whether or not the picture is autobiographical is of no consequence, nor is the actual texture of the dances which are manifold but repetitious. They are filmed with absolute mastery and the technique and imagination and invention of the film devices is on a par with the best Italian work of this period. Fosse has revealed himself what he promised to be in *Cabaret*, a great director in films, one of the best in the world today.

17.
THE MECHAN-ICALS: TELEVISION, VIDEO AND SOUND TAPE

U P to 1974 the situation in television, like the situation in movies, was very constricted. A few choreographers worked regularly in the medium, but generally not at things they really wanted to do. John Butler, for instance, had to create his ballets for early-morning shows and devote the rest of his time to hack service for big musical revues. He produced a few serious works for *Lamp Unto My Feet*, which, although it was a very interesting program, was shown on Sunday mornings at nine o'clock and therefore seen by only a small, select audience. It did, however, furnish the proving ground for Butler's early ballets, and with the money he made in TV he was able to pay for such distinguished scores as *After Eden*, which he otherwise could not have afforded. Herbert Ross was another TV choreographer who did whatever came to hand but nothing that really interested him.

In the mid-fifties, the *Omnibus* series, funded by Ford, initiated a series of dance programs. These included lectures and ballets and featured Edward Villella and me, but the series was discontinued when Ford withdrew its financial support. It went off the air and was replaced by nothing similar. A series called *The Seven Lively Arts*, which followed, included some good dance programs, but it was not of the same caliber.

Obviously TV producers assumed that the general public could not be interested in the dance and that the limited number of people who were interested were somewhat peculiar. But maybe they were wrong. A series called *The U.S.A. Dance*, sponsored by the Educational Broadcasting Company, began in 1965 and sparked some interest. Then in 1976 a remarkable series called *Dance in America* started on public television. This important, and for the most part good, series was funded largely by Exxon and was under the overall direction of Jac Venza. It began with a brilliant program on the American Ballet Theatre, filmed partly in Hollywood. It continued with monthly programs beautifully photographed and very ably edited, covering nearly all the big dance events of this country, expanding to embrace summer festivals and visiting artists, and climaxing in an hour and a half on Martha Graham that was one of the best programs ever produced for television. This series has gradually widened the public's knowledge and whetted its appetite for good dance.

Amahl and the Night Visitors, by John Butler, with Mary Hinkson, Scott Douglas, and Glen Tetley. CREDIT: Produced by Alvin Cooperman and Judith de Paul. Directed by Arvin Brown.

Christine Sarry rehearsing Eliot Feld's program for *Dance in America*. CREDIT: © *1979, Lois Greenfield*.

The great names in the field have now reached general broadcasting and perform frequently on commercial television, where they are able to command the best cameramen available. The costs for such programming are prodigious, and that is why there has been delay in bringing dance to the screen. However, the techniques have been mastered for sports, so given dance's present popularity, it is conceivable that the technique of filming dancers will very shortly approach the technique of filming tennis players.

Two mechanical inventions have transformed the craft of dancing and choreography—taped music and videotape. Taped music makes it possible to record instantly any kind of music, along with instructions, to stop the tape, to repeat passages as often as necessary, to go back to a particular bar of music just as a live accompanist would. This means that now the choreographer and the dancers can hear the sound of many instruments as well as the piano, something that was quite impossible before. It means that the choreographer can study the music aurally as well as visually while he is composing, and that he can work alone, without dancers and without accompanists. It means that the dancers can work by themselves whenever they want. All this spells a gigantic saving in money. Union pianists now get eighteen dollars an hour, so a three-hour session, which is the usual stint, is, of course, very costly.

The invention of videotape is perhaps even more significant. Videotape has made it possible to record movement instantly and play it back instantly, right in the rehearsal hall. The dances can be recorded at every stage of development and restudied on the spot. The finished product can be preserved and reviewed without all the paraphernalia, lights, and crew that filming requires (not to mention the cost). A single operator is required, and the action is caught for all time. Dancers will not now be forgotten or lost. We can have a literature of our art and an accurate record, by means of which we can develop beyond the primitive stage of rote. No performing art can mature or flourish until this happens because without it there is no means of studying the past exactly and of progressing. The young dance student or the young choreographer can learn the history of dancing and the great works while he or she is still young and formative, without endless travel and expense. This is a miracle, and I believe it will transform the art. The benefits are unforseeable.

But still the real teaching comes from the inspiration of direct contact and the immediate presence of personality, teacher to pupil, experienced performer to beginner, one human being talking and explaining and demonstrating for another human being. There is no substitute for this. This is the heart of inspiration.

18.
STATE ENDOWMENT AND THE UNIONS

THERE are certain kinds of theatrical arts, performing arts, which cannot support themselves—never have, never will, shouldn't be expected to, were not designed to. These include symphonic music, opera, ballet, concert dancing, and great repertory theater. They require lengthy rehearsal, large companies, and sumptuous production, and therefore they can't pay off the way commercial shows do by repetition. In Europe such art forms are never expected to succeed financially. In their early stages these forms were supported first by the Church and then by the State, whether it was a monarchy or a democracy. Usually the State also saw to it that there was in every city of size an opera house for grand opera, with a school attached, an *opéra comique* for light opera, and a state repertory theater to play the national classics. Moreover, these state-supported arts functioned right alongside all the commercial forms, beginning with the circus. One has only to read the theater history of Paris, Berlin, Rome, or London or to see European films and television to recognize how beautifully the commercial companies succeed even when there is a state-supported company in direct competition.

Enormous effort and money were traditionally given to sustain the arts. At one point in the eighteenth century, the Duke of Württemburg actually sold about two thousand of his subjects as mercenaries in order to support the ballets of Jean Georges Noverre. (That, by the way, is how the Hessians came to be in America during the Revolutionary War.)

Why haven't we, too, had state-supported art? After all, we are very rich and powerful, and usually we get what we want. Obviously, then, because we didn't want it.

What we needed we borrowed. We began by exchanging performing artists with other countries. Until recently there was a congressman from Brooklyn named Rooney, who didn't like art. He was not untypical of many in public office. He didn't want money spent on art and he highly disapproved of the State Department's program of exchanging fine performing artists for foreign stars. He couldn't actually halt the program, because it was an act of Congress, but he could delay it and confuse it and obfuscate it, because unfortunately he was the chairman of the appropriations committee.

However, he got his comeuppance under these

circumstances: Leonard Bernstein went with the New York Philharmonic to Moscow some years ago and was a historic success. Our State Department taped the reaction, a joyous and noisy one. But it recorded something not bargained for—Congressman Rooney's voice. He was standing near the machine, and he was heard to say in sheer astonishment, "By God, this is useful!"

We are, it has been lamentably proven again and again, probably the first people in history who have condescended to art. Other men have used art as magic, have worshipped it, cherished it, feared it, or forbidden it. We alone condescend to it. We neglect it. This is a remarkable historical fact. Who are we to hold these unique notions?

We are a diverse people. I don't mean the natives, who treat art most solemnly and fearfully and as it should be treated, but the later immigrants. We come from many places but we all came for one basic reason; because we couldn't stand it where we were.

First of all, we were English Protestants, who came here to worship God after our own conscience, to be free, to act as we saw best, and to rear our sons as free men, unbeholden to anyone. Then later we were Irish and Scotch Catholics, who came because we were persecuted by the Protestants, and *we* came in order to worship God after our own fashion. We were also French Protestants, who were persecuted by the French Catholics, and we came because we wished to conduct our lives as we saw fit, to be free, unbeholden, our own masters. And we were Dutch, persecuted by everyone, but mainly by the Spanish. And we were Quakers, *nobody* liked the Quakers, so we took over Pennsylvania. And we were many others. And all of us, no matter what we believed, had these goals: never to be beholden, never to have to act against our conscience, never to be indebted. The specter of debtor's prison haunted every poor man in Europe.

We were younger sons. In the old country the older brother got everything—the title and the money and the land and the seat in government. The younger brothers had to take what was left. They didn't like the arrangement. They took North America. This is a country of younger brothers. And over here we were not younger. We were governors and masters.

And we were craftsmen and we were farmers.

We were good workers, but we couldn't succeed at home because we couldn't own our own land and we couldn't rear up our children free. In order to come here we sold ten or fifteen years of our life to work as indentured servants for passage money. It takes five hours now to come from Europe. It took ten years then. But we knew when the service was over we could do what we liked and would be beholden to no one.

And we were boatloads of women. We came to find husbands we had never seen and knew nothing about. And this was a terrible risk, because there was no way back, morally, legally, or geographically. But our children would be free. We knew this. They would be their own masters.

And we were deported criminals. In the seventeenth century you could be hanged for stealing a farthing's worth of bread, and your sentence was commuted to transportation only in the case of the most piteous circumstances, for instance, if you were under twelve years old, or if you were pregnant.

We were ten million Africans, all kinds—kings, hunters, priests, artists, farmers, doctors—all nations. Only eight million of us survived the trip, but even we dreamed that someday somehow in this new land there must be a chance to walk free.

And we were white slaves, kidnapped off the streets of London or in the back alleys of the cities of Europe, mainly children, lonely people. It was called "Barbadoing." We couldn't stand the conditions. We perished.

But all of us, so diverse, so scattered, had the one idea—never to call any other man master, never to be indebted, never to be beholden.

You could do it in those days if you had your health and some courage. You took a horse and a sack of seed and a hatchet and a gun and a plow and your woman, and you went out into the wilderness and you broke it.

A pioneer once said, "When I was very young, the trees grew so thick and tall you had to look straight up to see the sky." The trunk of a three-hundred-year-old oak measures nine feet in diameter. You cut that down alone and then you dragged the roots out of the earth. (The roots of an oak stretch to the farthest tip of the longest branch.) And you dragged them out alone. And when you'd done that you fought your plow through the stony earth, your gun cocked in the furrow beside you, and you listened to the birds, which were more plentiful than now. You listened to what could not be heard—the soundless moccasin, the whistling thud of an arrow in the wall of your house, in the body of your child. Your wife coped, if she lived. There were no doctors.

Now, suppose someone came to you and said, "You cleared and plowed and planted your five acres; would you also plant my three, because I want to practice my violin?"

If such a request had been made of a German or an Italian farmer, I think he might have replied, "How well do you play? I can't live without music."

It was at this time in history that the American conscience became imbued with the idea that what was not *useful* was no good. If it had no practical, utilitarian purpose, if you couldn't mend the roof with it, or stuff a chink with it, or patch a boot, or wear it on your back, or put it in a stew pot, or manure your fields, or physic your child with it, what use was it? None, obviously. It was effeminate; it was trivial; it was un-American. And if at the same time it was pleasurable, then it was indeed suspect, because we are essentially and unforgettably the children of Puritans, and their point of view still shapes us.

We had arts, of course. We cannot live without them. We had literature, which travels light—a good thing in the days of big seas and little boats. And we had architecture. Architecture begins with the first rainstorm. And in those two arts we have held our own with any peoples on the face of the earth.

We also had house decoration and wonderfully fine artifacts. When one has to live for the rest of a lifetime with what one makes oneself, one is going to make it well. In those days obsolescence, the result of bad workmanship, was considered a disgrace and unacceptable, not an advantage.

Beyond this we had fine arts of a sort. We had limners, portrait painters. They traveled around with a cart full of male and female canvases with blanks for faces, and for a dollar and a good hot meal they would insert into the oval the face of your wife; it would look more like your wife than the Jersey cow, but not much more.

Music, alas, fared hardly. Eight or nine generations of men and women on this continent lived and died without ever hearing anything outside a fiddle tune or the melody of a hymn and the descant—no harmony, no development, no concert of instruments, nothing. Today we are deafened with music in every airport lavatory and supermarket. In those days in that Indian wilderness, an unaccompanied melody was an event.

The theater was in a class by itself. The theater meant patronage. All art needs patronage and protection, particularly the theater, which requires long periods of training and big investments in scenery and costumes. This was simple to arrange when the actors were kings or high priests. It was difficult when no single production or performance could be expected to pay back costs as it did in the popular theater of England and France. In early America there were no gentlemen rich enough to maintain private theaters, and no sponsoring organizations.

It was men from this background who gathered in Philadelphia at the end of the eighteenth century to write our Constitution. It was the best constitution to date in the world, and provided for nearly every contingency, with one startling exception: no provision was made for a secretary of fine arts or education. This was an omission of consequence. Every other civilized country had a minister of arts, and even countries that were relatively uncivilized had high priests who took care of these matters. The most ancient and primitive societies considered art, music, and the theater so important, so involved with their religion and well-being, that they always provided for someone close to the ruler to watch over these affairs. We alone did not.

But John Adams, despite the fact that he came from Boston, was liberal-minded and farsighted and sensitive to the arts. He wrote to his wife Abigail from Paris:

> The mechanic arts are those which we have occasion for in a young country as yet simple and not far advanced in luxury. I must study politics and war so that my sons may have liberty to study mathematics and philosophy, geography, natural history, navigation, commerce and agriculture, in order to give their sons the right to study painting, poetry, music, architecture, statuary, tapestry and porcelain.

We have surpassed the dreams of John Adams: We have achieved universal education. Almost anybody can get a primary or secondary education in this country. Indeed, almost anybody can get a higher education, something that a hundred years ago would have been considered impossible.

The state at first supported primary schools, then later libraries and museums and state universities, but never the theater, never orchestras or opera, which were all privately supported. As our population grew, our needs grew. The great dance companies of the twentieth century were the gifts of two or three individuals, notably Lucia Chase and Lincoln Kirstein. Even the two major ones in New York found it increasingly impossible to tour as costs mounted. Obviously other sources of income had to be discovered. There were other sources, which turned out to be the government once removed.

One of the most striking phenomena of the later nineteenth century was the development of big business, and one of the most striking phenomena of the twentieth century was the reluctant and enforced liaison between big business and culture. By the end of the nineteenth century there were about two dozen corporate monsters, so large and so powerful that they had to be considered as sovereign powers in their own right. They did not coin money and they did not maintain standing armies, but in all other ways they could have a voice in our state policy, and to a large extent they controlled our actions. These corporations amassed fortunes larger than the entire treasuries of small countries. Their power was very nearly without check.

Very nearly, but not altogether. The United States government took note of their growth and used the one single means at its disposal to curb their activities—taxation. The corporations, in turn, hit upon the escape of giving enormous charitable donations to scientific projects, which were supposedly for the public good. At first they were often in the chief interest of the corporations themselves, and the researches tended to be practical and of direct proven value. These charitable foundations were not taxed and were therefore used blatantly to escape the burden of taxation.

There has since been a slow but gradual pressure to force the corporations to endow certain educational institutions, and subsequently certain arts. This, of course, they were at first doggedly unwilling to do. "What use is art?" they asked. "And what good would it do us?" The pressure, however, continued.

The corporations found themselves in a quandary. The men who ran the big foundations were bankers or lawyers or businessmen, not scholars or artists. They knew very little about either field. They were interested in what would help them and increase the prestige of their product. So they did what they would do in business: they hired experts to advise them, but they frankly did not know where to get the experts. They did not know who had real taste and knowledge and who had only empty-sounding degrees and credits. As a result, the advice they got was generally not considered or experienced, and it very rarely came from men and women of culture.

The Ford Foundation was the first foundation to make a breakthrough. It began endowing music and theater as well as all forms of education and cultural experiments. Finally, in 1963, it gave more than seven million dollars to promote dancing in America. That was the first time that any such gift had ever been made to dancers by the government or even by private sponsors. It was considered unfortunate by some that the grant was made to one man, George Balanchine, who although undoubtedly a genius, was neither native-born nor interested in any of the native forms. He was, however, a leader in his art and the head of a very fine dance theater. Moreover, he spread a good bit of the gift around among his pupils, so geographically, at least, the money went to more than one spot.

Since then, other foundations and institutions have followed suit, although in an extremely cautious manner. They help endow ballet projects, opera projects, and symphonic music projects of unquestionable reputation. And by giving money to television they make possible the growing proliferation of music and classic theater and even dance. The costs, however, have overtaken the gifts. The pressure for government aid has therefore been overpoweringly strong. It simply had to come, or all of our arts would be stunted and even the old standard institutions would flounder.

Gradually, although it is repugnant to the American mind to consider patronage, we all came to the conclusion that we had to call in government help, on the civic, state, and federal levels. And although we had always feared that state sponsor-

Rehearsal in empty theater. CREDIT: © *Bil Leidersdorf.*

ship would lead to dictatorship in the arts, we could nevertheless observe that in those countries where there was freedom of government, there was also freedom in the arts, even if the arts were government-sponsored. On the other hand, those countries that do not have a free expression, as in the Iron Curtain countries, have no freedom in the arts either; they have no freedom of any kind whatever.

In 1961 New York State voted $450,000 to help the arts outside of New York City. In 1965 President Johnson signed the bill that gave us our first National Arts Endowment. I was fortunate enough to be appointed by President Johnson to the first national council. The night before the official first meeting, I met up with Associate Justice Goldberg in the driveway of Chairman Roger Stevens's house. He stopped me and asked, "Aren't you excited?" And I replied, "I'm shaking with excitement." And he said, "Let me entreat you, give us the best. Don't settle for anything less than the best for any reason whatever, the absolute best. You stand as representatives of the American people and that's what they want and that's what they should have and that's what the government and the people of the United States are paying for."

"We can't afford the best," I said.

"That's none of your business. You let us go up on the Hill and fight for that. Concern yourself with choosing well."

So with that as a guiding principle many of us, indeed most of us, proceeded. We selected the best, the absolute best. We were able to give them a pittance only, not enough for any project, virtually nothing. But it was to the best people that we gave it.

When Roger Stevens's successor, Nancy Hanks, took office as second chairman of the National Endowment, federal funds rose from $2 million for all the states and five protectorates to $100 million. Hanks and her aides achieved this by persuading the congressmen that all of the states would be represented equally and that no area of the states would be forgotten. And this was a different point of view. This meant that not only the best were the recipients of grants, it meant that everyone sincere and worthy got something and the best proportionately little.

But even today the government gifts and the private gifts together cannot keep up with costs, because we face the demands of the unions. The unions cut through every aspect of life in this country.

Everyone knows that there is not a union or labor organization in existence that wasn't formed as protection against exploitation and cruelty. The working conditions at the turn of the century demanded them. Men had to form these unions or be exterminated, and they learned their lesson with brutal thoroughness. They learned the value of force.

It is just and desirable that a man be paid fairly, even very well, for a job of work done. Everyone wants this. Justice demands it. But the extortionism and the blackmail that the workers have borrowed from the bosses is damaging—the featherbedding, moonlighting, all the little blackmail tricks that add up to levy toll on other people's labor and to force payment not earned. These dodges are not to obtain justice, but to make the bosses popular with the party members so that they can keep themselves in office. The result is very serious.

Whether we admit it or not, as a nation we are in economic civil war. On the one side are the people who own the natural resources, and on the other are those who control the labor blocks. It is a life-and-death struggle.

In our theater there are two kinds of unions. The unions of the performing artists are fairly good and on the whole reasonable, because the performers themselves govern the unions and therefore try to arrive at contracts that will get them better pay while at the same time protecting and continuing the art itself. The craft unions, on the other hand, the electricians, the grips, the carpenters, the painters, the people who sell tickets, the executants of costumes and scenery, the scene painters (not the designers), and the truckers all want to get as much money as they can, no matter what—even if the plays or ballets fail, even if the theater closes—and no matter at what price. To achieve their unreasonable goal they will resort to slowdowns and other harmful practices.

The basic wage for a chorus dancer on Broadway in 1943 was $45 a week, $20 a week for rehearsal. The basic pay today is $355 a week.

The pay for ballet varies with the different companies, according to AGMA (American Guild of Musical Artists). In 1939 Ballet Caravan paid its dancers $35 per week. Now the New York City Ballet pays $430 per week from 2 weeks to 45 weeks, Ballet Theatre pays $350 per week up to 36 weeks, and the Joffrey Ballet pays $345 per week up to 32 weeks. In the American Ballet Theatre the scale is (1979): first year, $235; second year, $259; third year, $285; and fourth year, $314. Soloists get more according to their ability to charge more: for instance, the meteoric Russian stars get between $2,000 and $5,000 a performance, depending on where they are playing and with whom.

Compare these dancers' salaries with IATSE (International Alliance of Theatrical Stage Employees) union wages for stagehands or members of the staff, as of January 1979. Rules and salaries vary with the size of the houses and the size of the companies, but for a company of, say, forty-five to sixty dancers and a house of about two thousand seats, they are approximately as follows:

1. The heads of departments, i.e., the carpenter, electrician, and prop man, get $438 per week, or about $15 an hour.

2. Overtime is time and a half, or $23, and double time, is, of course, $30. Overtime is deemed to be anything after eight hours or after midnight. Double time is any hour on Sunday or on the dark day, i.e., a day on which the theater is closed. There is a dark day every week.

3. Every call must be for at least three hours.

4. The head carpenter, electrician, and prop man must be called on each call. This is obligatory, except for the use of an empty stage without lights, props, or costumes. Then one electrician only is needed.

5. No scenery may be used, not a flight of stairs, or a platform, or a drop, or a bar of wood, nothing whatever that is used specifically in the show, without the three heads of the departments present. And if more than a drop is used, two men at $10 an hour (or $335 a week) must be called. If any of the show props is used, two extra men are obligatory, even if it is a broom carried by an actor.

6. If full scenery is used, six to eight men must be called.

7. The stage may not be used for any purpose, with or without props and scenery, during the lunch hour, which will be at either 12 o'clock, or 1 o'clock, or during the supper hour, six to seven.

8. The number of men used depends on whether or not the saving of man-hours puts any union members out of work.

9. If any costumes are used on the stage, two dressers at least are required. No part of a costume may be rehearsed in—no tutu, no long skirt, no difficult cloak—if it is the genuine costume designed for performance without the summoning of two wardrobe dressers and the prop man. Dummy costumes can be used on stage in rehearsal, but not the real ones, which are sometimes needed because of weight and the fall of material.

10. All scenery must be carried from the shops where it is made to the theater in union trucks, even small hand props. And they must be carried from the trucks to the stage by union truckmen and delivered to union stagehands. The reverse process, the hauling out from the theater, is also always enforced. The number of truckmen called and the hours they work vary with the requirements of the show. But the trucking union is notorious all over the United States for the stringency and severity of its rules.

These rules may be eased or adjusted depending on the goodwill of the men, but the book of rules can be enforced inflexibly if they so wish.

The lay reader may gather from the above that rehearsing a show is an expensive business, and he may begin to understand why the price of theater tickets is exorbitantly high.

In 1948 Ballet Theatre produced my *Fall River Legend*. When I first saw Oliver Smith's extraordinary set (on the afternoon of the opening), I gasped at its beauty and its possibilities. It consisted of one massive structured piece, which could be taken apart, moved about, and reassembled against different painted backdrops. "I haven't begun to use this," I said, "but I will have to work within the set." That meant, of course, a full crew call. In the thirty-two years since then (and the ballet has been fairly consistently in the repertory all that time), there has never been money for an experimental rehearsal, not even on tour in foreign countries. I consider this an enticing opportunity lost. For thirty-two years! And in one of our biggest companies!

In 1965 the American Ballet Theatre celebrated its twenty-fifth anniversary. All its children returned, many of them by then great stars. There was an unprecedented array of premieres, including Jerome Robbins's *Les Noces* with full orchestra, choir, four solo pianists, and Leonard Bernstein conducting; and a black group headed by Carmen de Lavallade and introducing Judith Jamison to New York, in my work *The Four Marys*; and everyone taken together, including guest stars, orchestra (which because of the constant change of repertory rehearsed daily for hours), choreographers, composers, conductors, regisseurs, designers, and dancers, did not equal in cost half that of the stagehands and technical staff. Since then, the ratio has worsened.

Such costs put limits on everything—the number of rehearsals, the number of new ballets mounted, the number of effects attempted, the number of scores commissioned. They also force up the price of tickets until ordinary people cannot attend the theater.

But the worst aspect of all is what is happening to the craftsmen themselves. If you spend your life doing bad jobs so that you will have to redo them tomorrow for some dough, where is your self-respect? Where is your joy? How can you face yourself? Well, you can't. You go home and get drunk. You have to keep telling yourself, "Don't be a sucker. If you don't get it, the next guy will. Do as

little as possible. Lie! Moonlight! Shift it to someone else! Go to sleep up there. They have to pay
you $15 an hour anyway—$22.50 for time and a
half—$30 for overtime."

Joseph Conrad wrote this about sailing:

The moral side of an industry, the redeeming and
ideal aspect of this breadwinning, is the attain-
ment and perfection of the highest possible skill
on the part of the craftsman. Such skill, the skill
of technique, is more than honesty. It is something wider, embracing honesty and grace and
rule in an elevated and clear sentiment, not
altogether utilitarian, which may be called the
honor of labor. The sort of understanding I mean
depends so much on love. And love, though in
a sense it may be admitted to be stronger than
death, is by no means so universal and so sure.
In fact, love is rare—the love of man, of things,
of ideas, the love of perfected skill. For love is the
enemy of haste. It takes count of passing days, of
men who pass away, or a fine art matured slowly
in a course of years, and doomed in a short time
to pass away and be no more.*

That is not what one hears in IATSE Local 1.
Nevertheless, all students, all artists, all good work-
men of every kind, know what Conrad means.

What have we got here in America that we
believe we cannot live without? We have the most
varied and imaginative bathrooms in the world,
we have kitchens with the most gimmicks, we have
houses with every possible electrical gadget to save
ourselves all kinds of trouble—all so that we can
have leisure. Leisure, leisure, leisure! So that we
don't go mad in the leisure we have color TV. So
that there will never, never, be a moment of silence,
we have radio and Muzak. We can't stand silence,
because silence induces thinking. And if we
thought, we would have to face ourselves.

We wear more clothes than any people who
have ever lived. We eat more different kinds of food
than anyone since Louis XIV. What goes on in the
corner drugstore the bazaars of Arabia couldn't
match! What we find piled up in the supermarkets
is the harvest of the world for all seasons at the
same time. And as we push through the aisles,
grabbing this and that from every corner of the
globe, with the Muzak sludge overhead, we should
be the most contented people in the world. Are we?

We have other things. We have death on the

* *Mirror of the Sea*, 1906.

highways. We have alcoholism. We have matricide,
patricide, fratricide. We have LSD. We have dope
pushing, murders, mugging in the high schools,
mugging in the streets, mugging in the parlors.
We have suicide. We have mass suicide. We have
infant murderers. We have insanity. And over and
above all we have total disrespect between the
generations—and lack of hope and lack of faith.
We have loneliness.

Now we don't like these things, but we have
got them. And we have got them, I think, in direct
consequence of believing that we cannot live without the other things, the luxuries, the gimmicks.

As the mother of all the goodies and as an
antidote for all the bad things, we have science. We
have given our entire trust to science. We have
given our faith and hope. We believe that science
can do everything, will fix everything for us. Will
it?

Science can put a telephone in our hands, but
it can't tell us what to say. Science can get us a
symphony orchestra playing on the dashboard of a
car going down the road at ninety-five miles an
hour, but I defy all the IBM machines in the world
to strike up a tune that will set our feet tapping.
Science has got us doing cartwheels in outer space.
We have reached the moon. Can we reach the face
across the breakfast table, or over the back fence, or
across the railroad tracks? Have we ever thought
of investigating the wilderness in the seat next to
us? Or exploring the constellations locked up in our
own skulls?

We are in orbit, all right, alone, sealed off as
no astronaut ever was—out of communication, all
our lives calling out, "This is my name! This is my
name! Can you hear me? Do you hear my voice?
Who are you? Speak!"

How do we break through?

Through art, because art is the radar communication of the human spirit. Somebody wrote
to our first astronauts, "I heard your heart beating."
Whose heart do we hear beating when we listen to
Beethoven? Whose voice do we hear when Hamlet
speaks? Ours, yours, mine—ours together, forever.

It is dawning on us, the richest and most
powerful people in the world, that there are some
things we are lacking, that we perish for want of,
that we are spavined, that we are deprived, that
there are some things that we must have or we are
lost.

Such as religion, not altogether utilitarian.

Such as education, and I don't mean training in a craft or a trade or a business. I mean exploration in depth.

Such as pride of craft, which is another word for self-respect and hope.

Such as beauty.

Dancers know beauty, and dancers know the pride and the joy of beauty which are in essence the love, without which no art exists.

Dancers, after poets, have been the worst paid artists. No matter. They may make millions, they may make a barren subsistence. This is not germane to the meaning of their function. They know power and the delights of refining communication, refinement upon refinement as one approaches the awesome, holy act of perfecting, as one locks spirit to beholding spirit.

No trade unions can ensure this or protect it. It is a gift and should be cherished.

To take the air. To challenge space. To move into space with patterns of shining splendor. To be at once stronger and freer than at any other time in life. To lift up the hearts of those who watch. To be carried on their response. And to walk once more in majesty, with an ancient glory breathing around, united to the spirits of the dedicated dead. For dancers this is enough.

Untitled. CREDIT: *C. A. Tripp.*

BIBLIOG-RAPHY

Amberg, George. *Art in Modern Ballet*. New York: Pantheon Books, 1946.

———. *Ballet in America*. New York: Duell, Sloan and Pearce, 1949.

Arbeau, Thorinot. *Orchesography*. Translated by Mary Stewart Evans. New York: Kamin Dance Publishers, 1948.

Bach, Richard. *Das Mary Wigman-Werk*. Dresden: C. Reissner, 1933.

Bland, Alexander. *The Nureyev Image*. New York: Quadrangle Books/The New York Times Press, 1976.

Blum, Daniel. *A Pictorial History of the American Theatre: 1900–1950*. New York: Grosset & Dunlap, Inc., 1953.

Carner, Mosco. *The Waltz*. New York: Chanticleer Press, 1948.

Castle, Irene. *Castles in the Air*. As told to Bob and Wanda Duncan. Garden City, N.Y.: Doubleday & Co., Inc., 1958.

Castle, Vernon and Irene. *Modern Dancing*. New York: World Syndicate Co., 1914.

Cohen, Selma Jeanne, ed. *The Modern Dance*. Middletown, Conn.: Wesleyan University Press, 1966.

Dickens, Charles. *American Notes* and *Pictures from Italy*. London: 1841.

Desti, Mary. *Isadora Duncan's End*. London: V. Gollancz, Ltd., 1929.

Dolin, Anton. *Alicia Markova, Her Life and Art*. New York: Hermitage House, 1953.

Dreier, Katherine Sophie. *Shawn, the Dancer*. New York: A. S. Barnes, 1933.

Duncan, Irma. *Duncan Dancer*. Middletown, Conn.: Wesleyan University Press, 1966.

——— and Macdougall, Allan Ross. *Isadora Duncan's Russian Days*. New York: Covici-Friede, 1929.

Duncan, Isadora. *My Life*. New York: Boni and Liveright, 1927.

Dunham, Katherine. *Island Possessed*. Garden City, N.Y.: Doubleday & Co., Inc., 1969.

———. *Touch of Innocence*. New York: Harcourt, Brace, 1959.

Elssler, Fanny. *La Deésse, an Elssler-atic Romance*. New York: Carvill & Co., 1841.

Engel, Lehman. *The American Musical Theatre*. New York: Macmillan Publishing Co., Inc., 1967.

Enters, Angna. *Artist's Life*. New York: Coward-McCann, 1958.

———. *Silly Girl*. Cambridge, Mass.: Houghton, Mifflin Co., 1944.

Gamez, Tana de. *Alicia Alonso at Home and Abroad*. New York: Citadel Press, 1971.

Gard, Alex. *Ballet Laughs*. New York: Greystone Press, 1941.

Genthe, Arnold. *Book of the Dance*. New York: M. Kennerly, 1916.

———. *Isadora Duncan: 24 Studies*. New York: M. Kennerly, 1929.

Graham, Martha. *Notebooks of Martha Graham*. New York: Harcourt, Brace, Jovanovich, 1973.

Green, Stanley. *The World of Musical Comedy*. New York: Ziff-Davis Publishing Co., 1960.

Haskell, Arnold. *Ballet Retrospect*. London: B. T. Batsford, Ltd., 1964.

Hering, Doris, with the writings of Rudolf Orthwine. *Wild Grass*. New York: Dance Magazine, 1967.

Howard, Ruth Eleanor. *The Story of the American Ballet*. New York: Ihra Publishing Co., 1936.

Humphrey, Doris. *The Art of Making Dances*. New York: Reinhardt Publishing Co., 1959.

———. *An Artist First*. Middletown, Conn.: Wesleyan University Press, 1972.

Hyden, Walford. *Pavlova*. Boston: Little, Brown and Company, 1931.

Kendall, Elizabeth. *Where She Danced*. New York: Alfred A. Knopf, 1979.

Kirstein, Lincoln. *Blast at Ballet*. New York: Marstin Press, Inc., 1938.

Lawrence, Robert. *Victor Book of Ballets and Ballet Music*. New York: Simon and Schuster, 1950.

Leatherman, Leroy, and Swope, Martha. *Martha Graham*. New York: Alfred A. Knopf, 1966.

Lloyd, Margaret. *The Borzoi Book of Modern Dance*. New York: Alfred A. Knopf, 1949.

Magriel, Paul, ed. *Chronicles of American Dance*. New York: Henry Holt and Co., 1948.

Magriel, Paul. *Isadora Duncan*. New York: Henry Holt and Co., 1947.

———. *Pavlova*. New York: Henry Holt and Co., 1947.

Martin, John J. *The Dance*. New York: Tudor Press, 1948.

———. *Introduction to the Dance*. New York: W. W. Norton, 1939.

———. *The Modern Dance*. New York: A. S. Barnes and Co., Inc., 1933.

———. *Sybil Shearer*. Robert Morrison: 1965.

Moore, Lillian. *Images of the Dance*. Brooklyn, N.Y.: Dance Horizons, 1977.

Morgan, Barbara. *Martha Graham*. New York: Duell, Sloan and Pearce, 1941.

McCracken, Howard. *George Catlin: The Old Frontier*. New York: The Daily Press, 1959.

Payne, Charles. *American Ballet Theatre*. New York: Alfred A. Knopf, 1977.

Philip, Richard, and Whitney, M. *Danseur: The Male in Ballet*. New York: McGraw-Hill, 1977.

Quirey, Belinda. *May I Have the Pleasure*. London: BBC Publications, 1976.

Seroff, Victor. *The Real Isadora*. New York: The Dial Press, 1971.

Seymour, Maurice. *Ballet Portraits*. New York: Pellegrini and Cudahy, 1952.

Shawn, Ted. *The American Ballet*. New York: Henry Holt and Co., 1926.

———. *Dance We Must*. Pittsfield, Mass.: The Eagle Press and Binding Co., 1940.

———. *Every Little Movement*. Pittsfield, Mass.: The Eagle Press and Binding Co., 1954.

———. *1000 and 1 Night Stands*. Garden City, N.Y.: Doubleday & Co., Inc., 1960.

Shearer, Sybil. *Creative Dance*. Robert Morrison: 1943.

Steegmuller, Francis, ed. *Your Isadora*. New York: Random House and The New York Public Library, 1974.

Taper, Bernard. *Balanchine*. New York: Harper & Row, 1963.

Terry Walter. *The Dance in America*. New York: Harper & Row, 1956.

———. *Frontiers of Dance: The Life of Martha Graham*. New York: Thomas Y. Crowell & Co., 1975.

———. *Isadora Duncan*. New York: Dodd, Mead & Co., 1963.

———. *Miss Ruth*. New York: Dodd, Mead & Co., 1969.

———. *Ted Shawn: Father of American Dance*. New York: The Dial Press, 1976.

Vaillat, Léandre. *La Taglioni*. Paris: A. Michel, 1942.

Van Vechten, Car. *The Dance Writings*. New York: Dance Horizons, 1974.

Walker, Katherine Sorley. *Dance and Its Creators*. New York: The John Day Co., 1972.

Other sources include:

Theatre Magazine, New York, 1905–1926.

Theatre Arts Monthly, New York, 1932–1946.

Miscellaneous ballet programs and souvenir programs, 1936–1979.

"Notes on the Lectures by Lillie Bess Campbell." Ph.D. dissertation, unpublished mss., in collection of the author.

INDEX

Academy of Music (New York), 34, 35
acrobatics in dance, 125–27, 153
"Acrobatics in the New Choreography" (de Mille), 126
Adam, Adolphe Charles, 45
Adams, John, 205
After Eden, 162–64, 201
Afternoon of a Faun, 141
AGMA (American Guild of Musical Artists), 208
Agon, 153
Ailey, Alvin, 110, 159, 167–68, 178
Ailey, Alvin, Company, 119, 167–68
Airs, 166
Ajello, Salvator, 186
All American, 194
Allan, Maud, 56–58
Allegro, 191, 192
All That Jazz, 200
Amahl and the Night Visitors, 165
American Ballet Center, 186
American Ballet Theatre (Ballet Theatre), 116, 124, 128–41, 144, 150–51, 168, 171–72, 180, 181, 182, 185, 186, 200, 201, 208, 209
  stars and soloists of (list), 129–30
American Ballet Theatre School, 128, 185–86
American colonists, 2–3, 23, 204–5
  dance forbidden by, 3
  European dances adapted by, 4–10
American Document, 159
American Primitives, 159
Annie, 194
Annie Get Your Gun, 193, 194
Apache dances, 21
Apollo, 127, 154
Arbeau, Thoinot, 3
Argentina, 81, 112
Arpino, Gerald, 165, 179
Arrow against Profane and Promiscuous Dancing, Drawne out of the Quiver of the Scriptures, An (Mather), 23
Artist's Life (Enters), 112
Art of Making Dances, The (Humphrey), 104
Asche, Oscar, 58
Ashton, Frederick, 178, 180, 200
Astaire, Fred, 40, 88–90
At Midnight, 180
Aureole, 165–66

Bach, Johann Sebastian, 107, 165
Baiser de la Fée, 182
Baker, Josephine, 70
Balanchine, George, 47, 75, 79, 99, 124–28, 132, 138–41, 144, 151–55, 158, 165, 176, 180, 182, 183, 185, 206
  acrobatics used by, 125–27, 153
  on Broadway, 187–88
  pure dance as goal of, 152–53
Baldina, Maria Alexandra, 73
Bales, William, 161–62
ballet, 23–36, 37, 40, 43–44, 45, 59–62, 71–80, 94, 99, 112, 123–58, 177–86, 196
  acrobatics in, 125–27, 153
  acting in, 96, 112, 146–50, 153
  colloquialism added to, 144–48, 153–54
  early American, 26–36
  early critics of, 25–26

male vs. female dancers in, 25
pointe work in, 24–25, 26, 62, 64, 116
tap dancing in, 135, 144
tap dancing vs., 63–64
see also dance schools; *specific artists and companies*
Ballet Arts, 186
Ballet Ballads, 193
Ballet Caravan, 128, 144, 158, 208
Ballet Export U.S.A., 158
Ballet Intime, 75
ballet-jazz, 187
Ballet Russe, 77–80
Ballet Russe de Monte Carlo, 135, 186, 188
ballet slippers, 24–25, 45–46, 62
Ballets U.S.A., 194
Ballet Theatre, *see* American Ballet Theatre
Balling the Jack, 16
Ballroom, 195
ballroom dancing, 3–12, 16–22, 52, 59, 63, 90, 195
  black dances adapted for, 16, 21
  clothing for, 3, 5–11, 12, 16, 18, 19, 20
  touching in, 3, 5–10, 19, 20
  of young, 19–22
Bal Nègre, 119
Barker, Barbara, 34
Barnes, Clive, 173
Barnett, Bobbie, 172–73
Bartered Bride, The, 76
Bartok, Bela, 144, 165
Baryshnikov, Mikhail, 116, 150–51, 171–72, 181–82, 200
Bates, Peg Leg, 40
Bauer, Elaine, 182
Bayadère, La, 51, 150
Beatles, 20
Beatty, Talley, 119
Beau Danube, Le, 79
Beebe, William, 90
Beethoven, Ludwig van, 45, 46, 79
Bennett, Michael, 195–96
Berkeley, Busby, 86
Berlioz, Louis Hector, 79
Bernstein, Leonard, 191, 192, 204, 209
Bettis, Valerie, 110
Big Apple, 16, 20
Billy the Kid, 128
Birch, Patricia, 195
Bitter Weird, The, 135
Black Bottom, 16, 19
Black Crook, The, 31
blacks, 97, 116, 168, 182, 209
  dance styles of, 13–16, 21, 37, 116–19
  Dunham's troupe, 116–19
  music of, 13–14, 18, 21
  in popular theater, 37–40, 67–70
Blasis, Carlo, 31
Bloomer Girl, 191
Bluebeard's Castle, 165
blues, 21
Bolender, Todd, 158
Bolger, Harry, 40
Bolger, Ray, 40, 188
Bolm, Adolph, 74, 75, 123
Bolm's, Adolph, Ballet Intime, 58
Bolshoi Ballet, 126–27

Bonfanti, Maria, 31, 32–34, 185
Boogaloo, 21
boogie-woogie, 20
Booth, Edwin, 28
Booth family, 24
Boris, Ruthanna, 80, 128, 186
Boston Ballet, 182
bourrées, 5
Bowman, Patricia, 75, 77, 123–24
Brahms, Johannes, 79, 153, 180
Bridegroom Called Death, A, 135
Brigadoon, 191
Broadway, 187–96
  ballet-jazz style for, 187
  dance and drama fused on, 188–89, 192
  see also theater, popular
Brown, David, 182
Bryant, Dan, 40
buck-and-wing, 16, 40, 144
Bunny Hug, 16
Butler, John, 159, 162–65, 168, 201
Butler, John, Dance Theater, 164
Bye-Bye, Birdie, 194
Byrne, James, 28

Cabaret, 200
Cage, John, 161
Cage, The, 141
Cakewalk, 16, 25
Cakewalk, 128
Caldwell, Sarah, 165
Camargo, 24, 59
Camelot, 193
Canadian National Ballet, 151
Can-Can, 192
cane dance, 40
Canto Hondo ("Deep Song"), 114
Capital Theatre Ballet, 64
Caprichos, 144
Carib Song, 119
Carmina Burana, 164, 165
Carnival, 194
Carousel, 191
Carrol, Elisabeth, 158
Cassidy, Claudia, 109
Castle, Irene, 16–18, 48
Castle, Vernon, 16–18
Castle walk, 16
Caton, Edward, 186
Catulli Carmina, 164, 165
Cavalazzi, Malvina, 34, 71, 185
Cerrito, Fanny, 30
Champion, Gower, 187, 193–94
Champion, Marge, 194
Chaplin, Charlie, 173
Charleston, 16, 19, 63, 86, 90
Chase, Allison, 172–73
Chase, Lucia, 123–24, 128, 129–30, 151, 206
Cherokee ant dance, 2
Choo San Goh, 180
Chopin, Frederic, 45, 56, 142
Choreartium, 79
Choreographic Offering, A, 107
chorus dancing, 62, 64–67, 86–88
Chorus Line, 195, 196

Christiansen, Lew, 128, 183
Circular Descent, 104
City Portrait, 128
Clarke, Martha, 172–73
Cleopatra, 71
clog dances, 14–16, 22, 62
clowns, 40–42, 119, 173
Clytemnestra, 166
Cochran, Charles, 128
Cole, Jack, 138, 165, 168, 187, 194, 197
Coles, Honi, 40
Collins, Janet, 38, 116
Commedia dell'Arte, 40
Compositions in Dance Forms, 111
Concert, The, 141
Conrad, Joseph, 210
Conrad, Karen, 123–24
Consort, 180
Copland, Aaron, 97, 128
Coppélia, 59
Coralli, Jean, 30
Cornell, Katharine, 187
Cortege of Eagles, 98–99
costumes and clothing, 25, 34, 43, 45, 48, 51, 97, 99, 120, 173
    in ballroom dancing, 3, 5–11, 12, 16, 18, 19, 20
Cotton Club, 21, 70, 116
Coulon, Jean François, 24
Cragun, Richard, 183
Craig, Gordon, 99
Cranko, John, 180, 182
Craske, Margaret, 76, 185, 186
Crawford, Joan, 19, 84–86
Crutch, Robert, 186
Cunningham, Merce, 159, 160–61, 170, 176
Curtis, Margaret, 185

Dabney, Ford T., 18
Daddy Was a Fireman, 104
Dafora, Asadata, 119
Dalcroze, Emile Jacques, 43, 108, 111
Damn Yankees, 194
Dance in America, 201
Dance Machine, 196
Dance Players, 164
dancers:
    lack of respect for, 31–34, 196
    profit-sharing for, 195–96
    wages for, 189–90, 208
Dances at a Gathering, 141–42, 144, 153
dance schools, 34, 35–36, 71, 77, 102–3, 104, 110, 128, 185–86
    see also specific schools
Dance Theater of Harlem, 182, 185
Dancin', 194
Daniels, Danny, 194
Danilova, Alexandra, 79–80
Da Ponte, Lorenzo, 26
Dark Elegies, 131
Deaths and Entrances, 167
de Basil, Colonel, 77–80, 128
De Lappe, Gemze, 186
de Lavallade, Carmen, 38, 110, 164, 186, 209
Dello Joio, Norman, 107
Delsarte, François, 43

de Mille, Agnes:
    American folk styles used by, 116, 132–35, 144, 184
    as arts administrator, 188–89, 207–8
    storytelling as concern of, 112, 132, 148–50, 188–89, 192
    works of, 67, 112, 116, 126, 128, 132–35, 138, 144, 148–50, 178, 184, 186, 188–91, 192, 193, 195, 200, 201
De Mille, Cecil B., 84
Denham, Sergei, 79–80
Denishawn, 52, 58, 67, 91, 99, 103, 111, 159, 186, 187
    see also St. Denis, Ruth; Shawn, Ted
Denishawn Era, The (Hastings), 52
de Rham, William, 12
Devi, Ratan, 58
Dexter, John, 76
Diaghilev, Sergei Pavlovich, 73, 74, 126, 127, 128
Diaghilev Ballet, 47, 71, 74–75, 77, 79, 91, 123, 141, 154
Dickens, Charles, 37
Dim Lustre, 132
discotheques, 20–21, 22
Dishrag, 21
Diversion of Angels, 167
Dollar, William, 128
Don Quixote, 150
Douglas, Scott, 164
Draper, Paul, 40
Druckman, Jacob, 108
drums, 1, 3, 13
Dudley, Jane, 161
Duncan, Isadora, 43–50, 51, 56–58, 81, 91, 97, 107, 108, 109, 110, 111
    barefoot dancing of, 45–46, 48
    lifestyle of, 49–50
    natural movements as source for, 44
    public acceptance of dance and, 43, 47–48
    simple sets and costumes of, 44–47, 48, 96
Dunham, Katherine, 38, 116–19, 168, 184
Dybbuk, The, 167
Dying Swan, The, 82

Early Songs, 180
Echoing of Trumpets, 132
Educational Broadcasting Company, 201
Eglevsky, André, 80
Eglevsky, Maria, 186
Ellington, Duke, 168
Elssler, Fanny, 25–26, 27–30, 31, 62
    in America, 28–30
Emerson, Ralph Waldo, 28
endowments for arts, 71, 123, 157–58, 182, 196, 201, 203–8
Enters, Angna, 111–12
Esplanade, 165–66
essence, 40
ethnic and folk dances, 63
    American, 116, 132–35, 144, 184
    American Indian, 1–3, 13, 21, 55, 173
    in ballet and modern dance, 25, 26, 51, 55, 63, 112, 116–19, 144, 187
    black American, 13–16, 21, 37, 116–19
    Indian, 51, 58
    Irish, 14–16
    Oriental, 51, 55, 91, 96, 97

Spanish, 26, 63, 112

Fables for Our Time, 104
Fairbanks, Douglas, 67, 81
Falco, Louis, 175
Fallis, Barbara, 186
Fall River Legend, 135, 209
Fancy Free, 141, 144
Feld, Eliot, 180–81
Felix, Seymour, 64
Fiddler on the Roof, 192
film, 81–90, 197–200
    camera technique in, 84–86, 197–99
    dance on stage vs., 82–84, 86, 90
    dances preserved on, 81–82, 100, 197
    see also television; videotape
Finian's Rainbow, 192
Fiorello, 194
Firebird, 154
First Person Plural (Enters), 112
Fisher, Nelle, 186
flamencos, 90
Flora, the Red Menace, 194
Flying Colors, 67
Fokina, Vera, 75, 80
Fokine, Michel, 47, 73, 75, 77, 106, 123, 128, 135, 138, 153, 154, 155, 185
Fontanne, Evan Burroughs, 58
Ford Foundation, 157, 182, 201, 206
Forty Thieves, The, or Stealing Oil in Family Jars, 31
Fosse, Bob, 187, 193–94, 200
Four Horsemen of the Apocalypse, The, 81
Four Marys, The, 135, 209
fox-trot, 16
Foy, Eddie, 40
Franklin, Benjamin, 10
Frug, 16, 21
Fuller, Loie, 58, 81, 120–22
Fuller, Margaret, 28
Funny Thing Happened on the Way to the Forum, A, 192

Gaité Parisienne, 79
Gala Performance, 131
Galaxy, 120
Galli, Rosina, 71
galop, 11, 12
Gambarelli, Maria "Gamby," 64
Gautier, Théophile, 25–26, 31
gavotte, 5, 16
Genée, Adeline, 59–62, 64, 71, 73
Gennaro, Peter, 187, 194
Gentlemen Prefer Blondes, 191
George White's Scandals, 19
Geva, Tamara, 67, 125, 188
gigue, 5
Giselle, 30, 59
glide, 16
Gluck, Christoph Willibald von, 45, 75
Goldberg, Arthur, 207–8
Goldberg Variations, 142–44
Golden Apple, The, 193
Goldwyn Follies, 188
Goldwyn, Sam, 188
Good News, 19

Goslar, Lotte, 119
Goya, Francisco José de, 144
Graham, Martha, 47, 58, 91–99, 104, 106, 107, 110, 111, 128, 144, 152, 159, 160, 161, 162, 164, 165, 167, 181, 187, 195, 201
    classic ballet vs., 94, 96
    ground used by, 91, 96, 104
    Oriental dance and, 91, 96, 97
    sets and costumes of, 96–97
Grahn, Lucile, 31
Grand Kabuki, 91
Grauman, Sid, 67
Grease, 195
Greenwich Village Follies, 58
Gregory, Cynthia, 116
Grisi, Carlotta, 31, 51
Grisi, Giulia, 24
Guérard, Roland, 80
Guimard, Madeline, 59
Guys and Dolls, 192
Gypsy, 192

Haakon, Paul, 75
Hale, Chester, girls, 64
Half Real Half Dream, 98
Hamilton, Lady Emma, 43
Hammerstein, Oscar, 112, 188, 191
hand dance, 40
Handel, George Frederick, 165
Hanks, Nancy, 208
Harbinger, 180
Harkarvy, Benjamin, 158, 182
Harkness Ballet, 162, 187
Harkness, Rebekah, 158
Harrison, Lee, 172–73
Hastings, Baird, 52
Hawkins, Eric, 128, 175
Haydn, Franz Joseph, 166, 180
Hazard (ballet teacher), 28
Hello, Dolly!, 194
Hendel, Henrietta, 43, 46
Heritage Dance Theater, 116, 184
High Button Shoes, 192
Hill, Martha, 186
Hindemith, Paul, 79
Hinkson, Mary, 164
Hodes, Stuart, 175
Hoffman, Gertrude, 71–74
Holm, Hanya, 91, 159, 181, 193
Hopi dances, 1
Horan, Eddie, 40
hornpipes, 23, 25, 28
Horse, 21
Horst, Louis, 186
Horton, Lester, 110, 116, 167, 168
Hully-Gully, 21
Humphrey, Doris, 47, 91, 99–104, 106–7, 108, 109, 110, 159, 161, 173, 187
    style of, 99, 104
    as teacher, 102–4, 106, 108, 186
    training of, 99
Hunting Ballet, The, 64
Hurok, Sol, 76–80

IATSE (International Alliance of Theatrical Stage Em-

ployees), 208–10
Ichinohe, Saeko, 179–80
I Married an Angel, 188
Immortal Swan, The, 82
Imperial Ballet, 125
improvisation:
   in ballroom dancing, 18, 20–21
   in black dancing, 16
   by Duncan, 46
   in Indian dancing, 1, 2
India, dancing of, 51, 58
Indians, American, 1–3, 13, 21, 55, 173
   buffalo dances of, 1
   paint and masks used by, 2
   rain dances of, 1
   women in dances of, 1–2
Inside U.S.A., 193
Intermezzo, 180
Interplay, 141
Irish immigrants, dances of, 14–16
Irma la Douce, 195
Ito, Misho, 111

Jack-the-Ripper, 21
Jamison, Judith, 38, 168, 209
Janin, Jules, 26
jazz, 16, 21, 37, 40, 63, 138–41, 164
Jazz Hot from Haiti to Harlem, Le, 119
Jeanne au Boucher, 165
Jehan, Ghoor, 58
jigs, 14, 23
jitterbug, 16, 20, 144
jive, 144
Joffrey Ballet, 135, 177–81, 182, 185, 208
   leading dancers in (list), 179
Joffrey, Robert, 171, 177–78, 186
Joffrey, Robert, Company, 158
Johnson, Lyndon, 207
Johnston, Julanne, 67
Jooss, Kurt, 178
Juba (William Henry Lane), 37–40
Judgement of Paris, 131
Juilliard School, 186

Kahn, Otto, 75
Kani No Yama, 179
Karsavina, Tamara, 47, 71, 74
Kaye, Nora, 131, 197, 200
Keeler, Ruby, 88
Keene, Christopher, 180
Kelly, Gene, 40, 88
Kemble, Fanny, 25
Kendal, Elizabeth, 135
Kerr, Walter, 40–42
Keynes, Lady (Lydia Lopokova), 73, 74
Kidd, Michael, 128, 144, 187, 192–93, 197
King and I, The, 192, 197
Kirstein, Lincoln, 124, 128, 144, 151–52, 185, 206
Kismet, 58
Kisselgoff, Anna, 178
Kiss Me, Kate, 193
Kitt, Eartha, 119
Kodaly, Zoltan, 108
Koner, Pauline, 75, 108, 184, 186
Kosloff, Theodore, 73, 123

Krassovska, Nathalie, 80
Krupska, Dania, 123
Kung Fu, 21

Laing, Hugh, 131
Lament for Ignacio Sanchez Méjias, 104
La Meri, 111
Lami, 25
Lamp Unto My Feet, 201
lancers, 12
Lang, Pearl, 159, 167
Latouche, John, 193
Leaves Are Fading, The, 132
Lee, Mary Ann, 30
Lee, Virginia, 186
Lend an Ear, 194
Leonidov, Leon, 77
Leslie, Caird, 144
Letter to the World, 167
Levi-Tanai, Sara, 159
Lewitsky, Bella, 110, 168–69, 186
Lichine, David, 80
Liebeslieder Walzer, 153
lighting, 96–97, 120, 122, 161, 176
Lilac Garden, 131
Limón, José, 103, 106–8, 109, 159, 182, 186
Limón, José, Dance Company, 106–8
Lincoln Center for the Performing Arts, 35, 124
Lind, Jenny, 24
Lindgren, Robert, 80, 184, 186
Lindy-Hop, 16, 20
Littlefield, Catherine, 123
Littlefield, Dorothy, 123
Little Night Music, A, 195
longways, 5
Look, Ma, I'm Dancin'!, 192
Lopokova, Lydia, 73, 74
Lorca, Garcia, 104
Loring, Eugene, 128, 164, 186
Louis, Murray, 122
Lowski, Woytek, 182
Lucille of London, 16
Lynch Time, 104
Lysistrata, 187

McComber's Folly, 108
McCracken, Joan, 123
MacDonald, Brian, 158, 178
McKayle, Donald, 168, 187, 195
Mack Sennett Ballet, 192
Magdalina, 187
Mahler, Gustav, 180
Maids, The, 144
Makarova, Natalia, 116, 150–51
Malibran, Maria, 24
Mandan dances, 1
Mansfield, Perry, Dancers, 58
Mapleson, Colonel, 34
Maracci, Carmelita, 112–16
Marceau, Marcel, 173
Marie-Jeanne, 128
Markert, Russell, 67
Markova, Dame Alicia, 75, 80
Martin, John, 80, 103, 106, 109, 112
Mashed Potato, 21

Maslow, Sophie, 161
Massine, Léonide, 77–80, 138, 178
Mather, Increase, 23
maxixe, 16
Maxwell, Carla, 108
Maywood, Augusta, 30–31, 34
Mazilier, Joseph, 27–28, 30
mazurka, 12
Meadowlark, 180
Mendelssohn, Felix, 56
Metropolitan Museum of Art, 16
Metropolitan Opera House (New York), 34, 35–36, 61, 64, 71, 74, 75–76, 116
    choreographers at, 75–76
    destruction of, 35, 77
Metropolitan Opera House School, 76, 185
Milhaud, Darius, 100
Miller, Buzz, 164
Mills, Florence, 70
minstrel shows, 37
minuet, 5, 16
Missa Brevis, 107–8
Mistinguette, 70
Mitchell, Arthur, 182
Mitti and Tillio, 125
modern dance, 37, 91–110, 144, 159–76, 177, 196
    avant-garde in, 173–76
    dehumanization in, 175–76
    see also dance schools; *specific artists and companies*
Moiseyev, Igor, 177, 184
Momentum, 180
Monk, Meredith, 175
Monroe, Marilyn, 197
Moor's Pavane, The, 106–7
Mordkin Ballet, 123–24, 128
Mordkin, Mikhail, 71, 74, 123–24
More, George F., 40
Morgan, Marian, Dancers, 58
Morlacchi, Giuseppina, 32–33, 34
Moross, Jerome, 193
Morrison, Helen, 109
music:
    dance without, 173
    electronic, 173
    taped, 202
Music Is, 195
Music Man, The, 195
My Fair Lady, 193

Nahat, Dennis, 182
National Arts Endowment, 207–8
Navaho Eagle Dance, 1
Navaho Squaw Dance, 2
Nedleman, Elie, 124
Nemtchinova, Vera, 186
Neumeier, John, 182, 183
New Dance, 99–100
New Dance Group, 161
New York City Ballet (American Ballet), 124–25, 141–44, 151–58, 182, 185, 186, 187, 188, 208
    stars and soloists in (list), 158
New York School of Ballet, 186
Nijinska, Bronislava, 79, 141
Nijinska, Romola, 124
Nijinsky, Vaslav, 47, 74, 124

Nikolais, Alwin, 119–20, 122, 173, 176
Nimura, Yeichi, 186
Nobilissima Visione, 79
Noble, Duncan, 184, 186
Noces, Les, 141, 209
Noguchi, Isamu, 97
North Carolina School of the Arts, 106, 186
Noverre, Jean Georges, 203
Nureyev, Rudolph, 116
Nutcracker, The, 150, 182, 183, 185

Oh Dad, Poor Dad, Mama's Hung You in the Closet and I'm Feeling So Sad, 192
Oklahoma!, 135, 165, 188–89, 191, 197
Oliver, 195
Omnibus, 201
110 in the Shade, 191
O'Neil, Zelma, 19
one-step, 16, 90
One Touch of Venus, 191
On Stage, 144
On the Town, 191
On Your Toes, 188
opera, 23, 24, 26, 31, 34, 165, 203
Orestes, 100
Oriental dancing, 51, 55, 91, 96, 97
Orpheus, 75
Otero, La Belle (Caroline), 81
Out of This World, 116

Pacific Overtures, 195
Page, Ruth, 75, 186
Paint Your Wagon, 191
Pajama Game, The, 194
Pan, Hermes, 88
Pankhurst, Emily, 48
Parade, 173
Paris Opéra, 24, 30, 36
Park Theatre (New York), 26, 34
Passacaglia, 99–100
passepieds, 5
Pavlova, Anna, 47, 52, 58, 61, 71, 73, 74, 80, 124, 185
    American tours of, 76–77
    dance films of, 81–82
pedestal dance, 40
Pell, Iris, 169
Pendleton, Moses, 172–73
Pennington, Ann, 19
Pennsylvania Ballet, 181, 182
Péri, La, 51
Perrot, Jules Joseph, 31
Petipa, Jean, 26–28
Petipa, Marius, 26–28, 77, 127, 132, 154
Philadelphia Ballet Company, 123
Picasso, Pablo, 91, 173
Pickford, Mary, 81
Pillar of Fire, 131, 132
Pilobolus Dance Theater, 172–73, 175, 176
Placide, Alexandre, 23
Pleasant, Richard, 128
Poe, Edgar Allan, 160
Pointed Ascent, 104
polkas, 11, 12, 16
Powell, Eleanor, 88
Pratt, John, 117

Presages, Les, 79
Presley, Elvis, 81
Primitive Mysteries, 159
Primus, Pearl, 119, 168
Prodigal Son, The, 127, 141, 154
Prokofiev, Sergei, 127, 180
prologues, in movie theaters, 67
Punch and the Judy, 167
punk rock, 21
Purcell, Henry, 107
Push Comes to Shove, 171–72

Radio City Music Hall (New York), 122
ragtime, 21
Raisin, 195
Rambert, Marie, 173
Rape of Lucretia, 187
Rasch, Albertina, 64, 67, 71, 86–88, 187
Ravel, Maurice Joseph, 144
Red Head, 194
Red Shoes, The, 197
reels, 5, 14, 22, 23
Requiem for Jimmy Dean, 187
Revalle, Flore, 74
Rhodes, Larry, 158
Rice, "Jim Crow," 40
rigaudons, 5
River, The, 168
Robbins, Jerome, 138–44, 148–50, 152, 153, 158, 180,
   187, 196, 197, 200, 209
   on Broadway, 191–92, 193–94
   humor used by, 138, 142, 180
   jazz incorporated into ballet by, 138–41
   musical sense of, 142
Robert le Diable, 59
Robinson, Bill "Bojangles," 40, 88
Rockettes, 67
rock music, 20
rock 'n roll, 16, 144
Rodeo, 128, 132–35
Rodgers, Richard, 188, 191
Roger de Coverly (dance), 5, 10
Rogers, Ginger, 88
Rogge, Florence, 77
Rogge, Florence, ballet girls, 67
Romeo and Juliet, 132, 187
Ronzani, Dominico, 31, 32–33
Rooney, John, 203–4
Rosemont, Franklin, 110
Roshanara, 58
rosin, use of, 25
Ross, Herbert, 144, 148–50, 187, 194, 197, 200, 201
Rothafel, S. L. "Roxy," 77
rounds, 5
Royal Ballet, 132, 151, 181
Royal Ballet School, 182
Royal Winnipeg Ballet, 135, 180, 182
Ryder, Mark, 186

Sacre du Printemps, Le, 77, 181–82
St. Denis, Ruth, 47, 51–55, 56, 58, 81, 91, 99, 103,
   104, 110, 173
   Oriental dances of, 51, 91
   style of, 51, 58
   see also Denishawn

Saint-Saëns, Charles Camille, 179
Sallé, Marie, 59
Sanasardo, Paul, 175
Sanctum, 120
sand dance, 40
Sanford, Terry, 186
San Francisco Ballet, 128, 183
Sangalli, Rita, 31, 32–33, 34
Sappington, Margot, 175
Sarazin, Anamarie, 182
Savage, Archie, 119
Scala, La, 31, 34
Scarlet Letter, The, 99
scenic design, 45, 96–97, 99, 120, 122, 131, 152–53,
   161, 176, 191, 192, 209
Scheherazade, 71
School of the American Ballet, 124–25, 151, 164, 185
schottische, 11, 16
Schubert, Franz, 45, 48, 99
Schuman, William, 97, 186
Scuola di Ballo, 79
Season in Hell, 162–64
Sebastian, 162–64
Seven Lively Arts, The, 201
Seventh Symphony, 79
Shadowplay, 132
Shag, 16
Shankar, Uday, 58, 173
Shawn, Ted, 52–56, 99
   see also Denishawn
Shearer, Sybil, 108–10, 132, 182
Siddons, Sarah, 43
Silly Girl (Enters), 112
slap-shoe, 40
Sleeping Beauty, 76, 150
Smith, George Washington, 16, 30, 31
Smith, Joseph, 16, 28
Smith, Oliver, 131, 191, 192, 209
Smok, Pavel, 76
Smuin, Michael, 183
social dancing, *see* ballroom dancing
softshoe, 40, 62
Sokolow, Anna, 159–60, 179, 184, 186
Soldier's Tale, 180
Solov, Zachary, 75, 116
Somniloquy, 120
Soto, Pepita, 30
Sousa, John Philip, 154
Spanish dances, 26, 63, 112
Square Dance, 154
square dances, 5, 22, 153
Stars and Stripes, 154
State Department, U.S., 203–4
Stevens, Roger, 207, 208
Stoll, Oswald, 59
Stone, Bently, 186
Story of Mankind, The, 104
Strauss, Richard, 58, 180
Stravinsky, Igor, 77, 127, 141, 144, 153
Streisand, Barbra, 197
Stroganova, Nina, 124, 186
Stuart, Muriel, 124, 164, 185
Stuttgart Ballet, 151, 181
Susie Q, 16
Svoboda, Josef, 76

Swan Lake, 64, 183
Swan Queen, The, 148
Sweet Charity, 194
Sylphide, La, 26
Sylphides, Les, 71, 153
Sylvain, James, 28
Symphonie Fantastique, 79
syncopation, 13, 153

Taglioni, Amalia, 26–28
Taglioni, Filippo, 24, 26, 59
Taglioni, Maria, 24–26, 31, 51, 59
Taglioni, Paul, 26–28
Tallchief, Maria, 80
Tally-Ho, 135
Tamiris, Helen, 193
tango, 16, 81
tap dancing, 16, 40, 52, 59, 62, 67, 90, 116, 117, 195
    in ballet, 135, 144
    ballet vs., 63–64
Taylor, Paul, 159, 165–67, 175, 176
Taylor, Paul, Dance Company, 166–67
Tchaikovsky, Peter Ilyich, 79
Tchelitchef, Pavel, 75, 124
television, dance programs on, 201–4, 206
Terry, Walter, 104
Tetley, Glen, 110, 150, 159, 164, 181–82, 183
Tharp, Twyla, 104, 170–72, 175, 176, 178, 195
theater, popular, 3, 23, 24, 153, 205
    blacks in, 37–40, 67–70, 116, 117
    clowns and jesters in, 40–42
    before 1900, 37–42
    1900–1930, 59–70
    see also Broadway; vaudeville
Théâtre Royale de Musique et de la Danse, 24, 36
Theodore, Lee, 196
There Is a Time, 107
Thief of Bagdad, The, 67
Thomas, Richard, 186
Thurber, James, 104
Tricorne, Le, 77
Tropical Revue, 119
Truitte, James, 110
Tudor, Antony, 47, 76, 131–32, 138, 141, 144, 148–50, 185, 186, 200
Turkey Trot, 16
Turnbull, Julia, 28
Turning Point, The, 197, 200
Twist, 16, 21
two-step, 16
Tyven, Gertrude, 80
Tyven, Sonia, 186

Undertow, 132
Unfinished Life, An, 104
Unfinished Symphony, The, 99
unions, 173, 202, 208–10

Unsinkable Molly Brown, The, 194
Untitled, 173
U.S.A. Dance, The, 201

Valentino, Rudolph, 81
Varsity Drag, 16, 19
varsoviennes, 12
vaudeville, 16, 40, 56, 59, 67, 90, 125
Venza, Jac, 201
Verchinina, Nina, 80
Verdon, Gwen, 194, 196
Vestris, Auguste, 24, 25
videotape, 202–4
Villa-Lobos, Heitor, 187
Villella, Edward, 201
Virginia reel, 5
Vivaldi, Antonio, 154
Viva Vivaldi!, 179
Volinine, Alexander, 61, 73
voltas, 4, 16

Walking Happy, 194
waltzes, 11, 12, 16, 20
Washington, George, 10, 23
Water Mill, 142–44
Water Study, The, 99
Watkins, Mary, 106
Watusi, 16, 21
Wayburn, Ned, 64
Weidman, Charles, 91, 99, 102–6, 161, 170, 187
Weisberger, Barbara, 182
Western Symphony, 154
West Side Story, 192, 194, 196, 197
White, Onna, 195
Wigman, Mary, 47, 91, 99, 110, 159
Williams, E. Virginia, 182
Williams, Lavinia, 119
Wind in the Mountains, 135
Wolken, Jonathan, 172–73
Works Progress Administration (WPA), 99–100
World War I, 18, 20, 21
World War II, 20, 55
Württemburg, Duke of, 203
Wyckoff, Bonnie, 182

Yarborough, Sara, 119
Yeats, William Butler, 111
Young, Laura, 182
You're a Good Man, Charlie Brown, 195
Youskevitch, Igor, 80, 186

Zemach, Benjamin, 111
Ziegfeld, Florenz, 59
Ziegfeld Follies, 56, 71
Zinneman, Fred, 197
Zorina, Vera, 80, 188
Zoritch, George, 80